What leaders are saying about "*Look Up America!*"

"Sociologists such as Max Weber and Karl Marx have noted the interplay between religion, economic development and the accumulation of wealth. Gary Moore does that too! In this book he transcends the easy answers of what is wrong with America being provided by those on the political right and finds that real sources of trouble lie in a moral deficit that has emerged in our nation over the past fifty years. Tapping into the rich treasure house of scripture he endeavors to explore what Jesus prescribed as the cures for our economic maladies. Rejecting "The Virtue of Selfishness" prescribed by Ayn Rand, Gary Moore demonstrates how a "Jesus Centered Economy" can rescue our free enterprise system and how, following the teaching of the "founder of our faith," the sufferings of this oppressed poor of the world can be alleviated. You may not like or agree with what he has to say, but you can't ignore his clear thinking. Good job Gary!"

Tony Campolo, PhD, Eastern University, St. Davids, PA

"America needs the wisdom Gary Moore delivers in his new book, Look Up America. As you're drawn into these pages, here's what you will learn about my friend: He's an intellectual, delivering these big ideas in plain English. He's a devout Christian proposing real world solutions for the real lives of all Americans. Just when you think you've got him pegged as a conservative ideologue, he'll turn that notion on its ear. He's a Wall Street veteran who has told the Emperor he's naked. Only someone who is well read, well-travelled, well-grounded and well-regarded could take intellectual honesty to the level you will find throughout his important history book about our future. And as Gary speaks to you from these pages, imagine you're hearing his stubborn Kentucky drawl."

Jim Blasingame, Small business expert, entrepreneurship thought-leader and host of The Small Business Advocate Show

"Gary Moore has been my mentor as much as anyone, providing a consistent and impeccably reasoned orientation in the middle of the economy's ups and downs. Over the years I have known him, his call to be a steward rather than socialist or capitalist, Democrat or Republican, keeps ringing. Some hear him as unreasonably optimistic. Others find him a pessimist they wish not to hear. It is their greed or fear that drives these contrasting reactions to Gary's consistent and important message. With this new book Gary's done it again."

Mark L. Vincent, Ph.D., Acting President, Christian Leadership Alliance

"Few people on the planet have the knowledge, experience, and expertise to write this book. Gary Moore does. But be warned: Gary's work will not just inform and enlighten you, it will also challenge and provoke you. He pulls no punches because what he's advocating is worth fighting for. Though some will dismiss him as being too far to the left, and others contend that he stands too far to the right, the truth is that words like 'liberal' or 'conservative' fail to do Gary justice. A more accurate description would be to call him faithful, and we are very well served by his faithful, provocative, and very important work."

David J. Lose, Ph.D., Center for Biblical Preaching, Luther Seminary

"If your mind is made up regarding the current political/financial/spiritual state of affairs in our country you probably shouldn't read Gary's book. It will be much too upsetting and counter to whatever conventional wisdom you may have subscribed. However, if you can approach the book with an open mind, you'll find thoughtful, biblically based and often unconventional thoughts from someone who has been 'right-on' with investment advice since back in the early 90s."

Dick Towner, Executive Director, Good $ense Ministries

"Gary Moore offers eye-opening insights and provocative perspectives on issues that confront all who seek to be faithful stewards of what God has entrusted to us. With a prophetic-like voice, Gary draws upon an impressive grasp of economics and his own spiritual journey to challenge frequently-heard views on financial matters and their impact on our daily lives. He also identifies pressing concerns for the faith community to consider. Gifted with a keen mind and a huge, caring heart, Gary offers a message that is worth hearing."

The Rev. Eric Wogan

"Gary Moore weaves the three stands of Christianity, politics and finance into an unbreakable cord. He reminds us that we exist only as the stewards of God's blessings and bear a responsibility to put our personal resources to work for the His Kingdom. Politicians on both the right and left benefit when they come together under the umbrella of The Christ."

Darren Ayres, Candidate for US Congress

"Gary Moore is direct, factual, and engaging. Even more, he reminds all those with ears to hear that we as Americans still live in a land of plenty, that as followers of Christ we are all blessed to be a blessing, and that faith (not fear!) should joyfully motivate us when it comes to stewarding the riches of God entrusted to us."

The Rev. Mark Bernthal

"In this age of increasing political polarization, Gary Moore steers a steady course that avoids the rocks and whirlpools on both the left and the right. As always, Moore offers an approach filled with both faith and practicality that offers hope and progress for any political or economic environment we may face."

John Santosuosso, Ph.D., Professor of Political Science, Emeritus, Florida Southern College

LOOK UP AMERICA

Financial Insights for
Tea Partiers Looking Right;
Occupiers Looking Left;
and All Americans Looking at a
Lower Standard of Living for their Children

by

Gary Moore

Wall Street Veteran,
Commentator,
and Founder of The Financial Seminary

Look Up America! Financial Insights for Tea Partiers Looking Right; Occupiers Looking Left; and All Americans Looking at a Lower Standard of Living for their Children

Author: Gary Moore

Published by Austin Brothers Publishing

Keller, Texas

www.austinbrotherspublishing.com

ISBN 978-0-9853263-1-9

Copyright © 2012 by The Financial Seminary

ALL RIGHTS RESERVED. *No part of this book may be reproduced in any form without permission in writing from the publisher, except in the case of brief quotations embodied in critical reviews or articles.*

Austin Brothers
Publishing

Books are available in quantity for promotional or educational use. Contact Austin Brothers Publishing for information at 3616 Sutter Ct., Fort Worth, TX 76137 or wterrya@gmail.com.

This and other books published by Austin Brothers Publishing can be purchased at www.austinbrotherspublishing.com.

Printed in the United States of America

2012 -- First Edition

Contents

Part Three: Trading the Compartmentalized Illusions of the Past for the Holistic Realities of the Future
Page 241

Dedication

"Blessed are the poor."

Jesus of Nazareth

This book aspires to be as moral as it is political and economic. It is therefore dedicated to the spiritually and financially impoverished.

The great faith of Abraham engages our hearts, minds, and souls to inform us of the "whats," "hows" and particularly the "whys" of life. When managing wealth, our minds have long told us the "what" is about rationally co-creating more wealth as there are more and more people. After the Great Recession, our hearts are increasingly telling us the "how" must be about co-creating that wealth prudently and ethically. Finally, our souls tell the truest believers that the "why" of wealth co-creation is that we love our families and neighbors, particularly those in need, both spiritually and materially.

It simply isn't right that those needy but blessed people were never mentioned, even once, during the presidential debates of 2008, by either interviewers or candidates. Too much economic theory also ignores the poor. Stephen Roach was chief economist at Morgan Stanley before joining the faculty at Yale University. He wrote these words recently in the *Financial Times* of being at the 2012 World Economic Forum in Davos and encountering Occupy protesters:

> *"I confess it was unsettling to engage a hostile crowd whose main complaint is rooted in Occupy Wall Street. I tried to stick to my expertise as an economist. First, **I bemoaned the irrelevance of economics for having little to say about income inequality. We are good at developing metrics that measure disparities but have no theory or analytics as to the whys** (emphasis mine)."*

Religion used to answer even the economic "whys" for us. And as this book will hopefully help you to better understand the reason Jesus told us the poor will be with us always is simply the self-centeredness of human nature. So this book is hopefully an introductory conversation between politicians, economists, Wall Street, moralists, and Occupiers, who might, to quote my dog-loving wife's bumper sticker, "Bark less; wag more." In other words, it's as much about Gross Domestic Happiness as Gross Domestic Product.

There is a deeply personal reason for dedicating this book to poor. I grew up in modest circumstances, with friends of modest means. For some reason we don't completely understand, several members of my immediate family have been troubled by various levels of depression over the years. For years I kept my relatively light case of depression as private as I did my humble origins. But I've recently grown to appreciate that it was a blessing to grow up as modestly as I did and that my depression was chemical.

I had seen two doctors, including a psychiatrist, for my depression. All they did was prescribe pills for my symptoms. Then a pastor friend told me about a doctor who takes a more holistic approach to medicine and specializes in helping us old geezers, er, senior citizens, live longer. When I described my depression, he immediately guessed I was low on a hormone. Blood tests, which one of my doctors had conducted for years when doing my annual physicals, affirmed the new doctor's guess. Once he prescribed the hormone, I was off one depression medicine almost immediately and was cutting down on the second until I was barely taking any. I felt like my old self.

There is a very important reason for sharing that personal medical history. The holistic doctor understood my mental depression was due to my body being low on a hormone. Similarly, this book will argue that many of the economic issues troubling our body politic, are actually moral and spiritual. Like my doctors who were unable to see my true problem as they were focused exclusively on the mind or body, our nation simply must be able to see the "mind/body connections" with which we were wondrously made.

I began discussing my depression years ago when serving on a Christian board with J.B. Fuqua. J.B. greatly helped me understand that paradox about blessedness taught by Jesus two millennia ago, which is so very seldom appreciated in our culture. J.B. suffered far more greatly from depression than I do, to the point of disability at times. But J.B. wrote honestly, even passionately, about his condition toward the end of his life. J.B. may have been the chairman of more New York Stock Exchange listed companies than any man in history.

The business school at Duke University is named for J.B., which is ironic and illustrative. My local paper once did a feature article on The Financial Seminary in which I questioned some of the things our business schools have been teaching our intellectually gifted young men and women. The paper also interviewed a professor of business ethics at Duke. He was a disciple of atheistic philosopher Ayn Rand and therefore argued "religion is incompatible with the profit motive."

It's a good thing the self-educated J.B. wasn't smart enough to know that, or the professor may not have had a job. J.B. gave Duke thirty million dollars. Much of that has likely gone to provide teaching jobs for young men and women with doctorates. I expect most of them have had little real experience in business, and particularly on Wall Street. Otherwise, they'd better appreciate that true religion, as opposed to the cultural type, has long incubated honesty and integrity. Those qualities incubate trust, and trust is the lubricant of the capitalism that produces profits to endow colleges.

As all college presidents know, they should be gracious toward their "A" students as they come back as professors but should be equally gracious toward the "C" students as they come back as donors. Making straight A's sometimes blinds academics to such realities. I've never understood why Jesus actually thanked God for hiding truth from the learned, but the Bible says he did. Regardless, Jesus clearly understood that humanistic education can interfere with divine wisdom unless we are very careful.

The religious board on which J.B. and I served would often discuss matters at length until J.B. would succinctly express his view, at which point we'd usually do what he suggested. Perhaps more importantly, J.B. was most gracious in helping me to understand that great leaders in human history, probably including St. Paul and maybe Jesus himself as he was described as "a man of sorrows," suffered serious depression, quite likely over the painful human condition.

It's one of the oddities of American public life, particularly at this likely turning point in history, that we consider depression to be a disqualifying disorder among our leaders. The July 30, 2011 issue of *The Wall Street Journal* contained an article entitled "Depression In Command: In Times of Crisis, Mentally Ill Leaders Can See What Others Don't." The article, by a professor of psychiatry, said Aristotle first noted the link between genius and depression. He went on to detail how Lincoln, Churchill, Martin Luther King, Jr. and Gandhi suffered serious depression, some to the point of considering suicide. He added this, which I found quite comforting, as should a lot of depressed Americans:

> *"Clinical studies have found that depression correlates with high degrees of both realism and empathy....Mildly depressed people tend to see the world more clearly, more as it is....Great crisis leaders are not like the rest of us; nor are they like mentally healthy leaders. When society is happy, they toil in sadness. When traditional approaches begin to fail, however, great crisis leaders see new opportunities. Their weakness is the secret of their strength."*

3

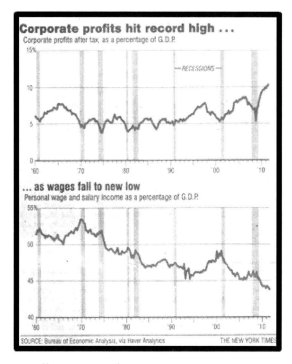

Corporate profits hit record high ...
Corporate profits after tax, as a percentage of G.D.P.

... as wages fall to new low
Personal wage and salary income as a percentage of G.D.P.

SOURCE: Bureau of Economic Analysis, via Haver Analytics   THE NEW YORK TIMES

Personally, I can't relate to the genius part; but I sure relate to toiling in sadness. During the nearly twenty prosperous years that began in 1990, more than a few conservative religious leaders suggested I was out of touch with reality to think that America's problems were moral and spiritual. One even called me a "tool of Satan" for believing our country had larger problems than credit card debt. I was routinely reminded that Jesus once chastised the Pharisees, who were also devout believers, for straining gnats and swallowing camels.

Today, a few more realize my concerns about the declining ethics and increasing speculation of Wall Street, the increasing inequality of income and wealth in our nation, that President W's Republican administration might not solve as many concerns as they'd hoped, and regarding other issues about which I was writing, may have been more problematic than credit cards. A few even believe I may have been right to have been concerned that so many conservative moral leaders seem to have taken their cue from conservative political leaders by placing too much faith in free markets rather than moral markets.

On the other hand, and I'll use that phrase often in this book in the interests of balance, confidence in government is still about as low as confidence in Wall Street and a few more progressive moral leaders better understand my reluctance to embrace coercive forms of management by the state.

Apparently, more Americans also no longer have faith in governments to save us, much less the poor. The January 23, 2012 issue of the *Financial Times* documented, "Faith in government plummets." I consider that to be a welcomed development. Religion may teach us to "honor and respect" government, but it also suggests we put our "faith" in an Entity more worthy of our highest beliefs. In short, I continue to believe that our deepest discontents are not with government, markets, the media or the church, but with humanism.

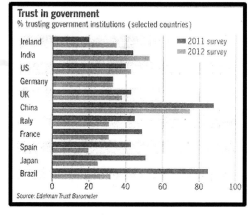

Still, many, if not most, of American conservatives unwittingly believe that "statism," or an economy largely managed by government, is the only known form of "socialism." But many European theologians do not equate the word "social" with "Social Security." They believe Christian forms of voluntary, loving community, as described in the *Book of Acts*, to be another form of socialism. I tell you that not only in the interests of global peace, but domestic as well.

A prominent mainline Christian theologian once said "any serious Christian must be a socialist" and many conservative Christians believe he was a "statist," which isn't necessarily so. My point is that our politicized culture makes it difficult for even conservative Christians and progressive Christians to understand each other, thereby further dividing the Church.

Regardless of how economic terms now create the modern Tower of Babel that is America and our world, I can think of far worse things to grace the tombstone of any leader, or any follower, than being described as realistic and empathetic. This is why I now devote much of the time I'm not engaged in investment counseling, writing or teaching to serving on the board of my local Samaritan Counseling Services, part of a national Christian mental health organization.

My passion at Samaritan, as when counseling investors and writing, is to share the good news with our dispirited but affluent donors and financially needy patients that we just might be walking a path together that has previously been traveled by giants of history. We are blessed indeed.

In gratitude for all our blessings, all profits, if any, from the sale of this book will be dedicated to teaching the holistic stewardship and improved mental health that might enrich faith-based lives.

Further, it is our hope that ministries, denominations, colleges and so on might enrich their own finances, as well as the spirits of their communities, by purchasing this book at quantity discounts and making the book available to their communities. You may inquire about that by contacting the publisher - www.austinbrotherspublishing.com.

Foreword

By David W. Miller

Mixing Faith with Personal & Public Finance

Christianity Today

It is often said there are three things that one should not talk about in polite company: sex, politics, or religion. If you add a fourth one to the list, money, you're sure to have a most lively conversation.

That is what you get when you read anything written by the ever-thoughtful and ever-provocative Gary Moore. As he said in a recent speech at Luther Seminary, "I talk about money, politics, and religion, any one of the three will get me thrown out of this church! But I propose we do it with humility and humor." I empathize with Gary, as I seek to discuss similar subjects through my teaching, research, and programs at the Princeton University Faith & Work Initiative.

I've immensely enjoyed reading the various meditations Gary Moore has written over the years. Whether I agree or disagree with where he lands, he inevitably forces me to think and grow in my relationship to faith and money. He is unusually well equipped to discuss the subject of finance and religion, as he is well credentialed and articulate in both spheres. In addition, he somehow manages to avoid the typical partisan trap into which many of us fall. Sometimes we get so absorbed by our political ideology or theology that we fail to see the inconsistencies or shortcomings of our own logic, let alone express a willingness to find common ground with the people or party we are railing against.

Yet Gary's admirable attempts to avoid partisan bickering can, ironically, sometimes land him in hot water, managing to upset both the left and the right. Or, as Gary once put it, "the truth of the Bible is that it is an equal opportunity offender, having a prophetic word for both left and right, for both Wall Street and Washington." It is in this spirit that Gary seeks to offer a word of constructive critique and eventual hope for all who care about the intersection of money, politics, and religion.

It is my hope that you will enjoy these meditations, and to the extent that they offend us, may we be offended into action and see what discoveries we make about ourselves and our relationship to money, politics, and religion.

David W. Miller, Ph.D.
Princeton University

Executive Summary

"Greedy bankers, overpaid executives, anemic growth, stubbornly high unemployment - these are just a few of the things that have lately driven protesters to the streets and caused the wider public in the developed world to become disgruntled with capitalism. The system, in all its different varieties, is widely perceived to be failing to deliver."

The "Capitalism in Crisis" Series of 2012
The Financial Times

"The biggest threat to America right now is not government spending, huge deficits, foreign ownership of our debt, world terrorism, two wars, potential epidemics or nuts with nukes. **The biggest long-term threat is that people are becoming and have become disheartened, that this condition is reaching critical mass.**"

Peggy Noonan

"When people in Washington talk about deficits and debt, by and large they have no idea what they're talking about - and the people who talk the most understand the least."

Paul Krugman
Nobel Economist & Syndicated Columnist

"The financial crisis is leading to a new model of capitalism... The propensity of modern economic theory for unjustified and over-simplified assumptions allowed politicians, regulators and bankers to create for themselves the imaginary world of market fundamentalist ideology, if government will only step aside. **Although the academic recommendations from the Left and Right differed in almost every particular, including on stimulus spending, they had one striking feature in**

9

*common — a detachment from reality that made them
completely useless for all practical purposes."*

The Wall Street Journal

*"Ethics, in the Judeo-Christian tradition, is the
affirmation that all men and women are alike creatures
— whether the Creator be called God, Nature or Society.
There is only one ethics, one set of rules of morality, one
code, that of individual behavior in which the same rules
apply to everyone alike. And this fundamental axiom
business denies.* **Business ethics, in other words, is not
ethics at all, as the term has commonly been used
by Western philosophers and Western theologians.
Business ethics assumes that for some reason the
ordinary rules of ethics do not apply to business."**

Peter Drucker

*"The people who created this country built a moral
structure around money. The Puritan legacy inhibited
luxury and self-indulgence. For centuries, it remained
industrious, ambitious and frugal. Over the past thirty
years, much of that has been shredded...* **The country's
moral guardians are forever looking out for decadence
out of Hollywood and reality TV. But the most
rampant decadence today is financial decadence,
the trampling of decent norms about how to use and
harness money."**

*Introduction to Enough
John Bogle
Founder, Vanguard Funds*

*"When you lose your way, go back to the beginning and
start again. I believe that everyone has lost their way in
handling the current financial crisis.*

*The "Capitalism in Crisis" Series of 2012
The Financial Times*

"If you wander off the road to the right or the left, you will hear his voice behind you saying, 'Here is the road. Follow it.'"

The Book of The Prophet Isaiah
Chapter Thirty, Verse Twenty One

"The true prophet does not engage in political diatribe to provide a rallying point for any particular course or action. He questions all the powers that be in the name of the one Power beyond them."

James Sanders
Torah and Canon

"In the face of intuition and anecdotal evidence, it is always good to look at the data."

The Economist

"Rather than denigrating Christianity and religion in general, socially conscious elites ought to be asking what the religious impulse can teach us."

Robert Bartley
Editor Emeritus
The Wall Street Journal

*"One absolutely essential prerequisite is: educate, educate, educate. It is really hard to see another way out of the growing sustainability problems that capitalism has given us...**If voters are uninformed and easily swayed towards demagogues peddling short-term, ill-considered policies, there is little hope for righting the course of capitalist countries.**"*

The "Capitalism in Crisis" Series of 2012
The Financial Times

About This Mixed-Up "Mini-Masters in Politics, Economics, Personal Finance, and Judeo-Christian Theology" and It's Equally Mixed-Up Author

"The world economy is made up of many tiny parts that are useful only when we combine them into more complex wholes. The higher the value of these aggregations, the more economic growth. The reason credit and capital have contracted for the past five years in the US and Europe is that the knowledge required to identify and join parts profitably has been unwittingly destroyed. Until this knowledge system is repaired, neither US nor European capitalism will recover."

Economist Hernando De Soto
The "Crisis in Capitalism" Series
The Financial Times
January 30, 2012

The following meditations are largely based on short articles I wrote for various religious and economic publications during and after the Great Recession. They will seem rather critical in places, particularly toward Wall Street. Kindly remember that I was writing them as respected economist A. Gary Shilling was confirming them in the March 2009 issue of his newsletter *Insights*:

"From 2002 to 2008, the five largest Wall Street firms paid $190 billion in bonuses while earning $76 billion in profits. Last year, they had a combined net loss of $25 billion but paid bonuses of $26 billion."

That doesn't mean Wall Street's problems are a thing of the past however. As we finish editing this book in the spring of 2012, a high level Goldman Sachs official has just retired and shocked Wall Street and investors with a scathing editorial in *The New York Times*, March 13, 2012 issue, about the shocking moral decline of the firm during recent years. That's most unusual as the code at Goldman has long been that the more senior the executive, the more secretive he or she is about the firm. Related articles revealed that fully 60%

of Goldman's revenues now come from trading, which is often against the interests of the firm's own clients.

I was therefore tempted to call these meditations "sermons." I decided against that as most Americans simply don't appreciate the art of a true sermon anymore, as good as sermons used to be for our souls. But if there's ever been a time America could have used a good financial sermon, it was surely during the past couple of decades. Still, even meditations require our hearts and souls to be involved in order to understand them, and that might be close enough for our purposes here.

Volumes have been written about the causes of the Great Recession. Most contain some truth; some contain significant truth. However, I take the rarely discussed perspective that our problems, so eloquently echoed by Abraham Lincoln during a time of previous crisis, are due to the biblical reality that a house divided cannot stand.

Even though the economy seems to be slowly recovering as I edit, the American house remains deeply divided, as witnessed by our House of Representatives in Washington. That causes me deep concern for the future, for I believe reality was created to be a very mixed up state, which is quite different from the confused state of our individualistic culture.

During more religious times, we often thought of the Church, and therefore society, as a body. We believed that God had the good sense to give us brains with two lobes to enable clear thinking about our present condition, two eyes for depth perception so we could better judge what's ahead, two legs for the balance we need to walk toward that future, and two hands to work together so that future is richer. Yet today, the "left" and the "right" seem to believe God was wrong to create reality in that fashion, so they are intent on turning the other into itself, or creating reality in their own images. That may not be a good idea.

You may have heard the modern joke about the body parts arguing over which was most important. The brain said it did all the thinking, so it was the most important. The eyes responded that without vision the brain was useless, so they were the most important. The backbone replied the brain and eyes would be helpless if not for its strength, so it was most important. At that point, the rectum made an equal claim of greatness, to which the others laughed. It shut down and three days later, the brain couldn't think, the eyes couldn't see and the body couldn't stand. The point is that a body can have brains, vision and strength, but one dysfunctional rectum can make the entire body quite sick. Reality is that body parts were created to respect each other and work together, without losing their identities as eyes, legs and hands. God only made one rectum so it always work alone.

It could be time for Americans to humbly confess that God may have known what God was doing. We might allow those gifted in government, those gifted in markets, and those gifted in ministry to cooperate. Unfortunately, sociologists tell us that we've closed our minds, closed our eyes and closed our hands, so we too often allow egotistical rectums to really mess things up in the political arena. This mixed-up book will therefore argue it's time for all of us to open ourselves to the idea of letting God mix things up a bit in order to enrich our grandchildren.

Please understand that as this book delves primarily into the moral dimensions of conservative approaches to political economy, its release was timed to avoid the 2012 Republican primary, but soon enough thereafter for the morality of that primary, dismal that it was, to still be fresh in our minds. It has no political agenda other than to suggest Alexander Solzhenitsyn was precisely correct when he said the line between good and evil does not run between political parties and nations but through the heart of every man and woman. He wisely emphasized the word "every."

Yet you should know that until a year or so ago, I was a life-long Republican who had even been on the board of advisors to Jack Kemp and Bill Bennett's Empower America. Jack was a vice-presidential nominee who believed tax cuts could cure cancer. But he was also a Christian and what we might call a "compassionate conservative." Jack had been an all-pro quarterback. He therefore understood that very large, and often black, linemen kept his handsome head from being torn off each Sunday afternoon. So Jack rightly believed in giving every American every opportunity we'd hope for ourselves. Not through governmental welfare necessarily but through equal opportunities for achieving whatever goals we set for ourselves.

I agreed to serve Jack's organization as he eloquently articulated two beliefs that I continue to hold very dearly. They are:

> *"Economics is more than a matter of interest rates and deficits. Morality is more than a matter of stained glass and hymns. Economic success is built on moral foundations.* ***An economy reflects the moral image of its people."***

> *"There are those who say that conservatives must make a choice between a message of economic growth and a message of cultural renewal. Take your side, we are told, and the fight can begin. Make your decision between economics and cultural values. Moments like this call*

*for clarity. So I want to argue as directly as I can: This choice is false; this conflict is destructive; and this decision, if forced on conservatives, would come at an unacceptable cost to our coalition. **It is false in the realm of ideas--because it ignores the full range of human needs.** And it is costly in the realm of politics--because it undermines the coalition of conscience that could transform our nation and renew our culture."*

Still, morality is always about taking the log from your own eye first, while politics is usually about taking the spec from the eyes of others.

As this book will explain, I believe the elites of the GOP made a tragic decision sometime during recent decades to prioritize economic values, almost to the exclusion of cultural renewal. I also believe Jack was proven prophetic as that decision was costly to our culture and is the primary reason the two major factions within the GOP, economic and social conservatives, are at war and the party is in near disarray. I became an Independent when the Tea Party prompted a rightward shift in the GOP, and perhaps America and the world, with the new atheistic and materialistic morality of Ayn Rand, which we will discuss at length.

Yet be assured that I most likely remain on the center-right of the political spectrum, at least as seen from the perspectives of everyone but the far right and the far left. I strongly agree with a recent issue of *The Economist* that said America "is being suffocated by excessive and badly written regulations." It added that for every hour a patient is treated in America, another half hour to hour is needed to do the paperwork; that general regulations add $10,585 to the cost of each employee; and that both parties are at fault:

> *"Republicans write rules to thwart terrorists, which make flying an ordeal and prompt legions of brainy migrants to move to Canada instead. Democrats write rules to expand the welfare state."*

I am also aware that since Democratic President Bill Clinton convinced this nation its primary problem was "the economy stupid," there has been a revolving door between Wall Street, particularly Goldman Sachs, and the White House, including Democratic White Houses. The Democrats' need of Wall Street money has continued with President Obama. While the President promised change, that financial reality of American politics seems to have actually changed for the worse during his administration, albeit largely due to the Supreme Court's ruling that campaign money is a form of free speech. That is likely one reason so many of his supporters believe that so many of his more populist campaign promises have gone unfulfilled.

It is therefore my guess that until we Americans understand and deal with the role of money in politics, which is a deeply moral issue, neither party

is going to make Americans very happy. As we will see, I believe that's been true since the Bible addressed the role of money and governance. This book therefore suggests that we need to look up rather than left or right, assuming we don't want our children to have a lower standard of living, defined both spiritually and materially.

The book's name was suggested by Garrett Moore, my son, best friend, and partner in business and ministry. He also designed the cover and did significant editing on the book, which I told him was a learning opportunity for him. (I don't think he bought that however being the young capitalist that he is!) The colors red and blue refer to the Republican and Democratic parties of course. The purple is a blend. It suggests Americans can overcome their political and economic differences, as well as their anxieties about the future, only through faith and love for one another. That is why purple is also associated with royalty, including the lordship of Christ Jesus.

I have no delusions of being a writer, which is why I'm so very grateful God created editors. My sister, Karen, helped a great deal in that regard. She was a high school English teacher before attending law school. So if you find errors, she would argue in a most articulate fashion that I'm the guilty party. She would be correct of course, as she's been all our lives. Yet informality is a southern disease that I enjoy having, so I do not care for the formal rules of writing, or anything else for that matter. Yet understand that I did not pay Karen for her work. So while she's far more intelligent than I am, I'm still persuasive enough to convince her that I get the snow sled going down the hill while she gets it coming back up! That, too, will likely be true all our lives, shameful as it might be on my part.

Also understand that I had no thoughts of compiling this book until very recently. I therefore do not always have dates for the graphs. I had simply filed the graphs for my use with our investment clients. I have used some of the quotes in my teaching seminars the past twenty years and also cannot date many of them. However, I would like to express my gratitude to *The Economist* who most graciously allowed me to use their graphs without cost as The Financial Seminary is a tiny non-profit. I paid a royalty to *The Wall Street Journal*, and was happy to do so. Still, that may reflect the reality, which you may notice over and over in this book, that the European financial media often seems to have more of a social conscious than does the American financial media.

It might also be important to you that I have a degree in political science from the University of Kentucky. I thought that would be quite useless upon entering Wall Street and contemplating seminary, but I was quite wrong on both accounts. Politics may not be omniscient but it's omnipresent, meaning it may not know everything but it's sure everywhere. I became an artillery officer during the seventies as I was quite good with mathematics. Be assured that while miscalculations about our political economy cause all sorts of long-term problems that are usually not seen today, miscalculating for artillery pieces causes very immediate, visible, and unpleasant consequences. So it was a good place for learning the need to be respectful of numbers.

I likely became a senior vice president of investments at Paine Webber during the 1980's due to the same ability with, and attitude toward, numbers. Unfortunately, the logic of mathematics will never help you understand Washington or human nature. I therefore thought about attending seminary. I quickly discovered seminaries no longer taught the moral dimensions of managing this world's wealth, despite such teachings being favorite topics of Moses, Jesus and the church fathers.

I began informal study of the subject and later founded The Financial Seminary, a non-profit educational group, to build bridges between the financial and moral communities. I also founded my own small, family-oriented investment firm as "counsel to ethical and spiritual investors." Desiring to model Christ to the best of our humble abilities, the company has no minimum requirements and provides counsel to anyone needing our help.

The last two of my five previous books on this subject were *Spiritual Investments and Faithful Finances 101* (John Templeton Foundation Press.) My views have appeared in publications such as *Christianity Today, The Wall Street Journal, The Christian Science Monitor, Money, Christian Ethics Today, BusinessWeek,* and have been expounded as classes for the *Good $ense Financial Ministry* which is affiliated with the Willow Creek Association.

I have served as a board member of the John Templeton Foundation; a trustee of Messiah College, serving on its investment committee; a board advisor to Bill Bennett and Jack Kemp's Empower America; the board treasurer of Opportunity International, a micro-enterprise organization; a trustee of Robert Schuller's Crystal Cathedral, chairing its endowment committee during its peak years; the board of my YMCA; the board of Samaritan Counseling Services of the Gulf Coast; a lay leader of both a Lutheran and an Episcopal church; and a financial commentator for UPI Radio and Skylight Radio. I live and work with my family in Sarasota, Florida.

You can learn more about us and our educational group at

www.financialseminary.org.

Part One

The Illusions of
Politics, Profits & Punditry

"What is Truth?"

Pontius Pilate

"If Jesus came back today and walked on water, the media would report that he can't swim."

Unknown

Preface

Illusions & Reality

"This is all an illusion. This is a lovely, tender illusion. We're all running around being busy and doing important things but this has nothing to do with anything. Up there God and the angels are looking down and laughing, and not unkindly. They just find us touching and dizzy."

Peggy Noonan
Life, Liberty and The Pursuit of Happiness

"Keep your face to the sunshine and you cannot see the shadow."

Helen Keller

Centuries before Jesus walked this earth, Plato taught his famous "allegory of the cave." If you're not familiar with it, you should be. It may be the most important parable outside the Bible for our media saturated society. It somewhat reflects the words of Solomon that "all is vanity."

Plato essentially said most of us confuse reality with shadows that are made by others, like politicians, the media and those who write popular books that tell us what we want to hear. The allegory adds that we grow quite attached to those shadows, rather than the light of enlightenment.

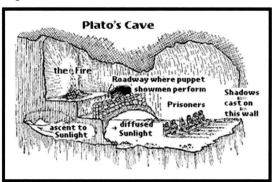

For this reason, we are often unkind toward well-intentioned attempts to enlighten us. Personally, I always tell my pastor I sit on the very back row not because I grew up Baptist, but because I'm always afraid he will hit me. I also tell him that if he doesn't stop preparing

Source Unknown

sermons specifically for me, I'm going to stop coming to services. Such is human nature.

Most of this book will describe how we have let human nature undermine our divine nature during recent decades, particularly in the areas of our nation's political economy and our personal finances. But the *Good Book* says there are two things we must do before curing culture of its ills: First, we must take the log from our own eyes before we can see to take the specs from the eyes of others, and second, we must confess that the judgment of a nation begins in the house of the Lord. I must therefore begin by confessing financial shadows cast by my investment firm and my American church.

As an independent investment planner, I am part of a national organization that handles my securities trades, custody of securities, legal issues, and such. I chose the organization as it specializes in helping brokers help individual investors. So it never promotes options, commodities, and other very speculative investments that, to me anyway, are little, if any, more than gambling. That doesn't mean we don't cast our own shadows on occasion.

For example, we annually have a national convention for our "top producers." There are literally hundreds and hundreds of us each year. When we last gathered, the president, who is a dear Christian lady, began by showing a touching video of "why we are here." It compassionately detailed that half of all Americans have no savings. There were few dry eyes in the place when the video finished. Unfortunately, we then spent the next two days listening to consultants tell us that to be "successful" in this business, we have to get rid of clients with few assets and focus on those with lots of money.

Emotions often prevent our understanding such tensions between perceptions and realities.

For example, my wife and partner Sherry was particularly impressed with one lady who delivered a key-note address. The speaker was marvelously humorous and truly entertaining, so I too enjoyed her talk. But Peter Drucker taught business leaders that the only criterion of successful meetings and talks is whether they change future behavior or not. Entertaining people is rarely a good reason for having business meetings and talks. So upon hearing Sherry say she was going to stay in touch with the speaker, I asked what she had said that would change Sherry's behavior in the future. Sherry couldn't think of anything. She added that she simply liked the speaker.

As I am also a speaker and like for people to like me, I went a bit deeper. Sherry finally said she wouldn't even listen to facts from someone she doesn't like. That hit me hard as my presentations are often prophetic and are typically factual, which means dull in places. And I've long known that I rarely impress Sherry in particular. But I now feel better as Sherry is a bubbly and emotional personality and, like most people, likes other people who are just like her. So she has largely avoided the economics that I constantly study as economics is often called "the dismal science" and economists are rarely bubbly and entertaining.

Still, there are good reasons for Sherry to know some of the things that economists know. I believe there are equally good reasons for you to know them as well, even if you too prefer emotions and entertainment to reason and facts. For example, if you are just beginning to establish a nest-egg, you should know that there are many planners at our company, like my son who is just entering our business, who are more than happy to help anyone put $25 away each month. But they are not usually among the experienced, top producers of Wall Street. Such is present-day capitalism. It seems so wonderful in concept that each of us can grow more financially secure with the assistance of experienced professionals like those at our conference; but the realities of capitalism tend to be more harsh in practice.

It's much the same with the Church. If you were to ask a hundred Christian ministers today how to pursue a more abundant life, defined as both material and spiritual, the odds are good ninety or more would tell you to seek out a good church. Yet Christ told us to "seek first the Kingdom of God," and there's a big difference in the Kingdom and a church. The Kingdom includes the Church, hopefully, but is much, much larger. The limited perspective of pastors has been ably documented by religious sociologist Robert Wuthnow of Princeton. He implied the four walls of a church can make a wonderful cave for casting financial shadows when he wrote this passage, which my experiences affirm:

> *"When we asked pastors to talk to us about stewardship, we encouraged them to tell us how they understood it in the broadest possible terms. Repeatedly, however, we found the church was their only frame of reference. They immediately talked about serving the church, doing church work, and giving money to the church."*

That's also not a very good prescription for making the Church relevant to a money culture. We church leaders might reflect on the original meaning of "sacrifice." In ancient times, people of faith literally burned the best of their wealth, which was usually livestock. Later prophets understood that wasn't doing much for the widows, orphans and needy; but such sacrifices had the distinct spiritual advantage of constantly reminding believers that God had graciously supplied enough that they had wealth to burn.

Today, the only such practice in our culture is when people smoke forty dollar Cuban cigars, which is a fairly reliable indicator that markets are getting speculative by the way. Absent that, even our churches unwittingly but routinely send the message that we don't have enough to get by. So I routinely counsel investors who have wealth that would have been unimaginable to the ancients who are living in anxiety, even fear, over the future. Such anxiety begins where faith ends. So in the interests of resurrecting faith while letting anxiety die, please notice from the following chart that even the contemporaries of Jesus lived on four hundred and fifty 1990 dollars annually, which would be about nine hundred dollars per year in today's dollars. Similarly, even today, the typical human being lives on about ten thousand dollars annually in today's dollars.

This book will therefore argue that if politics is too important to leave to politicians and the economy is too important to leave to economists, our faith is definitely too important to leave to the clergy. If the clergy are not going to help the laity build the Kingdom of God, at

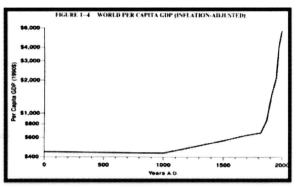

The World Economy by Agnus Maddison, p.264

the very least, they should not prevent the laity from doing so. And there is considerable evidence that most are doing just that, particularly when it comes to economics and our finances. In fact, my mentor Sir John Templeton, the mutual fund manager and major funder of religion around the world, used to say the Church has defaulted economic morality to the secular world. You will likely understand his perspective if you continue to read.

Second, most Christian clergy begin stewardship messages on pledge card Sunday with the illusion of asking us to give to God. But stewardship theology begins, and probably ends, by us acknowledging we humans cannot give anything to God. God has always owned it all, owns it all now, and will own it a thousand years after we're long gone.

Despite what our financial ministries pragmatically teach those in bondage to credit card debt, reality is that God has simply loaned a tiny portion of God's wealth to us for a short time to steward. Stewards never actually own anything; they simply manage what they've borrowed from the true owner, and for a very short period of time in the scheme of things. Contrary to what we're often told by Christian financial ministries, we're also to further lend what has been loaned to us when it is needed.

Reality is therefore that stewards can simply allocate some of God's resources to the moral, economic, and spiritual development of the Kingdom, which is far beyond the walls of our churches.

Until we embrace those realities, I do not believe God can ever bless America's churches, and therefore America's political economy and our personal finances. That doesn't mean we won't have more and more material wealth. It just means we won't ever be happy with it. Alexis de Tocqueville surveyed America during more religious times and famously said humankind was created with a desire for both heaven and earth. It is precisely that reason that I can hope, at this moment of seeming economic crisis that our taste for heaven is returning. Nearly a century ago, the controversial British economist John Maynard Keynes said:

> *"For at least another hundred years we must pretend to ourselves and to everyone that fair is foul and foul is fair; for foul is useful and fair is not. Avarice and usury must be our gods for a little while longer still."*

Time may nearly be up for the shadows that perverted capitalism into what is often referred to as "casino capitalism" or "winner-take-all capitalism," which has been further perverted into "loser-still-take-a lot capitalism." That will grow clearer as we proceed, but for the moment understand that Peggy Noonan was President Reagan's favorite speech writer. She is now a senior writer for *The Wall Street Journal* and one of its most spiritually insightful. She is therefore uniquely qualified to write passages, like the one at the beginning of this preface, about the intersection of faith, politics and economics.

As a conservative, Ms. Noonan probably agrees with little that Keynes taught, but she clearly agrees that we have been living in an age of illusion. Their agreement on that one subject, plus the disillusionment of so many Americans, is enough to make me more hopeful for the future.

Plato was collectivist in his thinking and is therefore often considered one of the world's first communists. He was actually both progressive and conservative, suggesting he might approve of America's "mixed economy." In *The Republic*, he suggested the ruling elite, who he called "guardians," should own no private wealth as doing so might interfere with their exercising responsibilities for the citizenry. As we will see, Moses rather agreed with him about that (Deuteronomy 17:17). Yet, Plato also thought it was fine for us common folk to own wealth. That mixed-up, or nuanced, way of thinking might go a long way in lessening the tensions between today's "1%" and the "99%."

Over the decades, I have grown to believe that the majority of our division and confusion is due to the fact that we live in a materialistic culture, which we call capitalism. As with people, the great strength of capitalism is also its great weakness. For example, psychologists have told me that my strength is my sense of insight, or being able to see what others often cannot. My weakness therefore is not being able to see what is apparent.

That is why my fashion-conscious wife used to tell me often to change the shirt I'd chosen to go with my slacks. I grew so weary of that I began wearing khaki pants with black shirts. I wore some white shirts until she told me black made me look ten pounds thinner. Now my friends think I'm trying to imitate Steve Jobs or a Catholic priest. But I even buy shoes and belts that mix black and brown so I don't embarrass Sherry by getting that wrong. We all have to know, embrace, and mix our strengths and weaknesses as both are God-given. An integrated life is simply less stressful than a life of dichotomies in tension. And stress can be as harmful and costly to you financially as medically.

Cultures are simply the sum total of the strengths and weaknesses of individuals, so we need to know, embrace, and mix with others. That is essential in our economy.

The great strength, as well as weakness, of capitalism is called the "division of labor." For example, few people any longer know how to build a house. One person knows how to pour the foundation. Another knows how to frame the house. Another knows how to install the electricity.

It's the same way with building a capitalistic culture. One person knows how to do politics. Another economics. Another morality. And so on. Unfortunately, that too often means politicians don't know anything about economics. Most economists, who tend to be the secular priests of materialism anyway, don't know anything about Judeo-Christian morality. Our personal financial advisors don't know much about politics, economics or morality. And so on. So we often get very conflicting advice about how to build our American home. It's also quite difficult to know who is sharing truth and who is making shadows. That is also the reason this book may be a frustrating, even difficult, read for many people, for three particular reasons:

First, we all make shadows as we're all human, even the best of the Church. For example, consider all those ministries that tell us they'll end global poverty if we'll just send a check. Reality is more difficult, which is why Jesus assured us that the poor will be with us always. You'll never hear it from a ministry of compassion but **there are actually four times as many people on earth today living on a dollar a day or less than there was when Christ walked this earth.**

25

Americans gave about three hundred billion dollars to charity last year. Half of that went to religious causes, and studies tell us very little of that was passed on to the poor. Reality is that in the scheme of things, that amount of giving to all the churches in America barely keeps the lights on. Much of the other half went to colleges and such.

In other words, a significant percentage of "charity" in America actually funds the business of teaching compassion, rather than actually goes toward practicing it.

I learned that difficult reality many years ago when speaking with Henri Nouwen. Henri had been a professor at Harvard, Yale and Notre Dame before moving to Canada to live with some of God's "special needs" children. Over breakfast, I asked him why the change. He replied he'd taught Christianity so long that he'd decided to give living it a try. I've been working toward that goal ever since, even as I've taught through The Financial Seminary. Maybe I too will one day live more as Jesus and Henri did and experience the bliss on earth that they knew by giving all they had. Until then, I'll content myself with the very mixed blessings of trying to give more financially blessed Americans what knowledge I have about God and God's world.

The Church is quite similar. The finances of my local church, and it's quite affluent, would not make a good case study in Christian stewardship. That's a confession on the part of a past president, but not anecdotal evidence. Studies by Empty Tomb and others reveal the difficult reality that a very small amount of even Christian charity goes to the global poor. That's quite ironic as Christ taught, "sell what you have and give it to the poor," rather than temples, evangelists, radio stations, charitable organizations and even foundations that spend enormous sums trying to learn why we haven't solved global poverty despite having more than adequate resources. As that great theologian Pogo taught, the enemy in the war on global poverty just might be us.

The world's markets had a total capitalization of $212 trillion in 2010, according to *The Economist*. So even if *all the charity* given in America last year went to the poor of our world, it would amount to about one one-thousandth of the capital sloshing around our world.

Let's put that word "trillion" in perspective. If a million dollars was a marble, a billion dollars would be a beach ball, and a trillion would be a hot air balloon. We can only wish that charitable giving had grown as quickly as the world's capital. I strongly believe that one reason it hasn't is that the Church likely has not created, and certainly hasn't taught, a theology for capitalism.

We should also understand that as huge as our accumulated $15 trillion or so of federal debt sounds, global GDP, or income, will be over $75 trillion this year alone. While the average American will enjoy $50,000 of purchasing power this year, the typical global citizen will enjoy $11,000, which is skewed upward by our incomes. We can also only wish that those financial ministries that lament the growth in debt, as serious as it has become, would occasionally put it into the context of our assets and income for better perspective.

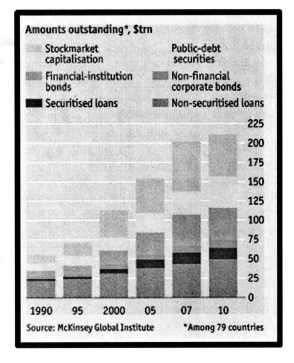

Amounts outstanding*, $trn

Stockmarket capitalisation

Public-debt securities

Financial-institution bonds

Non-financial corporate bonds

Securitised loans

Non-securitised loans

225
200
175
150
125
100
75
50
25
0

1990   95   2000   05   07   10

Source: McKinsey Global Institute   *Among 79 countries

To make matters even more difficult, some of that tidal wave of capital has been carelessly invested in industries and governments that aren't particularly sensitive to the needs of the poor. Some of that capital actually preys on the poor.

Reality is therefore that despite the good intentions, and we know where those lead, of those soliciting our donations for the most seemingly virtuous causes, we will never dent the plight of the poor until we invest more heart, mind and even soul in assuring the markets of the world are moral, as well as free.

The second reason this may be a difficult read has to do with self-deception rather than deceptions created by others. Whereas atheism teaches us that there is no God, "secular" culture teaches us that it's alright to believe in God as long as we don't let God meddle in politics, economics and our personal finances -- our earning, spending, investing and so on. This is far more dangerous than atheism as we seem to acknowledge God while living as "functional atheists," as one Christian sociologist says. This book therefore attempts to re-integrate what are normally "compartmentalized" dimensions of American life. It will therefore occasionally seem unfocused and repetitious as we moderns prefer to keep differing subjects in different compartments.

If you've studied the Bible, you know that connecting various aspects of life, and doing so repeatedly, is necessary to develop a more holistic way of thinking and living. If love is God's way of connecting people, thinking is God's way of connecting the various dimensions of our lives. Please don't let the repetition bother you as educators say we need to hear something six or more times before we even remember it, much less believe it. For example, my son Garrett has a degree in international finance and kept asking me whether I hadn't used a passage previously. The fact he couldn't remember suggests repetition of major points doesn't hurt. Still, each meditation has some new aspect of life about which we need to think or I wouldn't have included it. As with the Bible, this book teaches through stories, history, facts, myths which may be fictional but teach a reality of life, and so on.

Virtually every book in the Bible also seems mixed-up, or integrated, by talking about the connections between love, grace, peace, prosperity, and so on. The ancients never considered dividing those areas of reality as cleanly as we do. For example, the "wisdom literature" often attributed to Solomon teaches theology, politics, economics and personal finance. Despite all his earlier problems at balancing material and spiritual wealth, the more mature Solomon's way of thinking did not require four separate books on four different subjects. That meant he did not divide the way he lived into political life, economic life, religious life, and so on.

As do the meditations of this book, virtually everything Solomon inspired or wrote, and lived later in life, mixed those various dimensions of reality. It might even surprise you that the original authors of the books of the Bible found no need to break those books into chapters and verses for our convenience. Yet from the time we moderns enter school, we are taught to divide knowledge about life into focused "classes." This aids in our understanding of individual fields. Yet it too often keeps us from connecting dots that should be connected. Connecting those dots is what we call "thinking," rather than simply learning disconnected facts. As this book is rather questioning of how conservative Christians think, or more often do not think, it might resemble an economic version of Professor Mark Noll's book entitled *The Scandal of The Evangelical Mind*.

Though he wrote that book while Professor of Christian Thought at Wheaton College, Professor Noll began by saying the scandal of the evangelical mind is that there isn't much of an evangelical mind. If that is true in general, it is true in spades when it comes to political economy and personal finance.

The scandal, actually more of a tragedy, is that separating politics, economics, personal finance and our faith causes confusion in our thinking, even when attempted. That produces conflict in our spirits, usually making us anxious and angry, separating us from God's peace. That, in turn, often causes confusion and anxiety in our political economy, often separating us from the love of our neighbors.

A very simple example is that many of my politically conservative clients want to get rid of government, but they also insist on government-guaranteed investments and/or that our military prevent foreign threats as the border patrol secures our jobs for Americans. Unfortunately, to paraphrase President Reagan, any government big enough to guarantee our wealth and jobs, is also big enough to take all our wealth and jobs.

That is why, with the possible exception of Proverbs and Ecclesiastes, it is quite dangerous to simply pull a Bible verse out of context. Not to compare my writing to the Bible, but it will be much the same with this book. I hope you will read this book in its entirety before judging it. As with the Bible, you have a choice about how to read it, i.e., you can decide what you believe and find a few passages that agree with you, which is how most Christians develop their worldviews these days, or you can read it in its entirety and decide if it's the worldview for you.

The third and final reason this book may be a difficult read for many is its encouraging economic perspective will be quite different from the tribal drum-beat of negativity to which most Americans are accustomed. Capitalist culture, which is quite self-oriented and self-protecting, teaches us to count the threats to our material well-being. Christian spirituality teaches a less selfish approach and to count our blessings, or, more accurately, should teach us to do so.

Everyone I talk to therefore has repeatedly heard the size of the federal debt from politicians and the media, including Christian financial ministries. Yet I have never met a single American who has *even once* heard the size our nation's assets estimated. I've asked tens of thousands when speaking across America, including several professors of economics at Christian colleges. *So we've essentially worried about the size of our mortgage without knowing the value of our home.*

Yet the same people who estimate our federal debt each year also estimate the size of our nation's assets each year. It grows worse for Christians as St. Paul told us in Philippians 4:8 to "put your minds on the things that are good and deserve praise." Following culture rather than Scripture is precisely why so many of us are dispirited. I will therefore share economic facts you've likely never read or heard. I do not mean to imply that any reader is stupid, but studies do tell us that most Americans are ignorant of many facts discussed in this book. As I finish editing, the January 7, 2012 issue of *The Wall Street Journal* has just confirmed that by saying:

> "Americans Stumble on Math of Big Issues: Many Americans have strong opinions about policy issues shaping the presidential campaign,

from immigration to Social Security. But their grasp of numbers that underlie those issues can be tenuous. Americans vastly over-estimate the percentage of fellow residents who are foreign-born, by more than a factor of two, and the percentage who are in the country illegally, by a factor of six or seven. They over-estimate spending on foreign aid by a factor of 25, according to a 2010 survey. And more than two-thirds of those who responded to a 2010 Zogby on-line poll under-estimated the part of the federal budget that goes to Social Security or Medicare and Medicaid. 'It's pretty apparent that Americans routinely don't know objective facts about the government,' says Joshua Clinton, a political scientist at Vanderbilt University."

So now that we better understand our illusions, let's look at some more facts.

Introduction

Rationally, Yet Soulfully, Pursuing Economic Truth

*"Unless thought is valid, we have no reason to believe in
the real universe."*

C.S. Lewis

*"You can ignore the newspapers and be uninformed or
you can read them and be misinformed."*

Mark Twain

Politicians, the media, corporate advertisers, Wall Street, academics, televangelists and even many pastors seem to increasingly appeal to our emotions, often in order to separate us from our money. Perhaps you too have noticed that advertisements very rarely discuss the actual product anymore, but simply create a feeling of some type.

The Judeo-Christian tradition has long taught that prudent finance, both personal and public, is primarily rational. As examples, our Wisdom Literature, primarily Proverbs and Ecclesiastes of the Jewish Scriptures, contains considerable sound thinking about money. The ancient *Didache*, perhaps the earliest guide to living the Christian life, counseled that we should let our alms sweat in our palms for awhile before even giving, thereby giving us a period to think. I would suggest we might do the same before making political contributions, investments, purchases and donations to televangelists.

This could therefore be a good place to share a most important story. In ancient times, there was a great military commander who contracted a deadly disease. Just like today, someone told him there was a miraculous cure in a foreign land. So the commander asked his friend the king if he would introduce him to the king of the foreign land. The king did so by providing a letter of introduction that explained why the commander had entered the second king's land. Upon reading the letter, the second king grew very angry as the thought the first king had insulted him by expecting him to cure the commander. But someone told the king not to be angry as, unlike today, there really was a miracle cure in the land, in the form of a man of God. So the king sent the commander to the man of God.

The man of God told the commander to simply go and dip seven times in the local river and he would be cured. Now the commander was angry. Being patriotic, he reasoned the rivers in his homeland were better than the local rivers. Being accustomed to doing great deeds, he had expected to do great things in order to be cured. So he wouldn't do the simple thing the man of God told him to do. Fortunately, a lowly servant convinced him to do so. When the commander finally cooperated, he was cured. You can read the full account of that story in the Bible in the *Book of Second Kings* (chapter five).

I remind you of that story as there are parallels between that great, proud commander and modern America. We too have our illnesses. And we too look to the king, or politics, to cure them. So it makes no sense to most Americans, and angers many of them, when I've suggested over the years that **Judeo-Christianity has told us repeatedly through such stories that curing our illnesses is as simple as looking at what our IRA's, endowment funds, and so on are financing in our world.**

While our modern world is quite different than the ancient world in many ways, the root of all pathologies simply hasn't changed. Unfortunately, American religion has changed its attitudes about the root of all evil as we live in a money-loving culture. So if you are a conservative Christian, you are probably concerned with politicians' views on abortion; but it's equally likely that you never think about a problem of financing pharmaceutical and health care companies that profit from abortion.

This book therefore aspires to help you make *spiritual sense* of our world, hopefully enriching your life spiritually, and *possibly* financially, while making the world your children will inherit an increasingly moral place. That word "possibly" should indicate this book is most definitely *not* "prosperity gospel," perhaps the most un-Christian financial teaching in modern America, and therefore a source of considerable evil. For the uninitiated, prosperity gospel is the claim that Judeo-Christian morality must, and inevitably will, result in material riches for every believer. That claim was obviously soundly discredited by the financial ups and downs of the biblical Job, not to mention the fate of Jesus and his disciples.

We might therefore note that while Moses sometimes seemed to preach prosperity gospel to his band of ex-slaves, which is fodder for too many televangelists, Moses was always speaking to the Hebrew nation at large.

That's why he made quite adequate provision for poor individuals in the Promised Land. Some early Jewish people also missed that nuance and thereby questioned the faithfulness of Job, who had fallen on hard times. My father read that *Book of Job* over and over during the year before he died of cancer at the age of fifty five. *The Book of Job*, the *Book of James*, many teachings of St. Paul, and considerable church history are simply ignored by preachers of the prosperity gospel, usually as that gospel is quite good for the prosperity of those preaching it.

Instead, this book is a nuanced explanation of why Jesus himself suggested the truly moral and spiritual life is about "having life and having it more abundantly." It therefore seeks to enrich lives by providing ordinary, but thoughtful and truth-seeking Americans, particularly pastors and Christian leaders, with a multi-disciplinary, mini-masters in economics, politics, personal finance and Judeo-Christian morality.

Our subject is essentially holistic stewardship. Not the kind we usually hear about in church on pledge card Sunday as we pay those necessary bills, and certainly not the kind we hear from those television ministers suggesting God is a cosmic slot machine, wherein we insert a coin into their ministries and we immediately experience a "hundred-fold" return.

While I am hardly a decent disciple, much less prophet, this book intentionally seeks to share prophetic insights from those who may be prophets. Still, I might point out that Moses had to live in Pharaoh's palace before he could help the Hebrews understand how to free themselves from Pharaoh's oppressive rule. Jesus had to be Jewish to help his contemporaries understand how to free themselves of the oppressing legalism of the Law of Moses. While there's no comparison between Moses, Jesus and myself, I have had to live in the illusions of capitalism so I might help you to better understand how to free yourself of such illusions.

Such counter-cultural teachings are usually difficult reading for

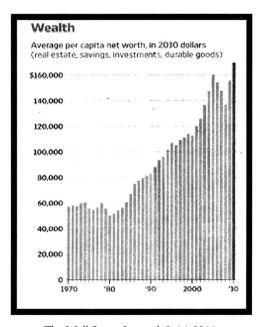

Wealth

Average per capita net worth, in 2010 dollars (real estate, savings, investments, durable goods)

The Wall Street Journal, 9-14-2011

all of us. They can be even tougher on the clergy as a primary role of the biblical prophets was to keep the priests on the right path. While I love many clergy, and respect them for the difficult, sometimes impossible, jobs they have, I have to admit that most clergy I know could benefit from a prophetic voice when it comes to America's political economy and our personal finances. Even many clergy seem convinced that America's primary problem is that it doesn't have enough wealth, a perception that is clearly disputed by facts.

As we'll explore later, it's definitely true that much of that wealth has gone to the so-called "1%." But it's also pure illusion that no one other than Wall Street financiers have prospered since 1980, when President Reagan took office. Politicians and the media too often leave that impression by focusing on manufacturing. But the February 23, 2012 issue of the *Financial Times* detailed the reality that "net farm income" in the United States has risen from around thirty-three billion dollars in 1980 to approximately eighty billion dollars in 2012. And that's in constant, or inflation-adjusted, 2005 dollars.

Studies also tell us the average American believes foreign aid is a major expense in the federal budget and that we might better balance our budget by cutting it. I'll leave the last belief to the political process, but I will argue we should make that decision based on facts and not illusions. America has long given a lower percentage of its GDP, at about 3/10ths of one percent, as official foreign aid than most major nations, and much of that goes for military and corporate purposes.

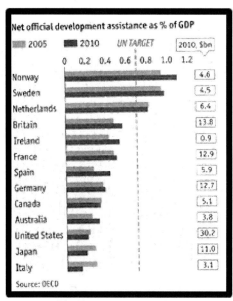

The Economist, 4-9-2011

This book aspires to help both religious and non-religious readers. If you are religious, you will hopefully better understand how to actually live your faith in a rather hostile culture of secularism and materialism. Religious sociologists tell us few Christians, the majority of religious Americans, do so today. Very simply, you cannot be a holistic, conservative Christian, particularly of the "Bible-believing" sort, and believe that government, abortion or homosexuality is the root of all evil. You cannot detest, rather than love, your political opponents.

You cannot believe it's actually quite easy to be rich and enter that old eye of the needle. Yet, you also cannot believe that Jesus was wrong to say that it's possible for the rich to do so "with God." My preferred interpretation of the eye, and there are several, is that it was a low gate in the wall surrounding Jerusalem. To enter, the camel had to hit his knees and bend his proud neck. In other words, it's not easy but can be achieved with sufficient humility.

If you are non-religious, you might better understand why Professor Robert Fogel, a religious skeptic with a Nobel Prize in economics, recently wrote a book entitled *The Fourth Great Awakening* which said:

> **"One cannot understand current political or ethical trends, or properly forecast future economic developments, without understanding the cycles in religious feelings in American history."**

This book might also help the non-religious reader better understand a major sector of America's political economy that often confuses, even frustrates, many Americans. You probably know that sector as "the religious right," though you may confuse it with "Evangelical Christianity," both of which can be more emotional than rational. If you are typical, you also probably think the religious right, evangelicals and conservatives are simply a homogeneous voting bloc. If so, you need a more nuanced worldview as badly as many members of the religious right do.

Leaders of the religious right met in Texas during January 2012 to anoint an "anti-Romney" candidate. After that group failed to do so the first day, Ralph Reed, a long-time leader of the religious right, told *The Wall Street Journal* that his fellow leaders couldn't agree on what to have for lunch, much less anoint a candidate. After those leaders eventually opted to support Senator Rick Santorum, conservative Christians in South Carolina played a major role in propelling Newt Gingrich to a surprising and decisive victory. This increasing political balkanization and independence of moral leadership, particularly among conservatives, was likely inevitable.

By definition, the further right you move on the political spectrum, from progressive to moderate to conservative to libertarian, the more you move from believing in the supremacy of the collective to believing in the supremacy of the individual. A major theme of this book is Christ's phrase "neighbor as self" is about balance, while also transcending the political term "moderate" by being about "how much love," rather than "how much government?"

Perhaps contrary to popular perception, particularly among conservatives, I believe this book will demonstrate that our country's thinking about political-economy has moved further right during recent years, even if it's debatable that our *activities* have. As that happens, we've thought less of ourselves as Americans and divisively thought of ourselves as progressive Americans, conservative Americans and libertarian Americans. Then we move even closer to a balkanized state by thinking of ourselves as conservative Christian Americans, progressive Christian Americans, and so on.

It was therefore inevitable that very conservative Christians would follow that trend to the point they'd think of themselves, and divide themselves, into economic and social conservatives. Then add that more and more Christians who believe they are conservative are actually libertarian, actually disdainful of government rather than simply wanting it relatively small, and even the Church begins to resemble a Balkan nation. Yet reality remains that any house divided cannot stand. I believe that is as true of the Church and political parties as of nations.

Extremism in anything but love is contrary to God's law, or at least natural laws like gravity.

Politics, economics and religion tend to be self-correcting, if only after considerable and avoidable impoverishment of the type we experience when we jump off a ten story building as we think we can fly. That could be a very short summary of Judeo-Christian Scripture and tradition, as well as the fate of nations.

This book also argues that we all have a religion, wittingly or unwittingly, when religion is defined as having a hierarchy of values. Therefore, this book aspires to put the seeking of truth, rather than winning of elections, getting you into the *Forbes* list of the four hundred richest Americans, or even the proclamation of truth, at the top of our values. That necessarily dictates a humble approach. It also dictates a somewhat slanted perspective for the book. As the book aspires to be moral rather than political, it primarily seeks a constructive critique of conservatives and their aspirations for our political economy.

The kind of holistic stewardship we therefore aspire to convey is the kind about which the Bible taught many centuries before Adam Smith unwittingly isolated what we call "economics" from moral philosophy.

He did so with his book commonly called *The Wealth of Nations*. Few people seem to have read it, but most businesspeople are familiar with its most cited passage: that bakers enrich society by simply acting selfishly in business. Recent years have clearly demonstrated why we transport money, rather than bakery goods, in armored cars. That's a way of saying the parasitic activities of high frequency traders and proprietary traders in our banks, as well as vulture-like activities of some sub-prime mortgage originators, hedge funds and private equity funds, indicate our economy needs a more relevant ethic than the one Smith provided for baking croissants and sticky buns. *Smart Money*, the magazine of *The Wall Street Journal*, even estimated in its February 2012 issue that simply the fine print utilized by businesses these days, which is a form of shadow-making, costs consumers $250 billion *a year*. For perspective, that is not far below total charitable giving in the United States last year.

The "casino capitalists" of our culture might therefore remember that Smith was actually a highly-regarded professor of moral philosophy who rose to fame with his previous book entitled *A Theory of Moral Sentiments*. Unlike most stewardship committees and televangelists simply raising money, Smith began that book by acknowledging this spiritual reality about humankind:

> **"How selfish soever man may be supposed, there are evidently some principles in his nature, which interest him in the fortunes of others, and render their happiness necessary to him, though he derives nothing from it except the pleasure of seeing it."**

Such nuanced and balanced realities are usually grayer than the simple black and white ways of thinking and living in our political economy that our culture seems to prefer these days. It may be ironic but it often seems to me that the more financial information bombards us 24/7, the more we simplistically think we just have to politically decide if it's government or business that's evil. That is precisely why the Bible did not come as *Cliffsnotes*. Yes, Jesus could make the really important foundations of reality as simple as a parable. Unfortunately, your author is hardly Jesus.

I'm also trying to explain some things that Jesus seemed to have had no interest in whatsoever. If Jesus didn't sweat the small stuff, our culture encourages us to sweat it 24/7. Jesus also asked his disciples not to worry about what they would wear, eat or drink in the future. Plan yes; worry no.

Yet most Christians take the cultural, which means materialistic, approach and worry a great deal about the economic future. As has been wisely said, the beginning of anxiety is the end of faith. I therefore need to explain why this three decade veteran of Wall Street now devoutly believes Jesus was quite right to teach us to focus on far more important matters and then have faith that economic matters will fall in line. My teachers tried to teach me that in Sunday School, but of course I had to learn it the hard and expensive way. Hopefully, this book will save you that spiritual and financial impoverishment.

That will hopefully help to save our nation. It could use our help. But several years ago, the conservative Heritage Foundation sought to prove religion is socially beneficial. It had to confess that there are two kinds of religion in America. It called the first "extrinsic" religion, meaning the kind that contents itself with wearing Christian t-shirts, WWJD bracelets, and so on. It actually found that sort of religion to be more socially harmful than atheism. The good news is that it also found "intrinsic" religion - the kind that softens the heart, transforms the mind, and quickens the soul to cause us to live differently - to be the most socially beneficial worldview. If this book aspires to anything, it is intrinsic religion that aligns believing and living. Theologians have termed the integration of what we believe and how we live as "praxis," which is also the name Mennonite Mutual Aid gave to their mutual fund group.

Despite having to use such ten-cent theological and financial terms on occasion, I take comfort that the Bible says Moses was not all that articulate. I hope you will forgive my occasionally poor grammar and focus on what I'm trying to say to your heart, mind and soul. If you do, I think you will be blessed by my amateurish efforts. I also take comfort that being an amateur did not keep Bobby Jones from being as great a golfer as any professional. Many golfers have since learned how to get out of the rough from his teachings. Maybe I can help you escape your own spiritual and/or financial rough so you can better help others out of their rough.

What this book therefore aspires to do is simply reduce the conflicts within the hearts and minds of Americans, among Americans, and *between* the peoples of the world. Moses was among the first to give that true meaning to the word "holy." He understood the ancients had many gods, and therefore many truths about reality. He, and the biblical prophets who followed, taught us there is only one God, one Truth and one reality. I simply believe they were quite right.

I hope you too will seriously consider their message after you read my case that we Americans also suffer from too many gods, too many truths, and too many perceived realities.

Meditation One

Faith & Reason

"To repent is to come to your senses."

Frederick Buechner
Wishful Thinking

"A system of morality which is based on relative emotional values is a mere illusion, a thoroughly vulgar conception which has nothing sound in it and nothing tr ue."

Socrates

It's more than a bit ironic that many Christians, and conservative Christians in particular, are skeptical of anything associated with Plato and Socrates, as well as believe faith and reason are dichotomous.

Many theologians argue that Jesus essentially "Hellenized" the Jewish faith and Hellenic culture, or Greek culture at the time of Christ, was largely based on the logic and reason of Aristotle, Plato and Socrates. Those theologians note that when Moses taught his great commandment, he said to love God with heart, soul and strength. Strength was highly valued in ancient cultures, as attested by the story about Sampson and his long hair. But Jesus taught us to love God with heart, soul, and mind, as long as that mind was the "mind of Christ." The Bible says that "God's thoughts are not our thoughts" and Jesus had no interest in having "evil geniuses" as disciples. So he essentially freed us of legalism by teaching us a lot of what his Jewish contemporaries were doing was irrational in the mind of God.

This might be a good time to pause and nuance, particularly for the uninitiated, the differences between conservative Christians, evangelicals, the religious right, and such. The media doesn't always share it but evangelicalism is much, much broader than the religious right. The word "evangelical" simply means one who wants to share the Good News of God's love for all creation.

There is no political statement in that. An evangelical can be progressive or conservative.

Even conservative evangelicals do not have to subscribe to the often extreme interpretations of politics offered by the religious right. Billy Graham has reportedly said that he may be a conservative Christian, but he's not a member of the religious right. In fact, it surprises most Americans, as even Reverend Graham was famously fooled by President Nixon, but Reverend Graham has long been a Democrat.

Such nuance is crucial to understanding the remainder of this book. I am a member of the *Evangelical* Lutheran Church of America. A recent book edited by my good friend Rick Bliese, the president of Luther Seminary, suggests our church may or may not any longer be either evangelizing or Lutheran. I believe my best friends would tell you that I am both, perhaps too much so. You'll understand why that's crucial to this book's perspective as we go along. Yet I have actively questioned many perceptions of the religious right, and even broader evangelicalism, for years. I have even written multiple articles and books about the need for conservative Christians to re-examine their perceptions of Y2K and politics for the magazine of the *National Religious Broadcasters, Christianity Today* and so on.

After studying what is usually thought of as evangelicalism the past twenty years, as admittedly something of an outsider, I'd argue that if there's a major fault among us, it is that we are cultural. It's been said of our culture that leaders can fool some of the people all the time, and fool all of the people some of the time, but they can't fool all of the people all of the time. You can therefore be assured that each time political or cultural leaders have very publicly taken us off a cliff, there have been evangelical leaders who have known better, even if they aren't always quick to disagree with other evangelical leaders preaching cultural perceptions and cultural religion.

It's probably right to hope that any believer who claims intimacy with God, or Ultimate Reality, might have better sense, but there's a reason Christ called us sheep. As any old farm boy knows, sheep are quite loving and loveable, but they aren't the brightest animals in the barnyard. And most evangelicals, Southern Baptists, Pentecostals and so on who constitute conservative Christianity are wonderful people of the heart, as anyone who's ever attended one of our spiritually uplifting services can attest.

For sure, there are times I wish I was more like the spiritually gifted. But it's been argued we Reformed Protestants have so immersed ourselves in the Scriptures that we have drowned the Holy Spirit. My road to God therefore remains primarily through a hopefully connected heart and mind. This has been termed "EQ," or "emotional quotient," rather than IQ. I therefore hope this book helps you to think most rationally about political economy without dampening your spirit, which is a quite difficult matter.

Still, more than a few of us evangelicals aspire to the "one mind" of Christ and long for greater community, at least among believers. We therefore think that when God drew a line, it was a horizontal line dividing good and evil rather than feel it was a vertical line dividing left and right. We also understand that being of "one mind" about political economy is primarily a rational matter, albeit one that enables the emotional act of loving one another. This book therefore argues the biblical root of all evil, defined as separation from God and neighbor, has long been in the economic realm and most of our separation is due to irrational political perceptions, which are typically due to a fight over money.

Very briefly, the best example of that argument might be the fact that the book-of-the-year in evangelical Christianity in 1992 was by a media personality who was at the heart of "the religious right" and prophesied our federal debt would soon destroy American society. Few evangelicals know it but a friend who chaired the economics department at Wheaton College, the hub of evangelical thought, wrote a response that was almost exactly the opposite perspective. So the only real line I've drawn between evangelicals during the past twenty years has been between "thoughtful evangelicalism" and "popular evangelicalism," which tends to be quite emotional. No less an authority than Richard Mouw, president of Fuller Theological Seminary, has lamented that line increasingly resembles a gulf.

I emphatically disagree with that old caricature that evangelicals are any more "dim-witted and easily led" than other Americans.

Survey after survey tells us that most Americans know little about our political economy. Other surveys tell us that Americans of all stripes are increasingly ignorant of biblical concepts and church tradition, perhaps primarily so in the area of political economy as those denominations with traditions don't speak of them much anymore. So even though Jesus asked us not to worry about the economic future, when Americans worry about Y2K, evangelicals worry about Y2K. When Americans worry about the federal debt, evangelicals worry about the federal debt. That cultural submission is a major focus of this book.

Our other problem is that our strength is our weakness, which is true of life in general. By its nature, evangelicalism has long relied heavily on popular media to spread the Good News of God's love. But most true experts, like my professor friend at Wheaton, do not have the time to both understand our complex economy and do the fundraising, staffing and so on that is required to do radio or television. In other words, minds aren't hands, and vice versa. That's why we must be the *body* of Christ.

The message most Americans therefore hear from us may be a mile wide, but it's an inch thick. Perhaps that is why Jesus was quite content to devote most of his time and talent to walking with twelve disciples rather than talking to millions. As Confucius said five centuries before Christ: "I hear and I forget. I see and remember. I do and I understand." The Gospel must be heard, but more importantly, it must be lived.

Still, the teachings of Socrates and Plato that we've read thus far, suggest that one does not have to be a believer of any particular persuasion to appreciate a primary concern of this book: that reality is less and less as politicians, the media and corporate advertisers are telling us. As rational truth has taken a beating the past few years, emotions seem to rule our times.

In some ways, we are becoming the "Amway nation." If you've ever been to one of Amway's stirring conventions, you know why *The Wall Street Journal* recently quoted Amway's leader in China as saying: "The most powerful weapon is to move someone emotionally." The *Journal* quipped the leader is, "the kingpin of emotional business."

I can attest after attending one such convention with friends. They wittingly or unwittingly made me *feel* rather badly when I *thought* it was good for my ministry and my family for me to continue counseling investors and teaching moral economics rather than launch an Amway business. As good as Amway has been to some of my other friends, and it has indeed changed their lives for the better both spiritually and financially, I also expect God is rather happy that I stayed put.

That's the only emotion any Christian should aspire to, whether within or outside Amway, as God's happiness is the only emotion that will make us truly and deeply joyful as a result. I've chatted with Rich DeVos who co-founded Amway and expect he would agree. Yet some of his managers occasionally get so passionate about their business that they forget the

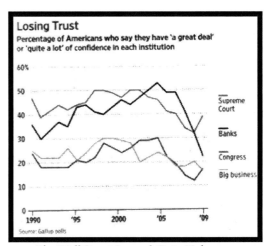

The Wall Street Journal, Date Unknown

42

bigger picture, which is true of American business, politics, and even religion, as well.

Drawing on the General Social Survey and the National Congregations Survey, Mark Chaves recently documented the continuities and the changes in American religious life and practice in a book entitled *American Religion: Contemporary Trends*. He showed that public confidence in religious leaders has declined and that "no traditional belief or practice has increased in recent decades."

Emotion often causes Truth to take a beating as well. As an old Army officer who was even a Distinguished Military Graduate of my college, I'm often surprised when surveys say the military may be today's most respected institution. Reality is that our job was to kill people. It's a dirty business, even if someone has to do it. Even General Eisenhower said it was the duty of every soldier to make war a thing of the past. He had clearly seen enough death and destruction to know that soldiering wasn't the highest calling to which humanity can aspire. But at least we did what we said we were going to do, which is quite unlike most institutions in modern America recently. That simple integrity, as well as the self-sacrifice that our young men and women practice daily, now seems to put the military heads and shoulders above other professions. That's just sad.

Even the Church has lost the confidence of many Americans, particularly in the area of finances. So in many ways, I believe **it might actually help to be a non-believer when discerning difficult moral realities about earning, investing and giving money. The church's emotional but reductionist teaching about Christian stewardship - that we are fine if we're donating a small percentage of our income to churches and ministries - too often conceals difficult realities.** This is precisely why people often tell me they trust highly visible Christians less than other businesspeople, and those with a fish on their business cards least of all.

I can personally attest the worst treatment I've gotten on Wall Street was from a supposed Christian brother who gave Bibles out at sales meetings and had one of those pictures of a smiling Jesus above his desk. We rarely chatted but that he didn't confess various sins of loving money rather than God and neighbor. That didn't keep him from preferring considerable money he owed to me above our friendship. Yet he still lives in a multi-million dollar waterfront home that I wouldn't buy if I won the lottery.

We hear such embarrassing realities in the markets quite often, but we rarely hear them discussed in church. We believers too often ignore the difficult reality that Jesus called the Pharisees - and we should remember the Pharisees were "good" men of God -"hypocrites" for tithing even the mint, dill and cumin from the garden while ignoring the "truly important teachings" of our faith. Jesus even taught that if we're about to offer our gifts to God at the altar in the Temple, which would mean church for most of us, and remember our neighbor has something against us, we can't give those gifts until we've made peace with that neighbor. We rarely hear that teaching in stewardship sermons around pledge card time either.

Jesus made it extremely clear that he was far, far more interested in love among people than giving to religious institutions.

Still, we must also remember he commended the faith of the widow giving her last mites in the Temple. On the other hand, he disdained those who made a show of giving. To paraphrase Harry Truman who wished for a one-handed economist, if only we had a one-handed theologian! But God gave us dual ears with which to hear the Truth, two eyes with which to see Truth and opposite hands with which to cooperate in doing the Truth. Reality, and especially Truth, is always about balance, even if that makes it less than simple. That's why God may have given us one brain, but it has a left lobe and a right lobe so we can be of one mind and think in a balanced fashion, as much as our two political parties might dislike that holistic notion.

Still, man-made, simplistic teachings frustrated Truth long before the Pharisees arrived on the scene. That is only one reason you don't have to be particularly religious to read on. As we will discuss, there are many secular philosophers in modern America who want to rid our nation of the Judeo-Christian ethic. Even if they succeed, they will not get rid of political and media illusions. They will simply do away with those claims to Truth that conflict with what they want to believe, and want you to believe as well.

We will later discuss the tensions between Judeo-Christian and "classical" Greek and Roman thought about political economy, which we often think of as conservative and liberal thought. But there is overlap. For example, the Roman philosopher Cicero added this comment to the observation of Socrates quoted above: "Nothing is so unbelievable that oratory cannot make it acceptable." That relates very directly to the political rule about telling "the big lie." It says that if you are going to tell a lie, tell a big one and tell it often enough that people grow to believe it.

As I began editing the manuscript for this book, I was reading respected but progressive economist Jeffrey Sachs' new book entitled *The Price of Civilization*. There's much for which conservative Christians may disagree in Professor Sachs' writings. For example, the "price of civilization" is a term for taxes generally favored by progressives. But we know the contemporaries of Jesus paid burdensome taxes to Rome without those taxes doing much for

Israel's civilization. So we need a realistic and nuanced understanding of taxes rather than a politicized and idealized understanding, on both left and right. Yet the professor was quite insightful when he wrote:

> *"The media, major corporate interests, and politicians now constitute a seamless web of interconnections and power designed to perpetuate itself through the relentless manufacture of illusions. The media peddle illusions, and those illusions lead to even more addictive behaviors, including the fixation on the media itself."*

A simple example of that power is your perception of Santa Claus. For centuries, Santa had been visualized as everything from an elf who really could get down chimneys to a stern old man who couldn't get down chimneys if the roof was on fire and he had no ladder. That changed during the 1930's, not for spiritual reasons but for purposes of corporate profitability. Coca-Cola had been almost exclusively a summer drink. Naturally, Coke wanted their fizzy sugar water, which is only consumable when cold, to be consumed during winter too. So while there had been a couple of depictions of Santa that resembled today's image, Coke's advertising department popularized the jolly old fellow with a Coke in his hand. Not only did consumers then associate the product with winter, but children, who are a very important market for Coke, looked most kindly on the old character, associating him with joyful times. That story can be affirmed on Coke's website.

So today, young mothers guard their babies from this other white bearded old guy as I love to give those babies their "first communions" of a sip of Coke and a piece of a M&M. I know that's shameful, but it makes me and the babies so very happy, even if for the brief moment until the mothers catch us. That's a perfect example of how even I, who am rather sensitive to such secular manipulations, manage to turn religious holy days into consumerist holidays. In other words, I too turn divine reality that brings eternal joy into secular illusion for a moment's pleasure. I should also confess that I enjoy the kids at church so very much that I was an embarrassment to my teen-age son. Just when I was having the most fun, he would interrupt it by saying in a stage whisper: "Dad, you know the judge told you to stop that." In effect, as much fun as I had harassing the kids, he had more fun harassing his parent.

There are other far more serious ramifications of confusing perceptions for reality. For example, consider our perceptions, and anxieties about China. On New Year's Day 2012, I asked my visiting mother if China's economy is larger, smaller or the same size as America's. She responded rather confidently, "larger." Yet I asked her the question as I'd just read these words in the December 31, 2011 issue of *The Economist*:

"In the spring of 2011 The Pew Global Attitudes Survey asked thousands of people worldwide which country they thought was the leading economic power. Half of the Chinese polled reckoned that America remains number one, twice as many as said 'China.' Americans are no longer sure: 43% of US respondents answered 'China'; only 38% thought America was still the top dog."

Yet *The Economist* went on to explain the reality that:

"In 2011, America's GDP was roughly twice as big as China's."

The article went on to explain that China's economy will most likely over-take America's as the world's largest later this decade, but that China has four times as many people so its *per capita* GDP will remain about one-fourth of America's. **There are nine hundred million people in China today who live on less than $2 per day**. Suffice it to say that China has plenty to occupy its time just feeding its people than to spend too much time conspiring against the average American.

Still, China seems to have replaced the old Soviet Union, OPEC, Japan, Y2K, and such as our obsession of the moment. So let me address the constant paranoia I hear about the Chinese yuan replacing the dollar as the world's foremost exchange currency. That's been crucial to our material well-being as having the dollar as the world's reserve currency means our Treasury can spend a dime printing a hundred dollar bill that can buy a hundred dollars worth of real goods and services around the world. Obviously, other nations would like to share in that good fortune.

A team of Cornell economists recently estimated that China needs five things to occur for that to happen. It only has one: a large economy. In particular, China is still a relatively insular country, with strict capital controls and therefore relatively little of the cross border capital flows required to be a reserve currency. The February 9, 2012 issue of the *South China Morning Post* estimated it only has about one-fourth of the currency flows that the U.S. and Eurozone do. That will change, but not over-night. When it does, the dollar will still be a major player in world trade.

The current paranoia over China, rising power that it is, is just one example of why this book argues that we're bombarded with unnecessary negativity. That is quite harmful as it lowers our spirits just so we might vote the right way or consume the right products in order to revitalize those spirits. Anyone who's ever been to Weight Watchers, as I have repeatedly, knows spirituality plays a huge role in over-eating. Anyone who's ever eaten or gone shopping when they're bored or feeling low, understands. Anyone who's ever purchased the right labels or driven the right car to improve his or her self-esteem can relate as well. Over-spending is not a wise way for our nation to remain a super-power.

In short, democratic capitalism is as good a system as humans have developed for living together. But it is not always enriching to our spirits. And the truly good life must be defined by both material and spiritual riches.

That's why it's so very essential for economies, and ironically affluent economies like America's, to look up on a regular basis. Economies should operate in harmony with religious and spiritual realities, not against them. That takes as much work on the part of our clergy, as well as the laity they lead, as it does on the part of our politicians and economists.

My approach is therefore largely based on the faith of my youth and common sense. Both seem increasingly scarce today. Yet my mentor and friend, the legendary mutual fund manager Sir John Templeton, used to also credit his faith and common sense, rather than his having been a Rhodes Scholar in economics, for his not only being an investing legend but perhaps the most ethically respected professional on Wall Street. While the business school at Oxford is now called Templeton College, John's belief also caused him to fund the Templeton Prize for Progress in Religion, the religious equivalent of the Nobel Prize. John essentially taught the holistic concept that while faith usually addresses the "why" of reality and reason usually addresses the "how," faith and reason are not contradictory, as is so often assumed, even taught, in our increasingly secular culture.

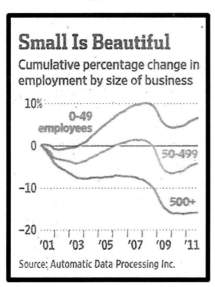

Source: Automatic Data Processing Inc.

CEO's rationalizing everyone's doing it
The Wall Street Journal, 11-8-2011

A more holistic way of seeing reality, particularly our economy, could serve us well at this divided and stressful point in history. For example, the election of 2012 appears to be yet another in which voters will focus on the economy, and particularly jobs, probably in the manufacturing sector. My clients usually tell me that we are becoming a nation of hamburger flippers as manufacturing has been off-shored. CEOs of our largest corporations are indeed being paid more than ever for making the lines in America's unemployment offices even longer. That's terribly important to understand as economists know the job-creating aspects of small business are overstated as they constitute 99.9% of all businesses. However, the number of jobs available is highly dependent upon the hiring and firing practices of major corporations.

Yet even that's not the full story. The accompanying chart from the January 12, 2012 issue of *The Wall Street Journal* graphically demonstrates our need for a more nuanced worldview, if for no reason other than to understand the contradictions in how we think about political economy. It shows that while the *number of employees* in the manufacturing sector has indeed shriveled, *actual manufacturing output* in the United States has steadily increased. In effect, we now pay politicians in the hopes they will create jobs as we also pay CEOs to cremate jobs.

Too often, cremating jobs is done with little more justification than CEOs rationalizing "everyone's doing it," which Peter Drucker said is the worst ethic a business can adopt. He clearly understood that American businesses can chop their way to next quarter's profits, but they can't chop their way to future growth for our children.

The tension between short-term profits and long-term growth was vividly demonstrated by the bankruptcy of Kodak, which once provided jobs to sixty thousand people in Rochester. Kodak invented digital photography. But it was slow to commercialize the technology as it was making so much money by selling film. So Fuji Film and others bet the future on digital, even though it seemed less profitable. Today, Fuji is soaring, and many Americans are myopically blaming politicians that jobs have moved overseas. The lesson is that regardless of what Wall Street, by which I mean all investors, thinks of next quarter's earnings, the future does arrive.

The irony is that we don't seem to have learned, which is normal for humanity but is particularly so for Wall Street investors who increasingly resemble casino gamblers. To be sure, what has been termed "short-term America," is often encouraged by the investment firms of Wall Street. During three decades of working just "off-Wall Street," I've learned that one of the great illusions of American life is when most Wall Street organizations call themselves "investment" firms. Trading firms, yes. Speculation firms, yes. Investment firms, not so much. Despite the fate of companies like Kodak, the short-term orientation of those firms' analysts remains a significant threat to our children's future.

Pepsi is a perfect example. It has been moving toward healthier fare for Americans for years. It knows very well that the future will also arrive for all those baby boomers who've been enjoying Paula Deen's down-home recipes and they too will develop type-two diabetes, with which I've flirted during recent years. According to a friend who worked at a very high level within Pepsi, its studies show that the more healthy Pepsi products, the more trust and allegiance consumers have in and to Pepsi. That's particularly true overseas. For example, there's a malted drink made from buffalo's milk, which is even more nourishing for young people than cow's milk, called Horlicks that still outsells Pepsi two to one in India.

Yet Wall Street analysts have been quite vocal recently that Pepsi is investing too heavily in the future and not enough with an eye toward next quarter's earnings. So despite its better judgment, Pepsi executives are trying to placate Wall Street analysts while they build a better company to serve our children far into the future. As Tocqueville predicted when surveying colonial America, as the light of faith, with its focus on the distant future, has dimmed, the more we've focused on gambling in every shape and form.

To nuance our role in such tensions even further, another primary reason for unemployment is that investors provide huge amounts of capital to American companies. CEOs invest much of that capital in productivity enhancing technology. Productivity is simply getting more and more from fewer and fewer people. CEOs are richly rewarded for increasing such productivity, even though it means fewer jobs for most workers. Still, even ever-advancing technology does not mean our economy is doomed. Nor does the equally jobs-challenging fact of globalization.

John Templeton, who was known as the dean of global investing, once told me about flying from New York City to his home in Nassau. As his plane was taking off, he noticed one American with a wide mower behind a tractor. After he landed in Nassau, he drove by six Bahamians cutting grass with sickles. There were six times more jobs cutting grass in the Bahamas as in the United States, but the one American, who was probably paid more than the six Bahamians combined, was cutting far more grass than the Bahamians combined due to technology.

Having spent a few days cutting grass on a Kentucky farm during my youth, I appreciate why it's long been the dream of humanity to have machines do mundane work for us. Yet that does not mean we are doomed to unsatisfactory levels of unemployment. It simply allows us to go the Y and work out on machines made by others. (That's after fighting for a parking place near the door so we can go in and exercise, of course!) The theory anyway, which seems generally true to me, is that people who used to have those jobs cutting grass, or working in today's manufacturing sector, need to transition to a more technological sector, or the financial sector financing that technology.

Think of how many people who tended stables and manufactured hand-crafted buggies lost their jobs with the invention and financing of the automobile industry. Yet today, many of my friends and relatives near Georgetown, Kentucky are working in an air-conditioned Toyota plant rather than cutting hay in the hot fields or spreading it to cattle in the frozen fields. If you've been through that plant, you know the ancients would agree with my friends that it is the eighth wonder of the world.

Economists tell us that ten to fifteen percent of all jobs now disappear annually for various reasons. That often seems to be speeding up. So most of us feel unemployment has gotten far worse. That's possible, particularly as we have more two-earner households in America these days. But official unemployment numbers, and I know how suspect many believe any government statistic is, actually indicate unemployment is no worse today than under Presidents Reagan and Nixon.

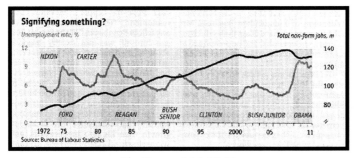

The Economist 9-10-11

It's also my guess that even if official statistics are inaccurate today, as I expect and groups like Shadowstats. com maintain, the statistics were inaccurate back then as well. What seems so obvious to me, but is missed by so many Americans, is that regardless of statistics, we are better fed, housed, and clothed, enabling us to live longer than those who walked this planet before us.

We should also understand that any official statistic in this book that relates an economic activity to GDP, such as the federal debt to GDP ratio, actually overstates the case. Ten to twelve percent of our national income is in the "informal" sector, or off-the-books, in order to hide from the IRS. Cash transactions, tips and so on constitute a lot of that activity, but so does crime. That's only one example of why economists are more humble about numbers than the media and politicians, as suggested by the headline in above chart about unemployment: "Signifying something?"

If you will excuse another personal story, I am a near perfect example of the need to change as our world does. When I was growing up on our tobacco farm not far from Georgetown, everyone said the business of manufacturing cigarettes was dying. We were wrong about that. Cigarette smoking has declined in the US, but has also picked up over-seas. Today, China is the world's largest market for cigarettes and the Chinese love American brands. Yet I essentially decided that if that particular manufacturing job was ending, I'd better find another profession.

I had no idea what I might do. But after getting married, Sherry and I loaded what little we had in the back of a U-Haul truck and confidently set out. We had no jobs or prospects for jobs. We had no money whatsoever. We had to find an apartment with a rebate program so we'd have money for the next month. I literally did maintenance on sizzling bulldozers for an earth-moving company when we first got to Florida. We could barely afford to eat, which was humbling after having been an Army officer.

Yet for a couple of decades, we've been in and out of the bottom of that seemingly detested club of the top "1%" of income earners in the country, despite my spending over half of my time doing financial ministry. Yet we're still working as we've seen too many retirees grow dispirited from having little meaning in their lives, plus we've given enough that we can't imagine retiring on our assets. It might interest you that the 1% club makes approximately 20% of our nation's income, pays 25% of its taxes, and gives 30% of its charity. None of that makes us good or evil.

We'll talk later about the need to nuance even the 1% club, but I feel little need to apologize for anything that God has surely and graciously bestowed upon us. I'm open to the idea that we may or may not pay enough in taxes. (We also may or may not give enough. We do forego some things we'd enjoy due to our giving, which is an acid test for me, but we do not forego anything we need.) It might surprise you but a significant percentage of the 1% agrees with Warren Buffett that our taxes are too low.

Yet I'm not open to the idea that any American should be subject to class warfare based on a simple quantitative glance at percentages. Before making such judgments, and I don't believe one human can judge the heart of another human, we need, at a minimum, a qualitative look at how his or her income and accumulated wealth was earned and is utilized. Even our all-knowing God did not set quantitative measures of virtue.

There was most certainly a huge measure of luck, or God's grace, in my entering Wall Street at the beginning of a thirty year bull market in stocks, bonds and real estate. Still, I believe my experience is testimony to why faith is so very integral to an economy. The age of faith essentially began when God told Abraham to go to a different land. I expect Abraham said, "But where?" It was then our God of faith essentially said, "I'll tell you when you get there." So while some of my best friends growing up are still growing tobacco and mowing hay, I've been counseling investors and writing books. While there are days I wish I was back on the farm, I know I wouldn't really go back.

I also know that as much as this recovering fundamentalist still respects the Bible, I have no interest in living on the nine hundred dollars, in today's inflation-adjusted dollars, on which the contemporaries of Jesus lived, or even the twelve hundred on which the Protestant reformers lived during the sixteenth century. If anything, I will therefore advocate we reconsider an ethic more similar to that of the 1960's, which of course was more biblical and reformed.

Economic progress means change, and we should remember that a scholarly author has termed progress as "the gift of the Jews." He convincingly argued that most ancients considered reality as going in circles until the idea of moving toward a better promised land entered the human conscious. Therefore, the difficult truth is that if change threatens us, we can do one of two things. We can elect a demagogue who promises that he or she will stop the economic progress that's been occurring since Abraham's contemporaries rode camels. Or we can have the faith to align ourselves with God's apparent plan for an increasingly abundant material life, while never forgetting the need for spiritual balance.

I won't pretend to know whether your goal should be material prosperity or spiritual tranquility, or even a balance, which I seek. When markets are in turmoil, I often aspire to the tranquility of a monastery or the river on the back of the farm on which I grew up. But I haven't moved back to the farm yet, and I doubt I will. So I'd better get real and tell you that I'm quite happy that I haven't had to work in the fields mowing hay and harvesting tobacco during recent decades. My transformation was difficult, but not impossible. Yet very little of true value on this old earth is easy.

Yet it's human nature, even among believers, to want it easy. That's why even **Gandhi made two of his "Seven Deadly Sins" wealth without work and worship without sacrifice.** It's also why we obsess on politics. What could be easier than simply pulling a lever to bring about enriching change, even if believing politicians can do so is most likely a form of idolatry? At the very least, that idea is illusion, pure and simple. It's been noted that the word "politics" comes from two Greek words: "polis" meaning "many," and "tics" meaning blood sucking insects!

I've also grown to believe that your reaction to the reality of economic change and material progress is often theological in other ways. If you believe God sort of set things in motion and mankind has been running everything in a rebellious manner since, you will have trouble seeing the economy as making any kind of progress. **But if you see God as a living force who is constantly**

shaping this world according to God's benevolent plan, you are more willing to see economic change and progress as God's plan. You are then more likely to align yourself and your future with that plan for a more abundant life, rather than resist it.

With that heady theological statement, I should confess that I am not a professional theologian, economist, politician, or educator. I am simply an investment planner who has spent nearly four decades trying to understand what the various pieces of our political economy and our morality *really* look like and how they can fit together again to make our thinking, and then ourselves and our nation, more whole rather than increasingly fragmented. That is actually more crucial in the investment business than most occupations. For example, politicians get to count many misperceptions as votes while the media get to count them as revenue, but investors have to tally them as capital losses each year.

Life-enriching connectivity was the original meaning of the word "holy," whereas we moderns usually think of the word only in terms of virtuous personal conduct. Yet Jesus taught the Pharisees that we can live a quite outwardly virtuous life and be most dichotomous, even stressed, in our hearts, souls and minds. Still, be assured that for two reasons, this book definitely isn't one that seeks to make you "holier than thou."

First, I wouldn't know how to do so as I am anything but holier than most people I know. My wife knows my temptations and sins more than anyone on earth. She attributes any knowledge I have in politics, economics, personal finance and religion to the fact that I've never decided what I want to be when I grow up. I usually reply I may have to grow older, but I never have to grow up. Didn't Jesus himself say the kingdom of God belongs to those like little children?! That's why he said we have to be "born again."

That's a term that causes confusion among many Christians, and even more among non-believers, as even the contemporary of Jesus expressed, being born again sounds quite irrational. But even the Buddhists understand the concept is necessary to the spiritual life. They sometimes compare life to a light bulb. We are born with a certain glow, but it begins to collect layers of dust, often pain, but just as often as we're taught self-protective measures like not talking to strangers, crossing only with the lights, and so on. Eventually, the light grows dim from self-interest.

That's when we need something, usually a crisis, to cause us to wash the dust away. The primary difference, as I understand it anyway, is that Buddhists believe we can do so ourselves through meditation and such, whereas Judeo-Christianity teaches we humans need the assistance of the Holy Spirit. **If there's one thing that costs investors quite dearly, it is the desire to protect**

oneself and one's money. If it is to earn good returns, it must be set free in our world to do good.

I've therefore had to learn how to "integrate" the spiritual and financial aspects of my life. The alternative would have been to go even nuttier than I was when thinking about escaping Wall Street for a seminary on a remote Tennessee mountain. Unfortunately, such "integration" can be confusing to modern Americans. For example, bookstores usually don't know whether to put my books in the religion, political, economic, or personal finance section.

This integration can also be quite inconvenient to our short-term financial self-interest. We don't hear much about this Monday to Saturday reality in church anymore, but Wall Street and the markets are great places for learning that **the Golden Rule often costs in the short-run, even if it just as often enriches in the long-run.** That's essentially my answer now to the eternal question of whether ethics and spirituality reduce or enhance returns for investors.

The second reason this book aspires to make you think more holistically without making you feel holier than thou is far more important however. **Prideful religion made Jesus quite angry on multiple occasions. He preferred a humbling religion. It was the Pharisees - worshiping, praying, fasting and giving in obvious manners - who preferred the kind of religion that makes one feel better than others.** Jesus wanted all those religious practices observed, but observed privately, where only God knows about them, even if he told us not to hide our good works for humanity under a basket.

The paradox, which is something factual that doesn't seem reasonable, is therefore that I hope to make you think and act more holistically, while better understanding our profound need for God's amazing grace.

Meditation Two

Re-Connecting with Truth

"I am a firm believer in the people. If given the truth, they can be depended upon to meet any national crisis. The great point is to bring them the real facts."

Abraham Lincoln

"Just as the 2008 election involved a debate on race relations, so the 2012 election will involve one on American capitalism. How ruthless, exactly do voters want it to be? The debate will be driven by emotions, not facts. The former are easy to inflame; the latter tricky to pin down."

The Economist

I began by suggesting most worries in our culture of democratic capitalism are due to others casting shadows in order to get some of our money, or some of our money so they can influence voters.

The essence of money is simply that it makes it far easier for us to exchange one thing for another. It is neither moral nor immoral. To use biblical imagery, it can be the thirty pieces of silver that Judas received for betraying Christ, or the "mites" the widow faithfully gave to the Temple, thereby earning the eternal commendation of Christ. The morality of money lies in how it is used, and not money itself. Hence the famous statement that the root of all evil is the love of money, and not money itself.

Unfortunately, studies suggest fewer and fewer Americans believe they are receiving a fair exchange on their money. That's because more and more shadow-makers, in both America and around our world, love money so much they are willing to use deception, even God, to get our money.

As the old theological statement goes, sin is simply using that which should be loved, such as God and neighbor, while loving that which should

be used, such as money. I'd simply add that if it's true that saints without dinners can be the worst of sinners, it's equally true that politicians without votes can be sinners of note.

If you are therefore interested in holding onto some of that money, redirecting some of it to where it might bring more real joy to your life and the lives of others, or investing it in a political process that might enrich the lives of your grandchildren, you must be free of the concerns created by shadow-makers. And they are quite prevalent today.

Only a few days after I read *The Economist* predict the 2012 election will be centered on how ruthless we want capitalism to be, there was a Republican presidential debate in New Hampshire. I was startled when Governor Mitt Romney, who was leading the primary process at that point, said taxes now consume 37% of our economy. Of course, the Governor was implying that President Obama was intent on turning the U.S. into "socialist Europe," as we hear quite often. So let this former Republican turned Independent get that political canard out of the way immediately. Let me also say that I believe Governor Romney is a moral person. But despite my family always being Republican, my sister was a staffer for Democratic Senator Walter Mondale years ago when he was considered a top presidential contender. He famously declined to run by saying he could not do the things he had to do to become president. Such is politics.

I also know better than to judge President Obama's heart, or any human heart for that matter. He may indeed aspire to make some portions of the American economy more like some European economies. Some of us who have been on Wall Street for decades do not think that would be terribly bad in *some ways*. Yet I also know the system of checks and balances instituted by the Founding Fathers made it quite impossible for any politician to take an informed and moral citizenry, which the Founders hoped would always be the case, of this great nation where it does not want to go.

I also know the August 21, 2010 issue of *The Economist*, the British equivalent of *The Wall Street Journal* that gets to observe European-style socialism quite closely, provided this perspective after the president decided to help, or bail-out, depending on your perspective, Detroit from the ravages of the Great Recession:

> *"An apology is due to Barack Obama: Americans expect much from their president, but they do not think he should run car companies. Fortunately, Barack Obama agrees. This week the American government moved closer to getting rid of its stake in General Motors when the recently ex-bankrupt company filed to offer its shares once more to the public...Many people thought this bail-out (and a smaller one involving*

*Chrysler, an even sicker firm) unwise. Lovers of free markets (including The Economist) feared that Mr. Obama might use GM as a political tool; perhaps favoring the unions who donate to Democrats or forcing the firm to build smaller, greener cars than consumers want to buy. The label "Government Motors" quickly stuck, evoking images of clunky committee-built cars that burned banknotes instead of petrol - all run by what Sarah Palin might call the socialist-in-chief. Yet doomsayers were wrong...**The lesson for American voters is that their president, for all his flaws, has no desire to own the commanding heights of industry. A gambler, yes. An interventionist, yes. A socialist, no."***

More recently, the January 10, 2012 issue of the *Financial Times* observed:

"While efforts to label Barack Obama a 'socialist' are silly, it is fair to label him a social democrat. The US president does not reject capitalism, but he does seek to soften its edges."

General Motors recently announced it will earn billions of dollars during 2012, so tens of thousands of American jobs were likely saved by President Obama's activism. Of course, he took credit for that, as he rightly should have, during his State of the Union address, which essentially launched the President's re-election bid. Yet the *Times* made this balanced observation:

"Any evaluation of Mr. Obama's record should start with the extraordinary turbulence he inherited in early 2009. Relative to the 'liquidate, liquidate, liquidate' stance of many Republican opponents, and the hair shirt some economists were urging, Mr. Obama's response to the crisis was effective. [His efforts to stimulate the economy] retrieved the US from the brink at a stage when many were urging it over the cliff. Mr. Obama did an efficient job of putting out the fire. Yet it was a stretch for him to suggest on Tuesday that the house is close to being rebuilt."

Rank	Countries	Amount ▼
# 1	Sweden:	54.2 % of GDP
# 2	Denmark:	48.8 % of GDP
# 3	Finland:	46.9 % of GDP
# 4	Belgium:	45.6 % of GDP
# 5	France:	45.3 % of GDP
# 6	Austria:	43.7 % of GDP
# 7	Italy:	42 % of GDP
# 8	Netherlands:	41.4 % of GDP
# 9	Norway:	40.3 % of GDP
# 10	Germany:	37.9 % of GDP
# 11	United Kingdom:	37.4 % of GDP
# 12	Canada:	35.8 % of GDP
# 13	Switzerland:	35.7 % of GDP
# 14	New Zealand:	35.1 % of GDP
# 15	Australia:	31.5 % of GDP
# 16	Ireland:	31.1 % of GDP
# 17	United States:	29.6 % of GDP
# 18	Japan:	27.1 % of GDP
	Weighted average:	39.4 % of GDP

We'll see later why even *Forbes* magazine has identified Denmark as a rather pleasant country in which to live and do business despite its government

OECD Revenue Statistics via NationMaster

taking 50% of its citizens' incomes as taxes. Yet as explained by the following chart, I'd never read anything close to Governor Romney's 37% number in *The Wall Street Journal*, *The Economist* or The *Financial Times* in recent years. So I went to FactCheck.org, which said:

> "Mangled Facts in Manchester: Truth took a punch or two at the first of two GOP debates before New Hampshire's critical presidential primary. Romney, talking about taxes, said federal, state and local government consumes 37% of the economy today compared with only 27% when John F. Kennedy was president. In fact, taxes now consume only 27.4% of GDP."

Since tax revenue has actually been in decline since the onset of the Great Recession, as we'll detail later, that 27.4% figure that Factcheck.org used is undoubtedly much closer to reality than was the figure the Governor used. Since the Governor was an investment banker and was likely reading the same economic literature I have been reading over the years, I would have hoped that he'd have known better. Perhaps just as sadly, none of the other candidates even attempted to correct the Governor, perhaps as that would be throwing stones in a glass house. Most conservative politicians create their own illusions about taxes spiraling "out of control" under progressive politicians. Of course, most progressive politicians create their own illusions about matters spinning out of control under conservative politicians.

The official budget of the United States for 2010 contained a table entitled: "Total Government Receipts In Absolute Amounts and As Percentages of GDP." I had my son summarize that table in the following graph. It shows that when this now senior citizen was studying political science in college in 1969, government at all levels, federal, state and local, consumed 28.5% of America's GDP. As these figures lag due to the time required for calculating past tax receipts, the table also showed the percentage for 2008, the latest available, to have been 28.1%.

In other words, despite the billions of dollars of campaign contributions spent and the billions of words expended in vitriolic politics, virtually nothing has changed during my adult years. I've therefore grown to view politics as being similar to the see-saws we used to ride as kids. We'd go up and down and get a little scared,

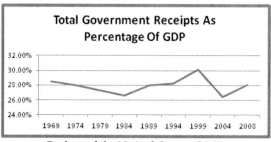

Budget of the United States, OMB

which would break our boredom, but when it was all over, we hadn't gone anywhere.

The only logical conclusion this Independent could come to is that Governor Romney, and perhaps his opponents, either didn't know what the Governor was talking about, or they allowed their political aspirations to trump their desire to be truthful with the American people. Neither struck me as what America needs at this point in history. So they all went a long way toward losing this Independent's vote, though I still have to see if the Democrats know any more facts about our economy, and are anymore willing to share them, than were the Republicans.

Before going further into how the election of 2012 is shaping up as a crescendo of our moral pathologies in the political arena, I should disclose that as an Evangelical Lutheran, I have no problem with electing a Mormon as President of the United States. Luther famously said it was better to employ competent pagans than incompetent Christians for mundane earthly jobs. Even Howard Hughes, who likely never had a religious bone in his body, knew that Mormons are most gifted at managing wealth.

As an investment professional, I have invested substantial client money with the W.P. Carey real estate trusts over the decades (see "WPC" on the NYSE). Sir John Templeton and Bill Carey, both now deceased, were friends and were cut from the same cloth. While John was a Presbyterian and Bill was an Episcopalian, Carey's chief acquisitions officer was a bishop in the Mormon Church. I didn't know that early in our relationship, which was quite mutually rewarding to Bill and my clients, but I later told Bill that I would have invested even more money with him had I known a Mormon bishop was making the investment decisions. My point is I vote for presidents, not popes.

Yet we also should not ignore the possibility that the Governor was simply telling affluent voters what they wanted to hear. There's an old Wall Street saying, which I'll undoubtedly repeat often, that we don't see reality as it is, but as we are. In other words, when your personal debts are burdensome, you're more likely to see the federal debt as burdensome. If you are affluent and "self-made," to use a cultural term that I find highly irrational knowing how interconnected investors and their neighbors are, you are more likely to believe others should need no help as well. It's crucial to understand that from the perspective of this book, this is actually a violation of the first of the Ten Commandments about creating God, or Ultimate Reality, in our own image.

I understand the temptation to do so. I was a relatively high earner while on Wall Street, by most people's standards if not Wall Street's. There were years when I paid more in federal income taxes than I thought I'd ever accumulate as net worth while growing up as a poor farm kid. As I need to share, though not bare, my soul as well as heart and mind in this book, I might tell you that we froze my personal net worth years ago, though we've allowed it to adjust for inflation.

There's nothing particularly virtuous about that as we have what we need and most of what we want. And I'm not necessarily recommending it for your consideration, though I've been known to tell clients to simply give their money away as: 1) they are poor stewards due to fear, greed or complacency and are unlikely be get better, and 2) they worry too much about their money. I simply share the fact because making that decision has produced enormous spiritual blessings for us.

We had just returned from a mission trip of teaching in Uganda after Idi Amin had raped that naturally blessed land of beautiful and spiritual people. That trip made it even easier to understand how blessed we were as Americans. But Sherry and I came from a place where millionaires were as scarce as hen's teeth. Still, a million dollars would have been a meager annual bonus had I continued my career trajectory on Wall Street. So we left an awful lot of money on the table in order to home school our son, engage in ministries, write books, teach, and so on.

Still, making our new Ugandan friends put faces on the reality that the net worth of the typical human on earth is about $2,300 dollars today, and we more deeply understood that we are tremendously wealthy. I therefore understand that most Americans who complain about our economy have never been outside our country. Traveling is a wonderful way for getting in touch with reality.

My point is that my personal experiences of paying high taxes should never blind me to the reality that the day after Governor Romney made his shadow, the January 9, 2012 issue of The *Financial Times* launched a new series on "Capitalism in Crisis." The first article focused on the growing inequality in American society and said:

> *"No one can be surprised that the legitimacy of capitalism is currently in question. And it would be wrong to call it a 'winner take all' form of capitalism, because privileged losers appear to be making off with the prizes too. **What is unquestionably novel is the ferocity with which US businesses shed labor now that executive pay and incentive schemes are more closely linked to short-term performance targets. In effect, the American worker has gone from being regarded as human capital to a mere cost...** Mancur Olson, a theorist on institutional economics, argued that nations decline because of the lobbying power of distributional coalitions, or special-interest groups, whose growing influence fosters economic inefficiencies and inequality. When he*

*was writing, the main interest groups were trade unions and business cartels. **Today, the pre-eminent interest group consists of finance professionals on Wall Street and in London. Through campaign finance and political donations, they have bought themselves protection from proper societal accountability.***"

It's therefore illogical, likely immoral, and surely non-spiritual, for affluent Americans - be they Republican, Democrat or Independent - to complain that half of all Americans pay no federal income taxes, while we also complain government is bleeding the economy dry.

According to the IRS, 46.4% of tax returns filed in the US for tax year 2009 reported less than $30,000 of adjusted gross income. At the very least, that means we affluent need to better nuance the reality that taxes may be too high on half of all Americans, and more likely twenty percent of us. There's no reason for us to impoverish the spirits of half our neighbors simply out of self-interest.

If there's a moral argument for raising taxes on moderate and lower income Americans while lowering taxes on the affluent, let's make it. If not, let's just be grateful we have among the very lowest taxes in the developed world, as documented by even *Forbes* magazine, not to mention Warren Buffett, as we'll see in the mediation on taxes. Even "The Capitalist Tool" has agreed with Buffett's famous complaint that very high-income Americans actually pay a lower percentage of their incomes in federal taxes than do many middle-class taxpayers.

Of course, I understand there are differing ways of measuring taxes, so I'm sure a crafty consultant will "spin" what Governor Romney said. For example, if I pay twenty dollars to enter and enjoy Yellowstone Park, is that a tax? Libertarian Congressman Ron Paul, for one, would likely say "definitely." But even he wouldn't call it a tax for me to pay one hundred dollars to enter and enjoy one of our theme parks in Florida. I've been to both Yellowstone and our theme parks and if that's a tax at Yellowstone, I'm happy to pay it as God's creation still trumps Disney's, in my opinion anyway. (Hopefully, I will differentiate my personal opinions from reliable facts throughout this book.)

Yet my point remains that even such relatively minor complications concerning taxes cannot explain the huge gulf that often exists between what I read in the economic literature and what I hear from politicians. I therefore suggest you read this book slowly, perhaps one section at time, followed by group discussion, personal reflection and even a little research. I encourage you to be as open-minded as possible, for your own well-being.

This investment advisor has seen as much money lost due to political illusion as any other factor, particularly in conservative Christianity.

The first question all Americans might therefore ask ourselves is: Why do so many politicians go on providing credence to that old political saying that we can tell when a politician is lying because it's when he or she is moving his or her lips? My answer is simply that "it works," for the politicians if not our union.

Governor Romney went on to win the New Hampshire primary. But former Speaker of the House Newt Gingrich won in South Carolina after a friendly "Super Pac" developed and heavily marketed in South Carolina what can only be described as an immoral video of Governor Romney's days at Bain Capital. Sadly, that stuff is contagious. Given the Governor's huge advantage in money, I fully expect him to remind the Speaker in my state of Florida that those who live in glass houses shouldn't throw stones, or that politicians with dirt under their own nails shouldn't go digging for it in the backgrounds of other politicians.

Super Pacs, or very large political action committees, are typically managed by former associates of the candidates. Too often, those former associates clearly understand the ethically-challenged work the candidate would like to have done, but doesn't want to do himself or herself. So the Pac does it for him or her. The candidate can claim that he or she has no control over those doing the dirty work. Of course, any candidate who is willing to disclaim responsibility as a candidate will also likely disclaim Watergate-type activities once elected.

People I respect have differing views on Super Pacs. A few days after the South

Carolina primary, CNN interviewed my friend Foster Friess, who founded the Brandywine Mutual Funds, on why he was giving generously to Senator Rick Santorum's Super Pac. The same day, the *Financial Times* contained an article by Martin Wolf, with whom I email on occasion, in its "Capitalism in Crisis"

series. Martin made the case that one of seven major changes needed to put the West back on track is "curbs to purchasing politics." Having studied political science as well as working in markets, I could see Martin's point when he wrote:

> *"Politics and markets each have their proper spheres. The market is based on the roles of people as producers and consumers. Politics is based on their roles as citizens. In the absence of protection for politics, the outcome is plutocracy [rule by the wealthy].* **Plutocrats like closed political and economic systems. But if they succeed, they undermine the open access on which democratic politics and a competitive market economy depend. Protecting democratic politics from plutocracy is among the biggest challenges to the health of democracies.** *What is to be done? The protection of politics from the market comes by regulating the use of money in elections and by the supply of public resources to those engaged in them. At least partial public financing of parties and elections is inescapable."*

My view is that there simply is no room in a democracy for political organizations, like Super Pacs, that are unaccountable to anyone. It's surely dichotomous for conservative politicians to detest the independence of the Federal Reserve, whose chairman is at least subject to the appointment of the President, when they are making use of Super Pacs. Such activities may also not raise confidence in the future of capitalism. *The Economist* described the video about Governor Romney as "vicious."

It was reported elsewhere that the video was financed by a fellow who became a billionaire while operating a Las Vegas casino of the nature evangelical leaders, like Jim Dobson, have long resisted. It was reported elsewhere that Senator Santorum was the only Republican candidate who had not dropped by to pay homage to the casino mogul. While that's a moral feather in the Senator's cap, it will undoubtedly hurt him politically as casino operators, pornographers and such have long been major supporters of prominent conservative think tanks. Obviously, they have major financial self-interests in getting government off our backs.

The ultimate irony, apparently invisible to the Speaker, was the video painted Governor Romney as an insensitive fellow who exploited his fellow Americans for money in his business. Yet the Speaker has been quite busy growing wealthy in Washington. **When Moses was laying down guidelines for future kings, Moses said a king "should not make himself rich with gold and silver. That will keep him from thinking he's better than others"** (Deuteronomy 17:16). That might mean God prefers leaders, like David, of modest means to rich leaders. But at a minimum, it suggests God didn't want anyone using his or her office to grow rich. In that, God and Plato agreed.

While political fact checkers should never be taken as gospel, they are generally more reliable than the propaganda put out by candidates. I therefore believe the *Washington Post's* political fact-checker was quite correct in awarding the video "four pinocchios." I may prefer markets to governments, but I do not place my faith in Wall Street, and, in particular, vehicles like private equity and hedge funds. Capitalism is a matter of "creative destruction" and private equity does more destruction, and possibly creation, than most financial instruments.

The Governor can claim he "created" tens of thousands of jobs at companies like Sports Authority and Staples by simply tallying the number of jobs before and after his involvement. Yet no one really knows how many owners and employees of local sports equipment and office equipment businesses had to go to work for the Governor's businesses after his companies squeezed them by making sporting goods and office supplies more affordable for consumers. In effect, **the real debate in this matter is whether capitalism should be "effective," in a broader sense by creating jobs and such, or whether it should simply be "efficient" in delivering the most goods for the lowest price. As always, I believe balance is the key. We must avoid extremes in both directions.**

Personally, I couldn't work in most private equity firms as I opt for quality of life over quantity of life, or more effective forms of capitalism over more efficient forms. Despite the enormous profits the Governor made for investors, *The Economist* has detailed few private equity firms deliver any better returns than a S&P 500 Index fund, particularly after fees. Yet I also know that over 11% of pension assets in the United States are invested with private equity funds, so many Americans who have no idea what a private equity fund is are the beneficiaries of them, for good or ill.

Morally, I also know that even Satan was once one of God's angels, which Governor Romney couldn't have been if the video was correct. The video appeared after the left-leaning *Post*, which has never-the-less awarded President Obama four pinnochios on occasion, had also awarded Speaker Gingrich four pinnochios for "highly misleading statements about the partisan nature of the ethics probe while he was House Speaker." The *Post* added this about the video:

> *"The 29-minute video "King of Bain" is such an over-the-top assault on former Massachusetts governor Mitt Romney that it is hard to know where to begin...At least some of the interviews of ordinary citizens appear to have been conducted under misleading pretenses and have*

been selectively edited to leave a false impression...Super Pacs will
cause endless headaches for fact checkers this political season. The
advertisements they produce are often insidiously inaccurate."

There were three things about Speaker Gingrich's surge in South Carolina that troubled me even more than his sinking American voters even deeper into our cesspool of cynicism. They essentially reflect *The Economist*'s statement that: "In a profession which specializes in hypocrisy, Mr. Gingrich's performance stands out." Politically active Christians might also reflect about this statement from a former congressman who worked with the Speaker: "He was the guy to lead us to the Promised Land. He was not the guy to manage us once we got there." In other words, its one thing to kick Pharaoh in the shins, and another thing do better when governing. Apparently, even Moses wasn't up to that job. And Mr. Speaker, you're no Moses.

So the first factor about Speaker Gingrich's surge in South Carolina that bothered me was that much of it occurred among evangelical Christian voters. As you will read, I had written later in this book, long before the video was produced, that evangelicals were badly fooled by the Speaker during the mid-nineties. We might remember the old saying: "Fool me once, shame on you; fool me twice, shame on me."

The second reason I was troubled was that evangelicals rallied around the Speaker largely due to his very public confessions of repentance. Jesus suggested most spiritual activities be conducted quite privately. Campaigns are not confessional booths.

The third reason was that a commentator for CNN explained to the American public that if evangelicals did opt for Gingrich, it would validate the suspicions of many that "family-values Republicans" fooled themselves during the past three decades by claiming they prefer morals to money. That too is unlikely to re-moralize American society, much less evangelize the world for Christ.

Even *The Economist* reminded readers that the Speaker was "indeed a serial adulterer" while noting that Congressman Paul described the Speaker as a "serial hypocrite." As if to prove them correct, while campaigning later in Florida as a "true conservative" who would cut government spending, the Speaker promised the "space coast" that he would put a permanent colony on the moon by 2020 and go beyond to Mars thereafter. My local paper stated the space coast was "thrilled," perhaps proving one man's pork remains another man's dinner.

I'd be the last person on earth to question biblical teachings about every human's need for repentance. Despite growing up in a devout home with

Southern Baptist parents, I've repented of more sins than the world's most elderly Southern Baptist quintuplets. Yet there are also very clear biblical teachings about discernment. One says that many will say "Lord, Lord" despite Christ never knowing them. So how do we balance such teachings, particularly with shadow-making so prevalent in the political realm, and make crucial judgments for our nation without judging the hearts of our fellow humans? Very simply actually.

There's another biblical teaching that says we'll know the true disciples of Christ by the loving fruits they produce for others.

The teaching does not say "by their claims of redemption ye shall know them." Nor does it say "by a single piece of fruit ye shall know them." We need to look at the *full range of activities* of a person in order to decide whether that person should lead a church, or a nation. As famed management consultant Peter Drucker so emphasized, the success of any effort to change hearts, souls and minds - be that effort in the political, academic or religious worlds - is simply and purely changed behavior. Go to the very best conference you've ever attended and if you don't change the way you live, that conference may have been fun and entertaining but it was also an utter failure. It's the same with redemption.

To be quite honest, that tough criteria made me even more skeptical than I have been over the years of Speaker Gingrich's claims of being more Christ-like. I once ate Sunday morning brunch next to the Speaker. I introduced myself as a friend of Jack Kemp. The Speaker was quite friendly and personable, but I've known a lot of friendly and personable people on Wall Street over the years that I would not want managing my IRA, much less the country my son's generation will inherit. *The Economist* has termed them "psychopaths" as what you see isn't always what you get. So I pointedly called him "Mr. President." I wanted to see how much Christian humility he had developed after losing his leadership of the House amid ethical concerns, for which he paid hundreds of thousands of dollars.

When I conducted the same test on Jack Kemp, he simply responded it would take a lot of work on both our parts to earn the title of "Mr. President" for him. But the Speaker simply smiled, rather broadly. Admittedly, that was probably before his marriage to his former mistress and repentance. But it turns out to have been quite illuminating. Just days before the South Carolina primary, *The Wall Street Journal* detailed how the Speaker had applied to be the president of his college during his first year as a professor. The *Journal* noted the Speaker's "confidence" caused a chuckle among the faculty. Then the January 21, 2012 issue of *The Economist* noted the Speaker's "gargantuan self-belief." As true Christianity is largely, perhaps primarily, about denying one's self so that one can better believe in God and more resemble Christ, the fruit grew rather distasteful.

I've been around politics too long to expect high-ranking politicians to resemble Mother Teresa, or even Billy Graham, Martin Luther King, and so on.

Maybe high-ranking politicians shouldn't resemble the more saint-like as it might require a psychopath, or at least a sociopath, to survive in Washington these days. But I believe we have the right to expect more humility and related virtues from politicians who make Christian repentance a major campaign theme. Sadly, conservative South Carolina voters have been known for political gullibility for decades. I have a friend named Gresham Barrett. He was a congressman from South Carolina and was almost its current governor. And he's a devout Christian. Yet *The Economist* article may have hinted as to why Gresham lost his gubernatorial bid by quipping:

> *"By the standards of the Palmetto State, where in the 1970's the notorious Republican strategist Lee Atwater honed the dark arts of character assassination, this primary has been downright gentlemanly. Consider the South Carolina primary of 2000, to the end of which someone spread the lie that John McCain (like Strom Thurmond, the state's arch-segregationist and favorite son) had fathered an illegitimate black child. 'We gutted McCain in three days,' a consultant working against him is said to have boasted."*

Most South Carolinians who attended their state's presidential debate seemed quite impressed when the Speaker, perhaps ignoring King David's humble reaction upon being reminded of his sexual indiscretion, began by shooting the messenger right through the heart. That moderator began by asking about the Speaker's second wife who had told a national television audience a couple days earlier that the Speaker had asked for an open marriage. The Speaker preached an eloquent sermon about how it was beneath the dignity of a presidential debate for the moderator to begin by asking that question. The Speaker maintained that quite arguable position even though his former wife had undoubtedly put the question at the very front of viewer's minds at the time and the moderator explained he simply wanted to get it out of the way. The Speaker clearly understands that Americans' cynicism toward politicians is only rivaled by their cynicism toward the national media, and he played that divisive bit of cynicism quite brilliantly, if immorally.

Yet you can't fool all the people all the time, even when they're your fellow conservatives.

The lead article on the January 23, 2012 editorial page of *The Wall Street Journal* said:

> *"The Gingrich Challenge: In the wake of his victory, Mr. Gingrich has his own challenge because he has always been at his worst when on top. The Georgian's main vulnerability isn't his failed marriages, as South Carolina proved. It is his penchant for over-the-top statements and sudden shifts of strategy or policy based on personal whim.... Media bashing may work when the questions seem unfair, but not when they are legitimate queries concerning his record at Freddie Mac or in Congress."*

Peggy Noonan, President Reagan's favorite speech writer, wrote these words for the December 10, 2011 issue of *The Wall Street Journal*:

> *"There are too many storms within him, and he seeks out external storms in order to equalize his own atmosphere. He's a trouble magnate, a starter of fights that need not be fought...What is striking is the extraordinary divide in opinion between those who know Gingrich and those who don't. Those who do are mostly not for him...He will continue to lose to his No. 1 long-time foe, Newt Gingrich. He is a human hand grenade who walks around with his hand on the pin, saying, 'Watch this!'"*

Ms. Noonan makes a crucial point about human nature, and not only politics but finances. Thirty years of investment counseling should entitle anyone to an honorary degree in psychology. Experienced advisors are quick to detect the storms within potential clients, for if there are no storms around them, they will create them. That's why **Jesus demonstrated that the calming of storms is an integral part of the abundant life**. The same principle applies to politics. If we want to reduce the number of storms around us, we'd better seek out leaders of spiritual calm. I can also virtually guarantee investors that if they have internal storms, they will create whirlwinds around them that will destroy their wealth or the wealth of neighbors.

Yet most voters in South Carolina had not had much time to get acquainted with the "new and improved" Speaker. He had just been resurrected by the "anybody but Romney" movement and the media's need to keep campaigns interesting. So it was morally questionable when the Speaker resonated with voters by later saying it was fair game for the video to question Governor Romney's business dealings as it was a matter of "character." It does not require a strong biblical worldview to wonder about that dichotomy in the Speaker's mind, as well as the voter's minds apparently. Yet the Bible also tells us that Jesus said those who have the most for God to forgive, will also be the most grateful.

This book suggests that gratitude for God's amazing grace is witnessed by how the affluent earn our money and how we utilize it. Again, that biblical criterion caused even more skepticism toward the Speaker on my part. The *Journal* reported the Speaker earned over three million dollars the previous year. Three hundred thousand of that, or six times annually what the typical American earns each year, came from supposedly "teaching history" to Freddie Mac, one of the giant mortgage agencies in Washington that conservatives so detest. Yet the repentant Speaker reportedly donated just two percent of his income to charity, which is almost exactly the percentage given by the typical American.

All in all, if the Speaker's stewardship activities, both pre-repentant and post-repentant, are weighed rather than his admittedly eloquent words, my fellow evangelicals might realize our children might be better off if we spend more time, talent and treasure on religion and less on politics. **Our leaders are always pointing out how much we could give if we stop paying credit card interest. And they're right. But we could also give far more if we stopped making so many political donations, which usually go to the secularizing media of course.** It's estimated just one presidential candidate this year will spend over one billion dollars getting elected. Try to imagine how much is spent by all politicians. And even that is a pittance in relation to the collective wealth of our nation's richest citizens, who are now free to buy as much unaccountable political propaganda as they wish.

I have no delusions after all these years of trying to share such rational stewardship concepts with evangelicals that this book is likely to change the minds of most modern Americans who make political decisions with their hearts. If we have few Abraham Lincolns in politics these days, it could be that we wouldn't vote for them as most of us no longer want to be bothered by the "real facts." The fact Lincoln had to use that term suggests political illusion was alive and well during his time. Still, even he might not understand why one of the most popular sayings in post-modern America is that everyone is entitled to his or her own opinion, just not his or her own facts. Perhaps it's time for all Americans to repent before we vote. As the Frederick Buechner quote in our last meditation suggested, such repentance simply means coming to our senses.

Given the confused state of our union, I will therefore appeal to beliefs for a moment in order to restore a respect for facts. We either believe in our hearts that Jesus was correct when he asked us to "observe the birds of the air," which suggests the more objective perspective that earlier prophets enjoyed from the mountain-tops, or we don't believe such things. We either believe in our hearts, or we don't, that we should "honor and respect" government, without relying on it to make us behave and love our neighbors as ourselves, as government was instituted by God, as St. Paul wrote in Romans 13, admittedly to smooth his trip to Rome by appeasing Roman authorities.

Likewise, in the economic arena, our hearts either believe that Jesus said on the Mount to lend to anyone in need without expecting a return, thereby ensuring plentiful and affordable credit, or they don't. They either believe the lead editorial in the January 25, 2012 issue of *The Wall Street Journal* was informed when it said the fact is that, "**the average effective middle-class tax rate is 8.2%,**" or they don't.

Corporately, we either believe, or we don't, that the "root of all evil" lies, for example, in shareholders of corporations like Playboy transforming human sexuality from marital bliss into extra-marital entertainment. My long considered perspective is that if we go with the modern capitalist notion rather than the ancient Christian teaching, we will endlessly argue about what the government should do about the symptoms of abortion, divorce, morning after pills, adoption standards, and welfare for unwed mothers.

During thirty years of futilely sharing facts, I've learned why Jesus said we must "train up" our children to believe in God's graceful and benevolent nature. Then they can objectively, rather than fearfully or greedily, observe the realities around us. And that could be a most important point. By definition, many evangelical Christians of leadership age were evangelized into our faith later in life. Few were "cradle Episcopalians" and so on. In addition, a major *Christianity Today* article has described how evangelicalism used to be the preferred faith of the lower income. So many evangelicals of leadership age have had to accomplish the most difficult transformation of materialistic worldview into Christian worldview; at the same time they have not had the stewardship traditions of the older faiths to help them.

So whether you are religious or non-religious, if you don't believe those things, particularly about the root of many of our social pathologies, and/or aren't sufficiently open-minded, it might be better stewardship of your time for you to go watch television. Given the state of the American mind, you are unlikely to ever see the world as Judeo-Christianity has taught us to do over the millennia, rather than as capitalism has during recent decades. Believe it or not, even *The Wall Street Journal* article I mentioned previously underlined the crucial nature of your core beliefs by commenting:

> *"Correcting misperceptions may not change beliefs about the underlying issues, according to several studies for which researchers tested the effect of supplying the right numbers...'People recall facts that support their beliefs, and don't recall facts that contradict beliefs,' says Leo Simonetta, a social psychologist."*

In the interests of stewarding the time of those who continue reading, I've attempted to screen out as much economic "noise" as possible and only bring to your attention truly important considerations. I do the same on my website www.financialseminary.org if you are interested in what you read here. My decades on Wall Street have taught me that *The Economist* was precisely correct in its December 31, 2011 issue when it said:

> *"Most commentary on social media ignores an obvious truth - that the value of things is largely determined by their rarity. As communications grows ever easier, the important thing is detecting whispers of useful information in a howling hurricane of noise. Everyone will need better filters - editors, analysts, middle managers and so on- to help them extract meaning from the blizzard."*

Finally, I am focusing primarily on conservative misperceptions for two reasons, i.e., I know more about them, and, second, our country, or at least the Republican Party to which I used to belong, has been moving to the right during recent years, at least in its thinking. Remember President Clinton telling us "the era of big government is over?" That could be because conservatives can claim more truths about the political economy. On the other hand, it might simply suggest conservative leaders have been more effective with political propaganda through outlets like Fox News. Every Christian needs to discern for himself or herself whether that movement in thinking is faithful or not. Personally, I'd rather see all of us think on a higher plane than from a right or left manner.

Christianity Today recently discussed a new study by religious sociologists at Baylor University. They concluded that frequent Bible reading can prompt more progressive attitudes about some areas of life. I found that painfully true when contemplating attending seminary and having to get really serious about Scripture and tradition. My experiences as an investment counselor since those days suggest that getting more serious about Scripture might particularly prompt a more progressive worldview in the areas of political economy and personal finance.

Let me share two quick examples that we'll expound upon as we go along in this book. I've found that most of my conservative clients think influential British economist John Maynard Keynes was an "anti-Christ" figure as he persuaded government officials during the Great Depression that activism on the part of government can enrich life. Yet Keynes also wrote:

> *"The day is not far off when the economic problem will take back seat where it belongs, and the arena of the heart and the head will be*

occupied or reoccupied, by our real problems - the problems of life and of human relations, of creation and behavior and religion."

On the other hand, most conservatives believe GOP stands for God's Own Party. Yet most have never even heard of Ayn Rand, much less understand her new atheistic moral philosophy.

Rand was a far right-wing philosopher who has greatly influenced our economy through former Chairman of the Federal Reserve Alan Greenspan, Congressman Paul Ryan and Justice Clarence Thomas. She literally *aspired* to be *the* "anti-Christ" by wanting to be remembered as the greatest ever enemy of religion, and particularly Christianity. Fox News, which many conservatives seem to believe is televangelism, recently ran an article by Rand's disciples claiming America's salvation lies in Rand rather than Christ.

Again, I ask conservative Christian readers to be particularly skeptical of such political propaganda, while understanding I'm well aware that Jesus did not depend on Rome to usher in the Kingdom of God. In fact, Jesus never bothered to even lobby Caesar, Herod, or Pilate. He thereby left an example of how to live a perfectly righteous life in a culture that was quite hostile to the concept of Truth. His example is surely relevant for Americans today.

Meditation Three

Render until <u>T</u>axed <u>E</u>nough <u>A</u>lready?

"In the face of intuition and anecdotal evidence, it is always good to look at the data."

The Economist

"Evangelicals have taken political stances that sometimes appear quixotic, sometimes heroic and often contradictory... Many rallied around President Reagan, the nation's first divorced President, who rarely attended church and gave little to charity, while viewing with suspicion Jimmy Carter, a devoutly religious President who taught a Baptist Sunday school class throughout his term in office."

Philip Yancey
Christianity Today

During the Republican primaries for the 2012 election, the Values Voters' Coalition, comprised primarily of evangelical voters, surprisingly favored libertarian Ron Paul in its straw poll. Congressman Paul has publicly supported the legalization of street heroin and prostitution for years. That caused this life-long conservative Christian to wonder if the only thing many of my fellow evangelicals now value is reducing government until it can be drowned in our bathtubs, as anti-taxer Grover Norquist famously quipped.

That seems odd considering Moses was a law-giver as well as prophet. As we'll see later, Moses sure didn't mind using his Law for "right-wing social engineering." David, who was admittedly an adulterer, and Solomon, the result of that all too human sin, were the purported authors of our Wisdom Literature and were kings. Jesus taught that every aspect of the law of Moses carved in concrete would endure for all eternity, even though he set his disciples free of legalisms by writing his spiritual laws of love on our hearts, minds and souls.

Jesus also told us to render taxes unto even Caesar, who would have never won a straw poll among Jesus' contemporaries. Saint Paul seconded that by commanding the Christians in Rome to "honor and respect" government, even if it was the psychopath Nero.

The apparent inconsistencies in our evangelical theology and politics suggest political humorist P.J. O'Rourke may have had a point. As I shared during the mid-nineties in my book *Ten Golden Rules for Financial Success*, O'Rourke wrote of what was called the "angry white man" years:

> *"Libertarianism is a philosophy of radically limited government. It is attractive to those well-off professionals who have nothing in common with the religious right but would just like to be left alone. The libertarians have also replaced the Marxists as the world's leading utopia builders."*

Even the conservative/libertarian *Wall Street Journal* said back then, in a passage I also quoted:

> *"Though most voters probably don't even realize it, much of the angry sentiment coursing through their veins today isn't traditionally Republican or even conservative. It's libertarian; utterly disdainful of government."*

Fast forward a decade and most evangelicals, in my opinion anyway, are influenced by the popular religious media as opposed to Christianity Today, and still can't nuance the profound theological differences between being conservative and libertarian. For example, consider Ayn Rand.

She remains such a god among libertarians that Fox recently featured an article by her disciples entitled, "Does America Need Jesus or Ayn Rand?" For that reason, Chuck Colson and Marvin Olasky of *World* magazine have recently challenged her views. It's about time.

As I also explained nearly two decades ago now, *The Economist* magazine called Rand "the heroine of America's libertarian right" in 1994. It explained that Rand's very close disciple Alan Greenspan, the former chairman of the Federal Reserve, deregulated most financial services due to Rand's notions that government is the problem and the moral purpose of our lives is to make money. For the reasons I cited above about government being an integral part of Judeo-Christianity, Rand therefore wanted to be remembered as history's greatest enemy of religion, and Christianity in particular.

Of course, that would make her the anti-Christ for us. If you missed it, you can read an article I wrote for *Christianity Today* on that subject for the

September 2010 issue. It should prompt all of us to reflect that the Bible says many believers will be fooled by such an anti-Christ.

If you've only read Rand's best sellers *Atlas Shrugged*, the second most influential book in America after the Bible, and *The Fountainhead*, you would indeed be tempted to believe utopia will result on earth once we rid ourselves of government. They are unparalleled in substituting shadows for reality. They contain no S&L scandals. No Enron scandals. No wayward sub-prime mortgage originators. No tobacco executives telling Congress that every mother in America is wrong about smoking. No inside traders. And no Mother Teresa's. Just virtuous CEO types who hate government. None of those virtuous types inherited their wealth and/or trade financial products for a living, as many of the "1%" do.

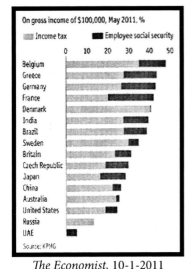

On gross income of $100,000, May 2011, %

The Economist, 10-1-2011

Rand's hatred of government creates a lot of misperceptions, particularly about the taxes the typical American pays. Americans have long been among the least taxed people in the developed world. It's a similar story when it comes to corporate taxation. Conservative politicians are always painting the illusion that our corporations are at a huge disadvantage as our marginal, or highest, corporate tax *rate* is "among the highest in the developing world." That's true of the tax rate. But it's also true that American corporations enjoy what are among the most numerous tax "loopholes" in the developed world, so the taxes *they actually pay* are among the lowest in the developed world. I'm not arguing that is right or wrong, only reality. But I can already hear libertarian readers calling me a "liberal!"

In addition, there are provisions in the tax code that allow more and more business entities, called "pass through businesses," to escape all taxes. In short, anytime voters pay a congressman to tax any business, there's a business paying a lobbyist to assure it doesn't happen. The

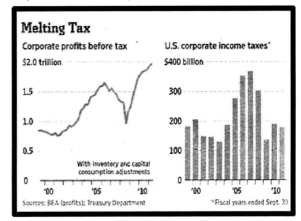

Melting Tax

Corporate profits before tax

U.S. corporate income taxes*

Sources: BEA (profits); Treasury Department   *Fiscal years ended Sept. 30

January 4, 2012

following charts from *The Wall Street Journal* attest to that reality:

I expect few affluent Tea Partiers want to believe it but even the September 2, 2011 issue of *Forbes*, The Capitalist Tool, contained a disturbing chart about federal taxes in America. It showed that tax rates rise until the taxpayer has an "adjusted gross income" of one million dollars per year. At that point, the percentage of incomes taken as taxes *actually declines* until the highest earning four hundred Americans, who are making over ten million dollars per year, are paying the same percentage of their incomes in federal taxes as are those making two hundred thousand dollars per year.

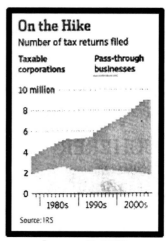

January 10, 2012

The very affluent don't really want to flatten their taxes, to even the level of those making five hundred thousand a year, as much as they want to lower them to what the average American is paying. That might be the just thing to do. But the electorate should not make that decision based on illusions.

The *Financial Times* has reported that tax payers with an income of more than $1 million dollars pay an average of 29.8% compared to those with an income of less than $100,000 who pay 34.9%. In other words, those with the lowest income pay taxes at the highest rate and those with the highest income pay taxes at the lowest rate. It's not my job to decide if the very wealthiest should be taxed at the same rate as the average American, but it is my job to suggest Judeo-Christian morality has long said that "much is expected from those to whom much has been given." Only you can decide whether that morality should be integrated with, or compartmentalized from, government and taxes. As Rand considered selfishness to be a virtue, she would obviously have you compartmentalize, or deny, that particular teaching.

So you might also read *My Years with Ayn Rand* by Nathaniel Branden, her one-time St. Peter turned Judas. He implies, if not states, Rand was a sociopath, if not an outright psychopath. She admired the fact that William Hickman, the OJ Simpson of her day, cast off all traditional morality when murdering a young girl and spreading her body parts over Los Angeles.

If you believe Branden had a score to settle even though he ditched his wife and Rand for a lovely young thing, you might read *Goddess of the Market; Ayn Rand and the American Right* by Professor Jennifer Burns. Burns wrote:

*"Rand was blazing a trail distinct from the broader conservative movement, as indicated by the title of her second non-fiction book The Virtue of Selfishness. Whereas traditional conservatism emphasized duties, responsibilities, and social interconnectedness, at the core of the right-wing ideology Rand spearheaded was a **rejection of moral obligations to others** (emphasis mine)."*

Rand once told *Playboy*: "My views on charity are very simple. I do not consider it a major virtue, and above all, I do not consider it a moral duty. What I am fighting is the idea that charity is a moral duty and a primary virtue." She also wrote: "I believe in complete, laissez faire, full, unregulated capitalism – not mixed economy." So as *The Economist* put it: "For her, government was nothing more than licensed robbery and altruism, just an excuse for power-grabbing."

Sadly, even today Rand's disciples paint the illusion that Christianity is purely about altruism, which is why they don't think our faith is compatible with business. Yet Christianity is built on the ethic of loving our neighbors as ourselves, while its *ideal* is to act selflessly in some spheres of life. After all, God loves us as much as God loves our neighbors. Again, you will have to decide whether that ethic involves government or not. I simply ask you to understand the selfish ethic from where Rand's disciples are coming.

Still, despite Americans receiving a lower percentage of their incomes from the government than any developed nation on earth, Rand's followers still want to shrink it far more, or at least they want government spending on others to shrink. In its "Capitalism in Crisis" series, the January 14, 2012 issue of the *Financial Times* said this in an article entitled "Caught between apathy and anger":

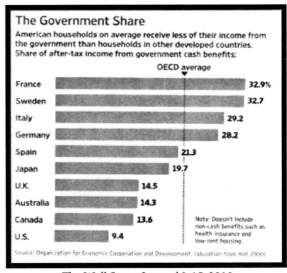

The Wall Street Journal 9-15-2010

"A recent survey of Tea Party supporters showed that more than three quarters wanted to leave untouched Medicare and Social Security, the public pension system - the largest items in the federal

budget. When Paul Ryan, the House budget chairman, unveiled a fiscal roadmap last year that would have rapidly slashed Medicare's largesse, fellow Republicans rapidly distanced themselves from his plan. Newt Gingrich, the Republican former speaker of the House of Representatives and now improbably anti-capitalist rival to Mr. Romney, attacked the Ryan plan as 'rightwing social engineering.'"

While federal spending that comes back to us is a relatively small percentage of our incomes, it is a very significant percentage of Washington's spending. Few seem to understand the following chart demonstrates that if money is wasted in Washington, it is likely wasted on us. I've even had several politically conservative physicians who pay a lot of taxes rail about the need for Washington to cut spending, at the same time they were expressing fears about cuts to Medicare, and so on. They simply haven't made connections between their political views and their professional lives, for it is actually medical spending that is "bankrupting" Washington.

Rand's selfish philosophy is shared by other libertarians. Nobel economist Milton Friedman famously influenced many CEO's of major corporations with

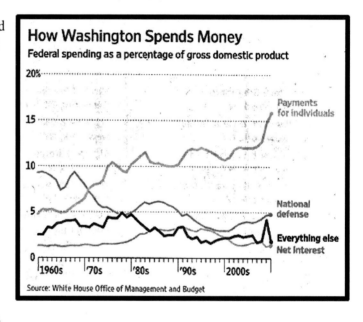

his teaching that "the only social responsibility of a corporation is to make a profit" for shareholders. It's a very small slide down the moral slope for a CEO to believe his or her only responsibility is to profit himself or herself. That moral perspective is likely a major reason that record corporate profits co-exist with high unemployment in America.

Corporate irresponsibility is why famed management consultant Peter Drucker, who once taught theology, wrote a book entitled *Post-Capitalist Society* during the mid-nineties. The book pointedly called Friedman's teaching "futile." Over and over, Peter told business publications that excessive

CEO compensation was "like watching pigs at the trough" and would ignite a backlash movement. Prophetic as always, Peter said that long before Occupy Wall Street became a global movement. Of course, CEO's ignored him, as people always do prophets.

Still, Rand and Freidman's philosophy was apparently adapted by the Koch brothers, owners of a multi-billion dollar private company, largely energy-based, who are reportedly major underwriters of the Tea Party movement. They were the recent focus of a *Bloomberg Markets* cover story that suggested the Kochs have recently skirted several federal laws while doing business in Iran and so on.

Their activities in the Tea Party are reportedly aligned with libertarian Dick Armey's FreedomWorks organization. As minority leader of the House during 1994, Mr. Armey helped to excite the "angry white man" with "Armey's Axioms," such as: "Social responsibility is a euphemism for personal irresponsibility." Another was, "Government is dumb while markets are smart." Apparently, Mr. Armey has never counseled investors, causing me to wonder who's really disconnected from reality. But David Koch was once a vice-presidential nominee on the Libertarian ticket. Presidential candidate Herman Cain once said he was the Koch's brother by another mother.

Such influential ideas seem reflective of the modern golden rule that "he who has the gold makes the rules," more so than the traditional parable of the Good Samaritan and the Bible's Golden Rule. It might interest Tea Partiers who detest special interests in Washington that Armey's lobbying firm has reportedly focused on energy issues lately.

So why would someone who was long a conservative until the GOP's right-ward shift turned him into a centrist and Independent, violate President Reagan's eleventh commandment and point out the logs in the eyes of Republicans? That's the difference in morality and politics, which is almost exclusively preoccupied with those specs in the eyes of others.

Plus, most Americans are conservative, respectful of the past, particularly in moral areas. Rand wanted libertarians to be "radicals for capitalism," in the over-throw of the past. Conservatives risk political as well as economic backlash due to libertarian excesses. Progressive economist Jeffery Sachs, who is so very influential in the developing nations, writes in his new book:

> "I decided early on in my career to devote my energies to the economic challenges abroad. Now I am worried about my own country.... At the root of America's economic crisis lies a moral crisis: the decline of civic virtue among America's political and economic elite. **Without restoring an ethos of social responsibility, there can be no meaningful and**

sustained economic recovery. (But) libertarians aim to absolve the rich of any social responsibilities toward the rest of society."

One of the reasons my more conservative friends hate taxes so much is they believe the political shadows that: 1) our country doesn't have enough, 2) it needs more, and 3) higher tax rates slow growth. Yet many economists are not as certain as libertarian politicians, who apparently believe if they tell whoppers often enough, they will become true. For example, Denmark takes half its citizens' incomes in taxes. But the country's economy has an admirable growth rate. Our Small Business Administration rates Denmark as the easiest country in the world in which to start a new business. And Denmark enjoys far more equality than does America. As a result, Danes are routinely surveyed to be the happiest people on earth. So even Joel Slemrod, who served as senior tax economist for President Ronald Reagan's Council of Economic Advisors has said:

"There's very limited evidence to support the claim that increased personal income tax rates on higher income people would reduce hiring."

I even believe the new golden rule is why the most popular evangelical financial advisors of the past two decades have actively discouraged the socially responsible investing movement that has exploded on Wall Street, even though its roots are in the teachings of Moses. It often seems we can make up our own rules as long as we say "God owns it all" often enough as we give a pittance to churches and ministries. Most do not seem to know what Moses said about the responsible management of wealth, though detractors say over and over that they are "Bible-believing."

Our confused syncretism, or the mixing of religions, is likely one reason that Mr. Sachs mentions the Dali Lama and Buddhism. But he's evidently similar to many Ivy League intellectuals, and progressives in general, in "knowing" little more about Christianity than that the religious right is a major voting bloc in the GOP. He seems totally unaware that while he was focused abroad, the Interfaith Center on Corporate Responsibility was sponsoring dozens of shareholder resolutions to clean up sub-prime lending. So repeatedly, Mr. Sachs advocates the federal government assume our responsibilities for us, thereby apparently preferring law and taxes to virtue and love.

On the other hand, Rand dismissed conservative Nobel economist F.A. Hayek because he thought government might play a role in the economy during a depression. Rand favored libertarian economist Ludwig Von Mises, who one-time presidential candidate Michelle Bachmann considers "beach reading." Yet it could also have been because Hayek once wrote:

"A movement whose main purpose is the relief from responsibility cannot but be immoral in its effects, however lofty the ideals to which it owes its birth."

I expect Hayek shot that arrow toward groups like Occupy Wall Street, which usually want government to assume responsibility for cleaning up markets, and so on. But it applies equally to selfish Tea Partiers who, wittingly or unwittingly, support avoiding the social responsibility of loving one's neighbor as self both voluntarily and through government.

If all this dualism in our thinking doesn't awaken values voters, we might note the inability of any Republican candidate to lead the party, much less our diverse nation. We might also note that as I write, the latest *Wall Street Journal* survey said a majority of Americans now favor returning Congress to the Democrats.

As a conservative Christian who may now be a political moderate, I can live with standing on principle in defeat. But I see little virtue in going down to defeat by refuting the principles that Moses and Jesus taught in order to advance the teachings of a radical anti-Christ figure. We Lutherans of German descent painfully remember that the German church made that huge mistake by baptizing another "ism" in the form of Nazism.

As with Rand's Objectivism, Nazism was largely built on the willful and humanistic morality of Nietzsche. Fool me once...

Meditation Four

Seek First a Debt Free Society?

*"Whenever I tried to become wise and learn what goes on
in the world, I realized that you could stay awake night
and day and never be able to understand what God is
doing. However hard you may try, you'll never find out.
Wise men may claim to know but they don't."*

Solomon
Ecclesiastes 8:16

*"I think there ought to be a club in which preachers
and journalists could come together and have the
sentimentalism of the one matched by the cynicism of the
other. That ought to bring them pretty close to the truth."*

Theologian Reinhold
Niebuhr

I'm going to risk my credibility - and most likely your anger if you're a
libertarian Tea Partier - by suggesting few of us, myself included, really
understand our nation's finances, particularly our federal debt. There are
simply matters that are too large for most human minds, even those with the
wisdom of Solomon. If he couldn't understand his simple economy, imagine
how he'd feel about today's complex financial instruments. Yet there remain
some "real facts," as Lincoln called them, that we ignore at our peril.

For example, odds are quite good that you know that the federal debt is
approximately fifteen trillion dollars as I write. There's even a billboard
about that in Times Square that is updated each second. But odds are even
better that you have never heard, even once, the size of our nation's assets.
Don't feel badly. I have asked two congressmen, both of whom served on key
financial committees in the U.S. House of Representatives, if either had ever
heard those assets estimated. Neither had. That's simply a limitation of our
republican form of government where we elect ordinary citizens to Congress.

You probably also do not know that although the federal debt has increased, we actually spend a lower percentage of our national income, or GDP, on servicing that debt, or paying interest, than we have in many years. That's simply as interest rates have dropped so sharply, contrary to the predictions of most pessimists.

I'll also suggest that the more burdensome debt is to you personally, the more you fear it on a national level. That's simply Jungian psychology. That can be explained very simply by pointing your index finger at someone. Notice that the three smaller fingers of your hand are pointed back at you. Very simply, odds are good that what bothers you most in this old world reflects an unresolved conflict within yourself. Otherwise, it wouldn't bother you. For example, my experiences on Wall Street suggest

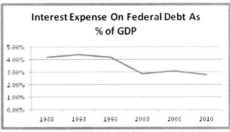

Budget of the United States, OMB

the most authoritarian business executives usually chafe most at regulations. The more they take from shareholders, the more they hate taxes being taken from them. And so it goes. But the following chart could bring enormous spiritual peace to millions of Americans who obsess over the federal debt, probably as they are too indebted personally, or in their corporations and ministries.

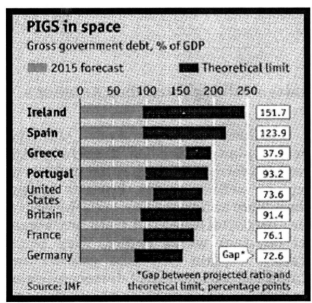

Despite what we hear constantly from the conservative media and conservative politicians, the above graph from *The Economist* shows actual economists at the International Monetary Fund, which is no dove on federal debts, have calculated America can likely handle

The Economist, 9-4-2010

an additional 73.6% debt to GDP. That is roughly ten trillion dollars of additional federal debt.

Of course, the economists added it would be silly to incur that additional debt unless absolutely essential for moral purposes, which, depending on tax policies, might include providing health care for an aging society, true defense of our nation, or enabling additional wealth creation for those in need.

During the Great Recession, I was asked by a conservative Christian radio host what I might do if king for a day. I said I'd have my advisors seriously explore borrowing an additional trillion dollars from the Chinese. The reasons are first, it could be borrowed at 1% interest, which means the real cost was a negative 2% as inflation was running 3%. Second, I'd use those trillion dollars to rebuild America's crumbling infrastructure, which would put a lot of unemployed workers from the housing industry back to work, meaning they'd be off the dole and paying taxes again. The host thought I was "touched." Such is how political illusions and perceptions frustrate economists, as well as a richer life for many needy Americans who could be in our work force.

The point, which I will stress again and again, is that true economists often strongly disagree with what most of us perceive as economics, but which is actually politics. As *The Economist* quipped years ago:

> *"Politicians earn much of their living by exploiting anxieties, encouraging people to feel worse than they should about the state of their country."*

Of course, the media does much the same, which is why they serve each others' interests so well, even if they don't always serve our nation's best interests. When I was in the newspaper business before doing radio commentary for UPI, our motto was: "If it bleeds, it leads."

I have nothing to gain by alienating you by questioning your intelligence and telling you such hard truths. I am quite ignorant in many areas in which you could inform me. I live a virtually debt-free lifestyle, so I'm not encouraging more consumer debt. Until recently, I was a life-long Republican who served on a board of advisors to Jack Kemp and Bill Bennett, so I'm not trying to provide political cover for the Democrats. Also, I've been a critic of Wall Street ethics longer than most of my libertarian friends have been critical of Washington's ethics.

The simplest reason for my suggestions is that more of us simply must begin to pursue, rather than claim, truth about mundane matters, primarily as judgment begins in the house of the Lord. I deeply believe the theological, political and economic truth that a nation divided against itself cannot stand. And today, the church may be divided as politically, economically, racially and sexually as our nation.

Such divide usually results in a huge deficit in grace, as demonstrated by the shouting in Congress, the rage on our roads, and the anger from our radio stations to our athletic courts. Grace is destroyed whenever prideful humans claim the Godly characteristic of knowing it all. Historic Christianity deplored that; humanism has applauded it…to our spiritual detriment, and increasingly to our economic detriment. It's time to come to our senses, at least as best as we possibly can.

Tap on a desk and ask students in your elementary school science class if it is a solid, and they should answer, "Yes." But ask students pursuing a Ph.D. in nuclear physics, and they should respond, "No. It's mostly space within rapidly vibrating atoms that are deteriorating according to the laws of thermodynamics." Both groups are "correct" despite giving seemingly diametrically-opposed answers. And despite many Christian's skepticism of higher science, the second answer is actually closer to the biblical truth that our material world is passing away.

Similarly, some verses of the Bible seem to advocate the enjoyment of alcoholic beverages (Deuteronomy 14:26) while others seem to advocate abstinence (Proverbs 20:1). So while we can quote the verses we prefer and claim that those who quote the other verses are wrong, in reality the Bible must say alcohol should be avoided by those for whom it is a problem but it can also enrich life for those with the maturity to enjoy it in moderation.

The same is true with debt. Most financial ministries deal with the very real pain that consumer debt causes. So they quote Bible verses that seem to discourage debt. I've even heard credit cards deemed "evil." I prefer ministries that can nuance the difference in consumer and productive debt, which is wise as credit can enrich life. If pessimists who decry rising debt levels can't also acknowledge rising levels of prosperity, perhaps they'll listen to Jesus and Moses.

In the Sermon on the Mount, Jesus said we should lend to anyone in need at any time, especially the poor (Luke 6:35). Moses also said God would deem it "evil" if we didn't lend to those in need (Deuteronomy 15:7). Both indicate considerable borrowing and lending, as Jesus demonstrated when he borrowed a donkey, the upper room and the tomb during Holy Week alone.

What was actually forbidden in biblical times was charging interest on loans, which no one now questions (Exodus 22:25).

Some ministries also suggest that if we do borrow, we have an absolute obligation as Christians to repay. Yet the true absolute of the Bible was seventh-year debt forgiveness (Deuteronomy 15:1; Nehemiah 5:10). A borrower simply cannot become even poorer when he or she borrows interest-free, repays when possible, and is forgiven when repayment is not possible. If the debt recommended by Moses and Jesus has indeed grown burdensome, we have the option of also forgiving some of it, as they recommended, or having natural law take effect by the borrower's default. The choice remains ours, as witnessed by subprime mortgage bonds.

It's difficult for us to see those biblical concepts through our cultural screens of capitalism, with its golden rule that "he who has the gold makes the rules." Most capitalists who lend various forms of wealth want it back, plus interest. Yet a truly biblical understanding of credit can have dramatically enriching consequences in the real world, particularly for the least of these, as demonstrated by the growing number of ministries doing micro-lending.

Those organizations, like Opportunity International, where I once served as board treasurer, make $200 loans primarily to women in the third world, which Opportunity says is actually "the two-thirds world." People use those loans to start tiny businesses. While the concept is as imperfect as people are, the people engaged in micro-enterprise must be better than usual people as it works quite well. The repayment rate has historically been better than most American loan repayment rates. Oxfam has conducted studies that suggest more than two people's lives have been dramatically improved with each loan. And it's now possible to lend to such organizations as well as give, an idea all affluent Christians and foundations might look into.

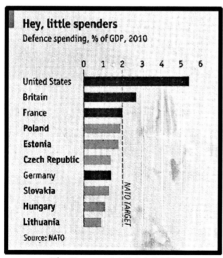

The Economist 5-14-2011

Pragmatically, as an investment professional, I often witness Christians doing considerable good with their savings by lending money to growing cities that need water and sewer projects, schools, airports, and so on. However, I'd also argue our banks would be more careful in their lending practices if they understood that more of us might default on loans that have become truly burdensome through no fault of our own. And one-half of bankruptcies are actually caused by medical emergencies. We need not add guilt to those pains.

Politically, rarely acknowledged in our age of cynicism toward government but remembered by some of us old timers, was that lending to our federal government by purchasing war bonds was considered quite patriotic during World War II. Some historians believe President Reagan, along with Margaret Thatcher and John Paul, wisely defeated the Soviet Union without firing a bullet by increasing defense spending. That spending, made possible by federal debt, bankrupted the Soviet Union when it tried to keep up. As an old Army officer, I believe in our troops being the best equipped in the world. But I'm also aware an awful lot of defense spending is for political rather than defense purposes.

If you've invested in a U.S. savings bond, Treasury bond or money market fund containing Treasury bills, you've owned part of the federal debt. That federal debt helped enrich our nation's future by winning World War II and the Cold War. You consider Treasury securities to be assets that will enrich your future, rather than a debt that will impoverish it. Nearly half of our federal debt is actually owned by Americans, who receive the interest payments to re-circulate through our economy, rather than owned by the Chinese, Japanese, and so on.

Morally, it is rather ironic that so many conservative voters have been made so angry over the growth in the federal debt over the years. Conservative leaders in particular made it possible for that debt to grow.

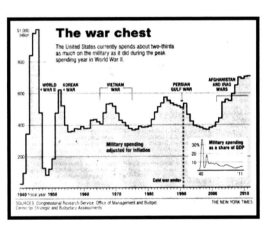

During the mid-eighties, we had special prospectuses for trusts of government bonds that we mailed to our clients in Latin America. In bright red letters at the top of the front cover, there was a statement that no one in America would report to the clients' governments that the clients had received interest. In essence, the United States needed to borrow for the Cold War so it became the largest off-shore tax haven ever for the rest of the world, with the exception of Canada.

I never read about that reality in the media until *Forbes* ran an article entitled, "Need A Tax Haven? Try America" in its September 2009 issue. The article essentially explained why there are unpleasant economic ramifications to conservative politicians and bankers painting the illusion that we need a wall across our border with Mexico. *Forbes* said:

> *"The US Treasury Department rails sanctimoniously against overseas tax havens and recently bullied Switzerland into naming American tax evaders of Swiss bank UBS. But who knew that the US itself is a tax haven?...The US allows nonresident foreign nationals to park their money in US bank accounts without having to pay taxes on interest or (in most cases) report it to the IRS. It also doesn't automatically exchange tax information with other countries, with the sole exception of Canada. Mexican Finance Secretary Agustin Carstens wants US Treasury Secretary Timothy Geithner to give his country the same favored treatment as Canada."*

Obviously, reinstating the so-called "reporting requirement" would have a significant impact on America's ability to borrow from abroad as foreign investors would have fewer reasons to invest here. One might assume that conservatives who want to reduce foreign borrowing would support that. However, the December 29, 2011 issue of *The Wall Street Journal* reported the Obama administration floated the idea of re-instating the reporting requirement and met with considerable resistance:

> *"US banks are trying to quash a proposed regulation that would require them to report interest income earned by non-US residents to the IRS, which could then pass the information to their home countries. Banks in Florida, Texas and California say the effort could drain the coffers of banks that rely heavily on foreign deposits."*

It is also generally believed that if the US does reduce its status as an off-shore tax haven to the rest of the world, our interest rates might rise rather quickly. So again, there is a tension between our desire to be the moral leader of the world, while also wanting to be the economic leader. Those two goals must be balanced.

Most of us can be forgiven for not understanding that financial version of nuclear physics. Yet for the sake of our spirits and finances, our Christian leaders, particularly stewardship leaders, simply must. Bruce Howard, who has chaired the economics department at Wheaton College, has written:

> **"If there is one element in the market economy that has caused more confusion in the minds of Christians than anything else, it is the issue of credit...While it can be grossly misused, credit at its best is entirely compatible with traditional Christianity."**

Most who see the world through political screens have been focused almost exclusively on the morality of federal and consumer debt. But the Great Recession was actually ignited by our Wall Street firms incurring excessive corporate debt, largely so they could underwrite excessive mortgage debt for Americans. This is why **Jesus taught the truth that we should remain on guard against *all forms* of greed, rather than simply politically-correct forms.** So despite credit cards causing some of us considerable pain and our federal debt threatening to increase sharply in the future, let me explain why some knowledgeable experts haven't lost all hope for the American economy. Because the self-interested shadow-making about our personal finances has probably matched that surrounding our nation's finances.

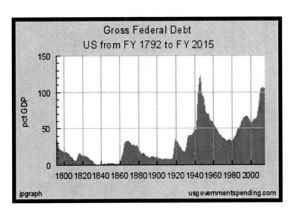

Most politicians seem as disinterested as the media in economic good news. Churches no longer teach good economic news. So our federal debt has been quite misinterpreted on occasion. Most everyone knows the federal debt is now fifteen trillion dollars. As a percentage of our national income (GDP), that is about half of what it was at the end of World War Two, at 60% versus 120%. **Notice from this chart how wars have been a primary reason for the growth of the federal debt since the American Revolution.** Also notice the chart extrapolates our growing debt out to 2015 in this chart.

The federal debt is indeed projected to rise to 120% of GDP, and possibly much more, during my expected lifetime, *assuming* our wars, taxes, and spending on retired boomers continue as is. The debt may even rise to the 240% of GDP level it was in Great Britain at the end of WWII. But there is hope that this figure is too pessimistic as the war in

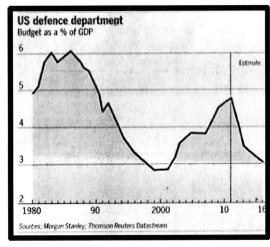

Iraq is apparently winding down and America may again experience a "peace dividend."

Again, we might remember that President Clinton ran on the campaign theme: "It's the economy, stupid." Years later, he claimed credit for balancing the budget. He never explained that a large measure of that had to do with the fall of the Berlin Wall and the end of the Cold War, with which he had little to do. Notice from the following chart from the January 26, 2012 issue of the *Financial Times* that the drop in defense spending after the Cold War ended amounted to fully 3% of America's GDP, a huge savings. As the old political saying goes: "Don't try to organize a parade of three hundred million people; find a parade, jump in front, and take credit for leading it."

More importantly, when we consider whether our family's mortgage is burdensome or not, we usually relate that debt to the value of our home, not simply our income. And I've never found one American Christian during twenty years of questioning who knows what the value of our American home is. However, that number is estimated each year by the same folks who estimate our debt. Such information simply isn't the kind of bad news favored by our media and politicians.

You can count your economic blessings as an American by studying the chart at the end of this section. It's from the Office of Management and Budget in the White House. In this case, it's from the last year of President "W's" administration as I know few conservatives would consider it legitimate if it came from the Obama White House. Unlike those charts we see from politicians and the media that only show our rising federal debt, this one shows the latest available estimate of our nation's total assets as having risen steadily to $125.5 trillion. It also shows we owe other nations $7.2 trillion more than they owe us. Again, that number is largely correct as one-half of our fifteen trillion dollar federal debt is actually owed to Americans, who consider Treasury securities to be assets crucial to their future.

So America's net worth, after paying off all debts, at the end of 2008 was $118.3 trillion, or $388,100 per person.

For some reason, hopefully not more shadow-making, that chart has not been included in Obama budgets. But an even fuller perspective shows we have more serious debt issues than the federal government, even if it's easier to rail against the financial sins of Washington than deal with our own.

Politically, we might "honor and respect" our government more if we notice that the last line of the OMB balance sheet tracks our federal debt as a percentage of our assets. After the debt-to-income ratio, that percentage may be the most important statistic for our policy makers in Washington to consider.

Notice the trend of our federal debt to our nation's assets has *actually been in decline* the past fifty years, from 10.3% in 1960 to 6.5% now.

In short, while the amount Washington has borrowed has soared recently, America's assets have increased more rapidly. I know that's small comfort for those who think of Washington as a foreign land, even alien land. **Economic reality is that Washington's finances can be better understood as a savings account that has been slightly over-drawn as our checking account and securities account have risen strongly in value.** That is not made clear by politicians who declare it's immoral for Washington to borrow money, as corporations and individuals do.

America **has not been spending more than it makes;** *Washington* **has been spending more than it receives in an admittedly inefficient effort to enrich our nation with various programs, including enriching our world with defense spending. That's the only way our nation's assets have increased as our federal debt has done the same. It's also questionable that Washington has been any more wasteful than corporate boards when paying CEOs and CEO benefits recently.**

To say otherwise and argue that Washington has "bankrupted" America might be the single most divisive bit of political propaganda in our nation during recent decades, as it has also impoverished many of my investors. It is also a form of class warfare as government borrowing often supports the neediest Americans while corporate and personal borrowing is usually done by the more affluent. I know that will irritate my more conservative friends but I think, actually believe, it is true. Everyone knows that banks only lend to those who don't really need the money.

It's always quite dangerous to compare our nation's finances to our own, as that can be creating Reality in our own image. But considering our assets as well as income is similar to the condition of our affluent retirees in Florida. Some have relatively small mortgages. As a percentage of their smaller retirement incomes, those mortgages are larger than they may have been a few years ago. As a percentage of the retirees' considerable assets however, the mortgages are quite manageable.

Furthermore, politicians may not know it, but true economists know that for every dollar of debt we owe to foreigners, we *own* **about a dollar's worth of foreign assets. Of course, those assets we own do not show up in the purely debt numbers the pessimists like to quote.**

els of government. The final section discusses a range of economic and social indicators.

Improving Tax Fairness and Federal Finances through Better Tax Compliance

The Internal Revenue Service (IRS) collects over 95 percent of total Federal receipts, including $2.5 trillion in 2008. However, not every dollar of tax legally owed is actually paid. The great majority of taxpayers comply with the law by filing returns and paying their taxes on time, but some do not comply, either because they do not understand their obligations due to the complexity of the tax law or because they seek to avoid those obligations.

Tax Compliance: In 2006, the IRS released updated results of its first large study in two decades of the difference between taxes owed and taxes actually paid—the "tax gap." The IRS estimated that taxpayers underpaid by $345 billion in 2001. This equates to a voluntary compliance rate of 84 percent. Late payments and IRS enforcement action reduced this to a net tax gap of $290 billion, raising the net compliance rate to 86 percent. The Department of the Treasury does not have es-

timates of the tax gap for the years after 2001, though current efforts are underway to provide a new estimate and subsequently update it annually.

Due to changes in methodologies, comparisons between the 2001 estimates and those from earlier studies should be made cautiously. However, it does appear that the voluntary compliance rate has not changed much since the 1980s. The IRS previously reported voluntary compliance rates of 87 percent in 1988, 86 percent in 1985, and 84 percent in 1983. While the overall compliance rate seems to have moved relatively little over time, each one percentage point change significantly impacts revenue. A one percentage point improvement would increase revenue by nearly $30 billion per year, based on recent revenue numbers.

The IRS compliance estimates, primarily based on random audits of individuals and businesses, are not precise, but give a good general sense of the size of the tax gap and patterns in compliance. This sort of information is critical for effectively targeting IRS enforcement programs to yield the greatest improvement with the smallest cost and burden on taxpayers. The IRS' estimates are most accurate for underpayments of known taxes as recorded

Table 13–5.   NATIONAL WEALTH
(As of the end of the fiscal year, in trillions of 2008 dollars) — *i.e., adjusted for inflation*

	1960	1965	1970	1975	1980	1985	1990	1995	2000	2005	2006	2007	2008
ASSETS													
Publicly Owned Physical Assets:													
Structures and Equipment	2.4	2.7	3.4	4.1	4.3	4.6	5.0	5.6	6.4	7.7	8.2	8.7	8.7
Federally Owned or Financed	1.4	1.5	1.6	1.8	1.7	2.1	2.2	2.3	2.4	2.5	2.6	2.7	2.8
Federally Owned	1.2	1.2	1.3	1.2	1.1	1.2	1.3	1.4	1.2	1.1	1.2	1.2	1.2
Grants to State & Local Gov'ts	0.2	0.3	0.4	0.6	0.6	0.8	0.9	1.0	1.2	1.4	1.4	1.5	1.6
Funded by State & Local Gov'ts	1.0	1.3	1.7	2.3	2.6	2.5	2.8	3.2	4.0	5.2	5.6	6.0	5.9
Other Federal Assets	0.5	0.5	0.5	0.6	0.9	1.0	0.9	3.7	1.0	1.7	1.7	1.7	1.5
Subtotal	2.9	3.2	3.9	4.8	5.2	5.6	5.9	6.2	7.3	9.4	9.9	10.4	10.2
Privately Owned Physical Assets:													
Reproducible Assets	8.1	9.3	11.4	14.7	19.1	20.3	23.1	25.6	31.1	38.0	39.6	40.2	40.2
Residential Structures	3.2	3.7	4.4	5.6	7.7	7.9	9.1	10.3	12.9	17.4	18.2	18.3	17.6
Nonresidential Plant & Equipment	3.2	3.6	4.6	6.1	7.8	8.6	9.6	9.5	12.7	14.6	15.3	15.7	16.1
Inventories	0.8	0.9	1.0	1.3	1.6	1.5	1.6	1.7	1.9	2.0	2.0	2.1	2.2
Consumer Durables	1.0	1.1	1.4	1.7	2.0	2.2	2.8	3.1	3.6	4.0	4.1	4.1	4.1
Land	2.4	2.9	3.3	4.3	6.6	7.5	7.8	5.8	9.5	18.3	18.8	18.8	14.1
Subtotal	10.6	12.2	14.8	19.0	25.7	27.8	30.9	31.4	40.6	56.3	58.4	59.0	54.2
Education Capital:													
Federally Financed	0.1	0.1	0.3	0.4	0.6	0.7	0.9	1.1	1.4	1.7	1.8	1.9	1.9
Financed from Other Sources	6.7	9.1	12.2	15.5	19.8	23.1	28.5	33.6	43.0	48.6	50.5	52.9	55.2
Subtotal	6.8	9.2	12.5	15.9	20.3	23.8	29.4	34.7	44.4	50.3	52.2	54.8	57.2
Research and Development Capital:													
Federally Financed R&D	0.2	0.4	0.6	0.7	0.7	0.8	1.0	1.1	1.2	1.3	1.4	1.4	1.5
R&D Financed from Other Sources	0.2	0.2	0.3	0.5	0.6	0.8	1.0	1.3	1.8	2.2	2.3	2.4	2.3
Subtotal	0.4	0.6	0.9	1.1	1.3	1.6	2.0	2.4	2.9	3.5	3.7	3.8	3.9
A. Total Assets	20.6	25.3	32.0	40.8	52.6	58.8	68.2	74.7	95.3	119.5	124.3	128.0	125.5
B. Net Claims of Foreigners on U.S. (+)	-0.1	-0.2	-0.2	-0.1	-0.4	0.0	0.9	1.7	3.4	6.1	6.4	8.2	7.2
C. Net Wealth	20.7	25.5	32.2	40.9	53.0	58.7	67.3	73.0	91.9	113.4	117.8	119.6	118.3
ADDENDA:													
Per Capita Wealth (thousands of 2008 dollars)	114.9	131.3	157.4	189.7	232.3	246.0	268.4	273.3	324.9	382.6	393.9	396.5	388.1
Ratio of Wealth to GDP (in percent)	671.3	656.6	694.8	778.5	842.6	782.2	766.2	735.8	758.5	833.6	845.8	836.7	821.6
Total Federally Funded Capital (trillions of 2008 dollars)	2.1	2.5	3.0	3.5	3.9	4.6	4.9	5.2	5.9	7.1	7.4	7.7	7.7
D. Percent of National Wealth	10.3	9.7	9.3	8.6	7.3	7.8	7.3	7.1	6.4	6.3	6.3	6.4	6.5

In essence, reality is that most Americans are too financially sophisticated to lend the American government money for decades at 2%, unless of course, they have been terrified by politicians. We therefore invest in equities. But if the Chinese decide to sell our Treasury bonds, as many pessimists fear, our mutual funds will simply sell our Chinese stocks. While globalization has its challenges, that economic version of "MAD," or mutually assured destruction that prevented the launching of nuclear missiles, is a primary advantage of cross border capital flows.

So yes, as with a reverse mortgage for individuals, I expect that our nation will mortgage some of those assets to care for retiring boomers. Just remember that a lot of that spending will go to the medical professionals in our

American family as, unlike cars, we don't buy much medical care overseas. The balance will go to our fellow Americans as inheritances, or to our American charities as bequests.

Now, after meditating on our nation's balance sheet, and particularly its assets, we need to take an equally balanced look at consumer debt.

A scholarly book entitled *Passing the Plate* explores the sub-biblical giving in our churches. Crucially, it suggests that economic perceptions can reduce giving as surely as economic realities. ("As a man thinketh…")

A recent study by two centers of philanthropy at European universities has also documented what America's Independent Sector said during the early nineties: That negative *perceptions* over the economic future prevent as much giving as economic realities.

Both said that *regardless of our actual financial situations*, the negative perceptions over debt, Social Security, Medicare and so on that is spread by our media, including the Christian media, as fear grabs our attentions, is quite destructive to charitable giving.

I've literally had clients worth several million dollars who've attended churches all their lives and are retired in Christian centers, tell me that they're not leaving anything to charitable causes through their estate plans as their first responsibility is to care for their children. And they believe their children will need every cent as the economy is about to implode.

Fortunately, *Passing the Plate* reiterates what the Financial Seminary has tried to say about credit card debt for years: "One commonly cited statistic in the media is that the average American owes $8,000 in credit card debt." Page 64 of the book concluded that reality is:

> *"In short, while many Americans are no doubt 'overspent,' the possibility of most people drowning in credit card debt as the explanation for lack of generous religious and charitable giving lacks empirical support."*

Between those two statements, the authors explained that the $8,000 figure is for those who have credit card debts they roll over each month. Yet, 52% of us have no credit card or pay our balances each month. The authors also explained that

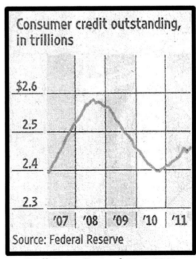

Consumer credit outstanding, in trillions

Source: Federal Reserve

Wall Street Journal 12-8-2011

the affluent - who pay for their taxes and for their BMW's with credit cards to get the frequent flyer miles - skewed the numbers higher so "the median balance was only $2,200." That's the reality for most of our members and suggests our moral leaders should be focused on far more serious financial problems.

The December 8, 2011 issue of *The Wall Street Journal* put consumer debt, and credit card debt in particular, in proper perspective. Total *consumer debt* at that time was just under $2.5 trillion. At the peak in 2009, total indebtedness in America, from our mortgages to our federal debt, was a bit over $50 trillion and it was slightly smaller when the *Journal* article appeared. When the article appeared, of our total consumer debt, which includes car loans and such, only a bit under $800 billion was credit card debt.

Credit card debt is actually under two percent of Americans' total indebtedness.

Few credit management ministries also share the fact, as stated by respected banking analyst Meredith Whitney in the October 2, 2009 issue of *The Wall Street Journal* after the credit crunch leading to the Great Recession, that:

> "Credit cards are the most common source of liquidity to small businesses, used by 82% as a vital portion of their overall funding. Thus, it is of merit when 79% of small businesses surveyed tell the Small Business Association that credit-card lending standards have tightened drastically and their access to credit lines has decreased materially."

Yes, credit card debt is burdensome to a few in our churches. But in general, I believe it's fair to say that our very negative perceptions of credit cards has more to do with the fundraising, or shadow-making, of credit ministries, than cards being a major problem for most Christians. If I asked you to give to my ministry as we're trying to reduce the portion of the 2% of America's indebtedness that is painful to a few Christians, it's unlikely you would be very generous. But you might be quite generous if I told you that "America is drowning in a sea of red ink" and we'd better do something immediately to save our children.

I was once called "a tool of Satan" by one of the best-known Christian credit ministries after I'd presented these facts at a church growth conference. I was trying to explain, as Independent Sector has done for years, that negative economic perceptions cause most people to hold tightly to the money that might fund more church growth. Apparently, some presenters were more interested in the growth of their para-church ministries than the growth of the Church and its members' finances, not to mention the pursuit of Truth. They might notice sometime that more and more ministries are increasingly using credit cards to secure quick funding in order to respond to natural disasters and so on.

There is no need to demonize credit cards simply as a small percentage of our citizens, including recent seminary graduates, are having trouble managing them.

So what can you do with these "real facts?" Simple: Proclaim the good economic news, perhaps simply by copying this chapter for your friends and/ or church members. One affluent businessman to whom I gave the nation's balance sheet keeps it on his desk to lift the spirits of his visitors.

By spreading such good news, the church might again become an oasis of gratitude and hope for our financially affluent but spiritually bankrupt culture that has grown so very cynical of politics, the media and Wall Street.

Meditation Five

Forget the Past, Despair for the Future

*"I am struck by the fact the prophets speaking about the
future of Israel always kept reminding their people of
God's great works in the past. They could look forward
with confidence because they could look backward with
awe to Yahweh's great deeds."*

Henri Nouwen
The Genesee Diary

*"The idea that economic crises, like the current financial
and housing crisis, are mainly caused by changing
thought patterns goes against standard economic
thinking. But the current crisis bears witness to the role of
such changes in thinking. It was caused precisely by our
changing confidence, temptations, envy, resentments and
illusions - and especially by changing stories about the
nature of the economy."*

Animal Spirits

One reason the Judeo-Christian ethos, and particularly the Calvinist spirit
that built America, has been decimated during the past thirty years is that
very few of us have any awareness of how blessed we are by historic and global
standards.

By definition, secular society is concerned with the here and now, which
affects our religious lives as well as political and economic lives. This is
particularly true when we attend contemporary churches that have had
few traditional anchors in the past. Ironically, those are the fastest growing
churches in America. Carolyn Arends described that conundrum in the June
2010 issue of *Christianity Today*:

"One of the quirks of growing up in certain streams of evangelicalism is a lack of historical context. In my youth, a church father was a dad on the deacons' board. If we had to summarize Christianity's history, we would probably reference the apostle Paul, Billy Graham, and our congregational building committee."

The other conundrum is that those denominations with traditions that could help us recover the better dimensions of Calvinism that built this country are in decline. They are primarily engaged in institutional survival so all we hear about money from them is usually about fundraising. Jack Bogle, the respected founder of the Vanguard Mutual Funds, is a Calvinist who remembers that tradition. On the front page of his book Enough, Jack shared this quote:

"The people who created this country built a moral structure around money. The Puritan legacy inhibited luxury and self-indulgence. For centuries, it remained industrious, ambitious and frugal. Over the past thirty years, much of that has been shredded... The country's moral guardians are forever looking out for decadence out of Hollywood and reality TV. But the most rampant decadence today is financial decadence, the trampling of decent norms about how to use and harness money."

If you have any doubts about how grateful we Americans should be with our material condition, or any illusions about our true poverty being spiritual and moral, the following passage, graphic though it is in places, should begin the process of erasing them. This was sent to me by a Lutheran minister who has been a friend for many years. My study of economic history, and particularly the period from the Protestant Reformation during the 1500's to the present, suggests that what you are about to read is fairly representative of economic conditions back then.

If you are a pastor or ministry leader and cannot see any reason to concern yourself with such history, you should. During the early nineties, when scarcity theology filled the Christian airwaves, as it is again, Independent Sector was saying negative economic perceptions were a major deterrent to charitable giving. Of course, those perceptions usually brought in donations and sold books for those spreading those perceptions as they usually promised solutions. I remember televangelist D. James Kennedy sending a fund-raising letter on which he grossly over-stated the federal debt but promised to use his influence to reduce it...if people would only send in enough money.

One book tied to the scarcity theology crowd was written by a well-known evangelical investment advisor. It even promised that the Bible had revealed to him how to prevent losses during market turmoil. I expect such teaching encouraged the naive to send money for his firm to manage. As for me, my Wall Street experience, and the *Book of Job*, caused me to prefer the realistic response of legendary mutual fund manager Peter Lynch when asked what would happen to his shareholders during such turmoil. He simply replied, "They will lose some money." Peter was a member of the Roman Catholic Church, which has enough tradition to understand such realities of financial life.

Regardless, the departments for the study of philanthropic studies at the University of Amsterdam and the University of Kent recently conducted a major study of economic perceptions and giving. The report, entitled "Feeling Poor, Acting Stingy," showed that *regardless of people's actual financial circumstances*, negative economic perceptions reduced charitable giving by at least one-third. So if nothing else, it's in our direct financial self-interest to realize that when Jesus spoke of "the rich," the average person on earth lived on the equivalent of nine hundred dollars per year.

The average American now lives on fifty thousand dollars per year, giving new meaning to the teaching about "hundred fold return." Perhaps God has already graciously granted one hundred times as much to Americans as God did to Jesus' contemporaries and we don't have to send money to a television minister to procure God's economic blessings. Come to think of it, that's likely why so many ministries seem so reluctant to help us count our blessings!

Politics may also prevent our understanding of that crucial reality about our material well-being. My friend Jack Kemp, who was a Republican vice-presidential nominee and a bit hot-headed on occasion, threatened to fight me over breakfast one morning if I ever used the words "the rich" again. When we had a private moment, I explained that I understood politicians, and conservative politicians who developed Reaganomics in particular, as Jack was a major force in doing, could never use those words. I explained however that no one hoping to share the Good News of God's love could avoid them. Jack graciously agreed.

From a historical and global perspective, the vast majority of Americans are very definitely rich, even if we're so spiritually poor we can't see that reality. Much like the ancient Hebrews wandering the desert, we just grumble so loudly we can't possibly hear God's directions toward the Promised Land.

Per capita GDP was barely twelve hundred dollars per year when Martin Luther launched the Protestant Reformation. Ironically enough, Luther did so largely because he disagreed with how the church of his day was procuring and using money. He penned his famous *Ninety-Five Theses* after hearing a creative, but misguided, fundraiser promising salvation to those who would simply give money to build the magnificent St. Peter's Basilica in Rome. Luther posted his theses on the door, or bulletin board, we aren't sure which, of Wittenberg Church and launched the Reformation, in addition to the eventual Counter-Reformation within the Roman Catholic Church.

We might also remember the first thing Jesus did during Holy Week was to cleanse the Temple of the money changers. Most of us don't understand the nature of that passage but Anthony Deane explained it this way in *The World Christ Knew*:

> *"By the Law a man was bound to maintain his parents when they became old and necessitous. But suppose he wished to escape this obligation? Then he would go through the form of making his possessions to the Temple authorities, with an understanding that later - less a fee for this service - they should be restored to him. His parents, compelled by extreme want, would sue him in the ecclesiastical court for maintenance. Then he would plead successfully that he had no available assets, all his possessions were now corban, dedicated to religious uses, and so the judge must dismiss the case...This example did not stand alone; 'many such things ye do,' Jesus said, 'making the word of God of none effect through your traditions.'"*

In other words, I strongly believe that our religious tradition is clear that our culture will never get religion, and therefore politics and economics, correct until the Church addresses money in a Biblically and traditionally sound manner.

Some economic sociologists, such as Max Weber, have famously, if arguably, taught that the Reformers made capitalism possible by allowing each of us to work for the glory of God outside the monasteries. We sometimes refer to that as the "Protestant work ethic." The Reformers also legitimated the earning of interest, which is the essence of banking and therefore capitalism. I can't see how those moral changes didn't play a role in the material enrichment of the world.

Still, some theologians now believe those changes went too far and resulted in the monastery becoming the world, rather than the world becoming the monastery. It would not be too far off-base to say that the purpose of this book is to help the world become more like the monastery again. This book essentially says our politicians can make - and break - all the contracts with America they can imagine; however, our future depends upon whether each of us contracts with all the virtues and spirit we ascribe to God as we contract with one another as our brothers' and sisters' keepers. Only gratitude to God and love for neighbor can help us to re-formulate that contract.

Now begins the email that I received from my pastor friend:

***

During the 1500's, most people were married in June because they took their yearly baths in May and they still smelled pretty good by June. However, since they were starting to smell, brides carried a bouquet of flowers to hide the body odor. Hence the custom today of carrying a bouquet when getting married.

Baths consisted of a big tub filled with hot water. The man of the house had the privilege of the nice clean water, then the other sons and men. Then the women and finally the children bathed, with the babies being last. By then the water was so dirty you could actually lose someone in it. Hence the saying, "Don't throw the baby out with the bath water!" The next time you are washing your hands and complain because the water temperature isn't just how you like it, think about how things used to be.

Where did the term "piss poor" come from? That's interesting history too. They used urine to tan animal skins, so families used to pee in a pot. Once the pot was full, it was taken and sold to the tannery. If you had to do this to survive you were "Piss Poor." Worse than that were the really poor folk who couldn't even afford to buy a pot. They "didn't have a pot to piss in" and were the lowest of the low.

Houses had thatched roofs, which were thick straw piled high with no wood underneath. The thatch was the only place for animals to get warm, so all the cats and other small animals (mice, bugs) lived in the roof. When it rained, the roof became slippery and sometimes the animals would fall from the roof. Hence the saying, "It's raining cats and dogs."

There was nothing to stop the animals and bugs from falling into the house. This posed a real problem in the bedroom where bugs and other droppings could mess up your nice clean bed. Hence, a bed with big posts and a sheet hung over the top afforded some protection. That's how canopy beds came into existence.

The floor was nothing but dirt. Only the wealthy had something other than a dirt floor. Hence the saying, "Dirt poor." The wealthy had slate floors that would get slippery in the winter when wet, so they spread thresh (straw) on floors to help keep their footing. As the winter wore on, they added more thresh until, when you opened the door, the thresh would start slipping outside. A piece of wood was placed in the entrance-way. Hence: a "threshold."

In those days, they cooked in the kitchen with a big kettle that always hung over the fire. Every day they lit the fire and added things to the pot. They ate mostly vegetables and did not get much meat. They would eat the stew for dinner, leaving leftovers in the pot to get cold overnight and then start heating it again the next day. Sometimes stew had food in it that had been there for quite a while. Hence the rhyme: "Peas porridge hot, peas porridge cold, peas porridge in the pot nine days old."

Sometimes people of those times could obtain pork, which made them feel quite special. When people visited them, they would hang up their bacon to show off. Thus, it was a sign of wealth that a man could, "bring home the bacon." They would cut off a little to share with guests and all would sit around and "chew the fat." Bread was divided according to status. Workers got the burnt bottom of the loaf, the family got the middle, and guests got the top, or the "upper crust."

Those with money had plates made of pewter. Food with high acid content caused some of the lead to leach into the food, causing lead poisoning death. This happened most often with tomatoes, so for the next 400 years or so, tomatoes were considered poisonous.

Lead cups were used to drink ale or whiskey. The combination would sometimes cause the imbibers to become unconscious for a couple of days. Someone walking along the road would take them for dead and prepare them for burial. The imbibers were laid out on the kitchen table for a couple of days and the family would gather around and eat and drink and wait and see if they would wake up. Hence the custom of "holding a wake".

England is old and small and the local folks started running out of places to bury people. So they would dig up coffins and would take the bones to a bone-house, and reuse the grave. When reopening these coffins, 1 out of 25 coffins were found to have scratch marks on the inside. The living realized they had been burying people alive! So they would tie a string on the wrist of the corpse, lead it through the coffin and up through the ground and tie it to a bell. Someone would have to sit out in the graveyard all night, "the graveyard shift," to listen for the bell. Thus someone could be, "saved by the bell" or was "considered a dead ringer." That's the truth.

***

Be assured your author understands most Americans are currently feeling as low and anxious about their economic prospects as they were twenty years ago during another recession. So they are again looking in every direction but up for answers. That's quite similar to looking for love in all the wrong places. In fact, it may be the same thing. Economic historians know we are quite well off economically. In fact, they often tell us we may be feeling spiritually impoverished simply because our material wealth has grown so high. Famed economic historian Robert Heilbroner wrote these words in his classic book *The Making of Economic Society*:

> **"It is a curious fact that as we leave the most primitive peoples of the world, we find the economic insecurity of the individual many times multiplied.** The solitary Eskimo, Bushman, Indonesian, or Nigerian peasant, left to his or her own devices, will survive a considerable time. Living close to the soil or to his or her animal prey, such an individual can sustain his own - more rarely, her own - life. But when we turn to the New Yorker or the Chicagoan, we are struck by exactly the opposite situation, by a prevailing ease of material life coupled with an extreme dependence on others."

Even *Forbes* magazine, often called The Capitalist Tool as it has no problem with people getting fabulously wealthy, has confessed to the spiritual challenges of wealth:

"Feeling down, anxious? Your problem may be that fat bank account. New research says the hell-bent pursuit of money can be hazardous to your mental health. It debunks the popular belief that having a goal, any goal, is psychologically beneficial. People

| Table 2.1 Total Wealth: Top-10 Countries, 2000 | | | | |
Country (descending order of per capita wealth)	Wealth per capita ($)	Natural capital (%)	Produced capital (%)	Intangible capital (%)
Switzerland	648,241	1	15	84
Denmark	575,138	2	14	84
Sweden	513,424	2	11	87
United States	512,612	3	16	82
Germany	496,447	1	14	85
Japan	493,241	0	30	69
Austria	493,080	1	15	84
Norway	473,708	12	25	63
France	468,024	1	12	86
Belgium-Luxembourg	451,714	1	13	86

Source: Authors.

World Bank 2006: *Where is the Wealth of Nations?*

who value extrinsic goals are more prone to behavioral problems and physical ailments...The gold diggers interviewed scored far lower on measures of vitality and self-actualization...There's no drawback in having money. You just need to remember the things that truly provide meaning in life."

You may never hear those preaching prosperity gospel say this. Their message is quite popular as mankind was created with a taste for both heaven and earth. However, prosperity gospel also keeps many on a never-ending treadmill in the misdirected pursuit of happiness from material prosperity alone. Even those pastors and stewardship leaders who go beyond giving to the church to address their member's finances usually dwell on paying off the credit cards. As those leaders are taught by Christian financial counselors, their hope is that people can then give more to build larger and larger churches. That is a very old problem within Christianity.

There is a story in the Bible where Jesus takes Peter, James and John to the mountain-top, where Moses and Elijah miraculously appear to stand with Jesus. I suppose that Peter didn't know what else to do in the presence of such holiness so he immediately offers to build three buildings. The voice of God simply says, "This is my son, listen to him." Of course, Jesus told us that even the Temple would fall. But our all too physical natures make it necessary for even the best of us to listen to such teachings about materialism.

Repeating that ancient mistake is unlikely to slow materialism in America. The more sophisticated will see credit card management for greater giving as simple baptized self-interest on the part of our members and churches. Since self-interested activities in Washington and on Wall Street are killing our spirits, culture and economy, I rather doubt those churches will save America.

Despite the other-worldliness and self-centeredness of our thinking, salvation has always been a primary objective of true religion, i.e., the kind that acknowledges that sustainable material riches - for us, all nations, and future generations - are always built on solid spiritual and moral foundations, rather than illusions and shadow-making.

Meditation Six

Attitude Begins with Gratitude,
Or Lack Thereof (Part One)

*"In normal life we hardly realize how much more we
receive than we give, and life cannot be rich without such
gratitude."*

Dietrich Bonhoeffer
Letters and Papers from
Prison

*"The heart never takes the place of the head: but it can,
and should, obey it."*

C.S. Lewis
The Abolition of Man

Twenty years ago, I agreed to a debate on Christian radio with a fellow who
had just participated in a "Christian" economic video. It was extremely
pessimistic, probably paranoid, largely because of debatable perceptions
over the federal debt. It showed rioting in the streets and other forms of total
societal breakdown.

My opponent seemed completely unaware that Americans have debated the
virtues and vices of the federal debt since Alexander Hamilton was early
America's Treasury Secretary. However, my opponent basically won the
debate when he began by telling the audience that I may have had all the facts,
but he had "the truth."

That approach was brilliant debate strategy. I would cite an economic statistic
to refute his vague feelings that the sky was falling and he would say, "See,
I told you he had all the facts." The more he did so, the more the callers
questioned my facts. That's famously called "telling the big lie" in politics.
The strategy is to say something outrageous, such as "the United States is

bankrupt," time and again until people believe it is true. I suppose the radio station considered the debate to be a success because heated discussions always seem to get people's attentions and increase their passions. Sadly, that is precisely what Lewis was getting at when he said mankind is becoming less and less as God created us.

I never advocated any government program whatsoever during the debate. I did suggest one private enterprise and one charitable method for helping the poor to help themselves. Yet the host told me the next day that Christian listeners had called to ask why "a socialist was on the air." Ironically, they complimented me. Christianity is indeed a form of socialism, as demonstrated in the *Book of Acts*. It's just not statist, as many of my progressive Christian friends believe. This is why a famous mainline theologian could say, "any serious Christian must be a socialist."

Before conservatives stop reading, let me clarify that Christianity *does not* suggest, much less teach, that the state has to mediate between us and the needy. The case can be made that Moses, being both law-giver and prophet, did so. But though Jesus was Jewish, he didn't appeal to the state as Rome wasn't all that friendly toward his movement and his people.

The Bible therefore provides guidance for living in cultures with friendly, neutral and hostile forms of governance. But we are usually so emotional about politics, we have trouble seeing such biblical realities.

Don't get me wrong. I very much appreciate emotion in the appropriate spheres of life, like my marriage. Discussions between my wife and me usually begin with her saying, "I just feel..." I usually respond, "But don't you think..." To which she responds, "No, I feel..." After thirty-five years, I've learned the key to a successful marriage is to let that end the conversation. Fortunately, we don't have many of those conversations. We agreed thirty-five years ago that I would make all the major decisions and she'd make all the minor ones. I'm still surprised that we've never had a major decision to make!

Still, even Sherry has grown to understand facts are crucial to our family's investment practice. Each day, clients tell us they "feel" something is dreadfully wrong about America. They usually feel our government "is out of control." They feel we "don't have enough" for college expenses, retirement, medical care and so on. They feel our country is no longer saving any money. They feel our kids' disinterest in math and science has killed our creative endeavors. They feel we have become a nation of "hamburger flippers" with no manufacturing base. So many feel America will soon be, or already is, financially "bankrupt."

I usually ask if these Americans know some very simple economic facts, such as the size of America's assets. None do. I ask if they know anything about our savings beyond our "personal savings rate," a negative that was much reported when it fell to near zero before the Great Recession. None do. I ask if they know the number of patents recently awarded to Americans recently as compared to previous decades. None do. I ask if they know the amount of manufactured goods we produce. None do. Finally, I ask if they know that richest Chinese prefer America as the land they would move to if they could. None do.

The "mind of Christ" is not like that. Observing the birds of the air, or doing a little scientific observation to inform our feelings, should prompt incredible gratitude for our material blessings. The irony is our ingratitude, and the hoarding it is producing, is likely harming our economy, meaning we are turning our fears into reality. I can make the case that our society would be better off without at least ten percent of our GDP attributable to adult literature, violent movies, cigarettes, alcohol, and so on. However, I'd hope we would make that choice from sound moral reasoning rather than moral confusion.

I have grown to understand that there is a very direct connection between my investment practice, as well as Americans' unease over the political economy, and Chuck Colson saying Americans are gravitating toward "a religion that is easygoing and experiential rather than rigorous and intellectual." There was a *reason* God had Moses conduct the census described in the *Book of Numbers*. The former slaves had little except what modern economists call "human capital," but that was sufficient once their minds were right and they thought of milk and honey rather than fearsome giants in their future. In essence, if your goal is to work to accumulate more assets in the future, and I'm not saying that must, or even should, be a goal for you, it helps to know with what you have to work and be able to see what you can achieve.

Despite that ancient counsel, few American Christians still seem to understand there have always been irrevocable connections between economics, politics and faith. But my friend and mentor Sir John Templeton, the Rhodes Scholar in economics turned legendary mutual fund manager and dean of global investing, did. Before he died, John told *Forbes* magazine:

> *"Religious views are important to whatever anyone does - investing, writing articles, anything. How you see yourself in relation to others and your Creator, why, it's the most important thing that there is because you think most clearly only if you're at peace with yourself and your Creator."*

True, we evangelical Christians have begun to re-connect with the real world again, something we rather lost after the Scopes Trial. Due to the efforts of Pat Robertson, Jim Dobson and others during the past two decades, many of us have made halting steps toward reintegrating faith and politics. How successful we have been is debatable, largely as we have virtually ignored the economic dimensions of life. And like war, politics is usually a fight over money. So it would be good at this point to nuance between popular evangelicalism and thoughtful evangelicalism, for they usually have quite different beliefs, particularly about economics.

Professor John Schneider of Calvin College has observed:

> *"It is possible to envision a time when evangelicals have the 'consistent Christian perspective tools' [or worldview] they require in this area of life. But it is probably best to expect Christian theology for life under modern high-tech capitalism to come mainly from where it now does - from Jewish, Catholic, Reformed, and Lutheran sources, in which traditions exist for relating doctrines of creation to matters of redemption in a modern economic context."*

I have long believed that the separation of politics and economics by conservative Christians has been a tragic mistake. There was a time when many "Bible-believing" Christians were Democrats because that party has long been more identified with what Jesus called "the least of these." But the Democratic Party's legislation of civil rights handed the South to the Republican Party, as President Johnson predicted on the day he signed the Civil Rights bill. Religious conservatives in the Bible Belt have had to sleep in President Reagan's "big tent" with the economic libertarians of the far right since. We will discuss the theological challenges of that in depth later, but suffice it to say it's hard to sleep with dogs without getting some fleas.

Conservative Christians may have gone along with economic policies that have been quite enriching to the libertarians of Wall Street and those affluent businesspeople who fund lobbyists on Pennsylvania Avenue. However, many of those policies have hurt the economic interests of Christians on Church Street and Americans on Main Street. I also do not believe that we receive adequate social return in exchange for our economic compromises. And it might not be far afield to suggest that's largely due to the sin of racism in our past, and perhaps present. Let's pray it won't continue to impoverish us into the future.

All in all, I'd judge our foray into politics as less than enriching to date. As the ancient prophets tried to tell us, compartmentalizing our faith off from other dimensions of life, particularly the economic, always has a price.

On the other hand, some of us have mixed faith and politics until many Americans complain, rightly in my view, that we can no longer discern traditional Judeo-Christian morality, which begins by taking the log from our own eye, from politics, which usually settles for taking the spec from the eye of others.

Painful as it might be to confess, those critics have a point. Sociologist Paul Froese recently discussed the latest Baylor Religion Survey. Crucial to understanding America's political economy, and particularly the election of 2012, the September 20, 2011 issue of *The Economist* magazine quoted Froese as saying:

> *"When Rick Perry or Michele Bachmann say 'God blesses us, God watches us, God helps us,' religious conservatives get the shorthand. They see 'government' as a profane object — a word that is used to signal working against God's plan for the United States. To argue this is to argue with their religion. They say the invisible hand of the free markets is really God at work. They think the economy works because God wants it to work. It's a new religious idealism invoking God while chanting 'less government.'"*

I hope you paid particular attention to those words "new religious idealism." The rest of this book will shock many social and political conservatives by suggesting our political alliance with economic libertarians has been just as secularizing to our faith, and therefore culture, as the alliance of progressive Christians with the secularizing sexual forces of Hollywood and such.

The *Financial Times* agreed about the role of this new religious idealism in our policy making when it said this in its August 1, 2011 issue:

> *"The astonishing battle over fiscal policy that has raged in Washington these past months, bringing the US to the brink of default, is a quarrel about the proper role of the state. But its intensity is impossible to understand unless you recognize that deeper values are also in contention. The fight has not been about politics alone. It is also a clash of values — worldviews whose adherents, lately, have no regard for each other. Religion is undoubtedly part of the mix."*

The crucial question of our times may be whether we're allowing our moral views to shape our politics, or allowing politics to shape our moral views.

Consider, for example, the common perception among my conservative investment clients that "government is out of control," as witnessed by the federal debt. Most of them therefore take a very conservative attitude toward politics, as well as investing. Yet most of them are not aware that a November

25, 2011 issue of MSN Money calculated that over the past fifty years, the stock market has gained 247.9%, or an average of 41.3% per term, under Democratic presidents but only 147.1%, or an average of 21.0% per term under Republican presidents.

Of course, that certainly doesn't mean investors should automatically vote for Democratic presidential candidates. It simply demonstrates how common political perceptions, created by political shadow-makers, can be so opposed to our economic interests at best, and very wrong at worst.

I can certainly argue we need to reduce some dimensions of government, particularly those policies that favor the rich, as they no longer serve legitimate needs of society. I work in one of the most heavily regulated professions. There are times I believe we counselors are not needed as well-intentioned financial regulators are going to tell my clients where they can invest anyway. Since the Great Recession, such financial re-regulation has undoubtedly played a major role in the over-all re-regulation of America, as illustrated from this chart from the December 14, 2011 issue of *The Wall Street Journal*:

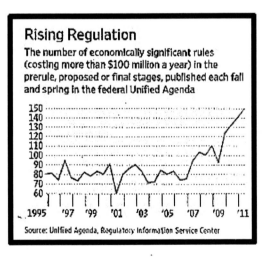

Still, we must honestly ask: "Why so much new regulation?" The *Journal* did not connect the chart with two other stories in that day's paper, but it could have. The top story on its investing page was entitled, "Boomers Wearing Bull's-Eyes. Post-crisis, Those Over 50 Targeted in Investment Scams; Problem is 'Rampant.'" The other headline story was about Jon Corzine of MF Global still not being able to tell Congress where a billion dollars of his clients' asset are now located. The less moral Wall Street behaves, the more government attempts to regulate. That's also true of business and culture.

We have also explored the reality that wars always increase the role of government in our lives, as those wars expand the federal debt. Political historians tell us that one of the major expansions of federal government occurred during the Civil War. It's not far astray therefore to say that many of the things political conservatives in the South detest have been the result of our "sins," which have often been economic, such as slavery.

That seems common sense as most of what government does is regulate behavior and transfer wealth. Obviously, if we behave ourselves and live in charity with our neighbors, we can save some overhead. The prophet Samuel made that very clear long, long ago when the people of Israel first wanted a king (1 Samuel 8:18-20).

But we still aren't angels. So in a passage that could have been written during the Great Recession, B.C. Forbes, the founder of the magazine that makes no secret of wanting more wealth and less government, confessed:

> "The 1929 breakdown was at its roots, a moral breakdown. We were not living right. We had become extravagant. We had become intoxicated by the alluring notion that the royal road to riches did not lie through sweat but speculation. **We discarded and scorned old-fashioned virtues.**"

Forbes added these words on July 1, 1944:

> **"The sins of Big Business and High Finance were responsible for the over-whelming voting of the New Deal into power. Therefore, any** and every act calculated to bring business into disrepute is infinitely regrettable."

We also shouldn't buy entirely into that shadow made by conservative politicians that they will unilaterally and drastically reduce government spending until they fix our budget problems. Contrary to popular perception, federal taxes as a percentage of our national income, or GDP, are already as low as they've been since I was born in 1950, as demonstrated by this chart:

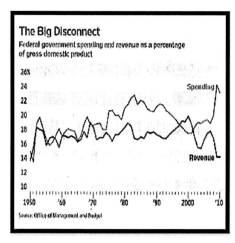

The Big Disconnect
Federal government spending and revenue as a percentage of gross domestic product

Source: Office of Management and Budget

Presidents and members of Congress actually have far less power to shape the federal budget than they let on, largely due to "mandated spending." The *Journal* recently ran the following graph on its editorial page. It affirms another graph and editorial that libertarian Congressman Paul Ryan, who is leading GOP efforts to dismantle much of the welfare state, discussed on the same page recently. Both clearly showed the current budget battle is not so much about the size of government, but whether we will pay taxes and/or borrow to provide medical care for aging baby boomers. Both showed total non-health-care spending was due to decline rather sharply. And that was before the "super-committee" on deficit reduction even reported its recommendations.

What's breaking the federal budget is actually health care spending. That's now politicized as health care has increasingly become largely a governmental affair.

However, we were going to spend more of our GDP on health care anyway due to aging baby boomers. And unlike the purchase of foreign cars, the vast majority of health care is purchased from domestic providers, which means the money stays in our economy.

I also no longer believe the two major parties care as much as they let on about health care being politicized. Public health care gives one party significant leverage with some voters to increase it, and the other party significant leverage with other voters to reduce it. Either way, politicians have greater job security and fund-raising appeal. But again, we see money is at the root of another evil bedeviling Americans.

Morally, one question arises when political pollsters ask us whether we want to reduce the size of a faceless, inefficient government and quite another when they ask if we want to provide healthcare for ourselves and our neighbors. Most Americans hate a faceless congress but love their own members of congress whose faces they know. So asking the right questions is as important as tabulating the answers. That has been a major weakness of so-called "voters' guides" often distributed in conservative churches. I've never seen one that shared candidates' views on the increasing concentration of wealth and layoffs by corporations earning record profits. Moses was careful to provide for the needy as he also assured as many as possible got their share of the Promised Land.

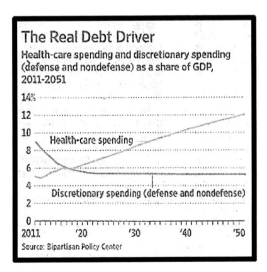

The Real Debt Driver

Health-care spending and discretionary spending (defense and nondefense) as a share of GDP, 2011-2051

Source: Bipartisan Policy Center

While earning a degree in political science, I learned something that you should always keep in mind when listening to politicians. The professor said that it's quite difficult for the five hundred leaders in Washington to really organize a parade. So the key is to find a parade already formed, jump in front and take credit for leading it. With most non-health care government spending already set to decline rather sharply, many conservative politicians could simply be jumping in front of that parade. Such is politics, but religion should never make such shadows.

Unfortunately, we probably are.

Meditation Seven

Attitude Begins with Gratitude,
Or Lack Thereof (Part Two)

*"The agenda of the world - the issues and items that fill
our newspapers and newscasts - is an agenda of fear and
power. A huge network of anxious questions surrounds
us and begins to guide many, if not most, of our daily
decisions. Clearly those who pose these questions which
bind us have true power over us. Jesus seldom accepted
the questions posed to him. He exposed them as coming
from the house of fear. They did not belong in the house
of God."*

Henri Nouwen
Professor, theologian, and friend to millions

One might assume that mixing a faith of wisdom and compassion might rationalize and civilize the discussion over most mundane and worldly matters. One might be wrong.

As others usually see us more clearly than we see ourselves, we might reflect that the British see those of us who lean toward the conservative side of things as a political and economic difficulty. *The Economist* shared the disturbing graph shown below. I know Jesus saw no reason whatsoever to lobby Herod, Pilate or Caesar in his quest to save the world. On the other hand, I also know his attitude toward the zealots of his day suggested he might cringe at hearing his modern disciples described as politically "recalcitrant."

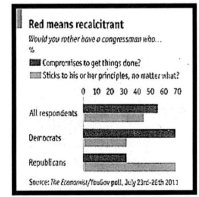

The Economist, 7-30-2011

Yet theology may play a major role in our recalcitrant attitude. "Certainty of belief"

113

is a defining characteristic of evangelical faith. Whatever the merits of that theologically, and I'll leave that to theologians, it can cause some very real problems in the political economy. Even our dearest and most thoughtful friends are not really sure we should be so certain of our own views about mundane matters.

Mark Noll was a professor of Christian thought at Wheaton College when he wrote *The Scandal of the Evangelical Mind*. He began by saying the scandal is that there isn't much of an evangelical mind. If that's generally true, it's true in spades when it comes to economics. I was once actually asked to give a keynote talk to the annual convention of the Christian Stewardship Association, comprised of about a thousand evangelical stewardship leaders, on the subject of, "The Scandal of the Evangelical Financial Mind." Whereas Professor Noll focused on theological issues, my task was to explain a great deal of what evangelicals believed about biblical and modern economics was also suspect. Yet I've also heard one influential financial commentator jokingly describe his views as: "Rarely correct, but never in doubt." That is not a joking matter, for our nation or our faith.

John Stackhouse wrote these soul-piercing words years ago for *Christianity Today*:

> *"One of the attitudes that is tearing us evangelical Christians apart is the insistence that everyone else better just agree with me when I give my opinion – and if some refuse to do so, then I'll write them off and associate exclusively with those who will. We badly need an attitude of Christian humility that affirms we don't know it all and that we'd like to know more. We badly need an attitude of Christian appreciation, one that recognizes that other people can give us what we do not have ourselves."*

Even Phillip Yancey, who wrote a regular column for *Christianity Today*, affirmed that need for humility with his book *What's So Amazing About Grace?* He detailed that the one word never associated with evangelical Christianity is grace. I grew up as an obstinate biblical fundamentalist before becoming an Evangelical Lutheran, a denomination that makes grace a very high priority. I suppose that's the primary reason I confound my friends by continuing to evangelize the evangelicals before they evangelize the world with their economic views. Like many fundamentalists, who have long been quite different than evangelicals when it comes to the Bible, I continue to be concerned about the pragmatism with which many evangelicals approach the Bible.

Too often, we evangelicals simply look for isolated verses that affirm our worldviews, when we should be allowing the entire Bible to shape our worldview. One of my favorite examples can be found in Romans 13. Debt counseling ministries often quote one of its verses which says "owe no man anything." Unfortunately, that entire passage is about politics. By taking the verse out of context, which Bible quoting Christians do far too often, we turn it into a financial teaching. Not only do we get our attitude about borrowing and lending wrong, we get politics wrong by getting too cozy with conservative politicians and then we're angry with politics again.

As we'll explore later, our lack of enthusiasm for the first President Bush over not being able to read his lips with confidence when he spoke about taxes, was a major contributor to the election of Governor Clinton. We then complained about President Clinton the next eight years. My guess is that had we been as concerned about morality as economics, we might have been more enthusiastic about President Bush. It's also my guess as I write that it's quite likely conservative's focus on economics is going to keep President Obama in office for another four years, during which we'll also complain.

Surveys tell us most Americans believe the current congress is a "do nothing" congress. Studies actually say it has passed less legislation than any in history. Surveys also tell us President Obama's favorable rating is very low. However, if we're fair, we simply must ask ourselves if we are ready to again "throw the bums out" as we're actually a "know-nothing" nation concerning political economy. Proverbs 28:2 told the ancients, and us: "When a nation sins, it will have one ruler after another."

Source Unknown

Several of the Ten Commandments are about desiring things that aren't ours and/or we don't really need, both of which are primary motivators of advertising. Then, the great conservative political philosopher Edmund Burke told us the people of modern democracies can only have the kind of government they deserve. Again, we seem to have campaigns built on raw emotion and perceptions, rather than calm reflection and realities.

Most of my conservative friends have emotionally blamed the government for the Great Recession. Such is a major weakness of a mixed economy, or one where government runs a portion of the economy and the private sector another portion. The private sector can blame the public sector for all our ills and the public sector can return the favor. Government certainly played a role. Yet common sense suggests that in a mess that big, there was enough blame to spread around. There's an increasing amount of evidence that hundreds of thousands of speculators pursuing a quick and easy buck, many from being tempted by all those "nothing-down," get-rich-quick real estate ads, must accept a good deal of that blame. As the Bible cautions, we're likely to be punished when we're in a hurry to grow rich. And a December 13, 2011 Associated Press story said:

> "Flipping caused housing bubble. More than a third of 2006 borrowers already had a home. A new federal report shows that speculative real estate investors played a larger role than originally thought in driving the housing bubble that led to record foreclosures. Researchers with the Federal Reserve Bank of New York found investors who used low down-payment, subprime credit to purchase multiple residential properties helped inflate home prices and are largely to blame for the recession."

Sir John Templeton often remarked on the irony that the internet bubble of 1999, which he considered the greatest *financial bubble of all time*, and he was a very serious student of bubbles, coincided with the greatest amount of financial information of all time.

For that reason, John always had his associates read *Extraordinary Popular Delusions and the Madness of Crowds*. Needless to say, the book does not suggest that participants in our markets, or voters for that matter, are always rational, as many ivory tower economic philosophers have taught recently. Being a great student of human nature, as well as actual practitioner rather than theoretician, John knew investors and voters are not angels. All Christians, and particularly conservatives, should remember that in the political arena. If we were angels, we'd need no government. But that's not a realistic description of the human condition.

Yes, I know that means government leaders aren't angels either, but the Founding Fathers didn't want us governed by leaders. They wanted us to be governed by laws that are the will of a hopefully moral and informed citizenry, subject to checks and balances, including judicial review. For better or worse, that's the best we have until humanity is redeemed and/or the Good Lord returns. Again, I'll leave that up to the theologians as to which will happen first. Until then, we have to act realistically, rather than idealistically, about political matters.

Though John was of the quite conservative "Austrian school" of economics, as an investment advisor he also understood the reality that there are times when government stimulates economic activity and times when government aspires for more austere measures. If we dogmatically seek leaders who only know one approach, we'll inevitably elect someone who: 1) will lie to us to get elected, or 2) be willing to do the wrong thing to remain true to his or her personal values when the economy changes due to changes in our "animal spirits," which are quite volatile. I believe it was David Stockman, President Reagan's budget director, who changed positions on the federal debt after America won the Cold War. He was asked about changing his mind. He replied something to the effect that: "When reality changes, I change with it." He then asked: "What do you do?"

Stockman knew that President Reagan, who virtually all conservative Christians adore, had once been a Democrat. (Yes, I know all puppies are blind before their eyes open!) Reagan was also divorced and had stormy relations with his children, but spoke fondly about family values. He ran on fiscal conservatism but raised taxes several times while still ballooning the federal debt. If there was ever an economically pragmatic president, it was likely Reagan. But no one accuses The Gipper of being a "flip-flopper." I'd therefore suggest he might tell us to be as dogmatic about our faith as we want, but respond to economic and political realities in a reasonable fashion. Moreover, Reagan and House Speaker Tip O'Neill were pretty good friends despite their political differences, something we could sure use more extensively in Washington today.

Finally, let me suggest that conservative Christian leaders have not done our nation any good by baptizing Reagan's famous "Eleventh Commandment" to: "Never speak ill of a fellow Republican." In the past few decades we have been quite good at holding progressives, immigrants and such accountable. However, we do actually practice amazing grace in one narrow area: ourselves.

During the past twenty years, I've had numerous conservative Christian leaders tell me privately that our thinking about the economy, federal debt, Y2K and so on has been seriously flawed. However, each adds that he or she could never publicly disagree with another conservative Christian leader, so they're grateful I have. That might be good politics; but the Bible commands exactly the opposite in the fifth chapter of Corinthians, verses nine through thirteen. There, St Paul says it's none of even his business to judge non-believers as God will do so; however, he then asks if we should not judge the activities of church members.

Apparently, we are faced with yet another paradox, the kind that typifies the Christian life as described in the Bible, such as: Seek first; the first shall be last; and so on. We have been called to live in a democratic republic in which we are to govern ourselves while we have an unprecedented amount of highly persuasive but secular information thrown at us. We must also integrate our faith with our political and economic lives, but our faith can never be forced upon anyone. Like Jesus, we must therefore understand the difference between living in a responsibly Christian manner ourselves, and coercing others to do so, which is what politics usually does.

Wall Street may be the most secularized segment of American society. But I still believe, even in a multi-cultural society, living a responsible Christian life without coercing others to do so can be achieved. We can live in harmony. Perhaps in two percent of collective human affairs, the will of the majority, with all possible protection for the rights of the minority, must govern. A good rule to remember might be: "In essentials, unity; in non-essentials grace."

For example, from both a political and theological perspective, having the Ten Commandments posted on court house walls is not so needed as having them inscribed on the heart of every believer. Moses actually subscribed to that approach as he tucked the covenant into the Ark. Apparently Moses had no reason to expect future Pharaohs to chisel God's commandments in concrete.

Of course, equally important is for all our citizens to be introduced to the loving spirit of the Ten Commandments which helped to shape this great nation. This is true even as they are also taught respect for the moral principles of true Islam, Buddhism and other faiths of our neighbors at home and abroad. Meanwhile, even our children should read *Terror in the Name of God* to realistically understand the always present "Christian" cults, zealots and terrorists, as well as their compatriots in other faiths.

If our faith is as true as I believe it to be, no harm will result from other faiths. That confidence only comes from knowing and appreciating the amazing grace and enriching works of Yahweh over the millennia. Anything less than that complete confidence leaves us insecure and overly sensitive in the face of other faiths and secularism. This is not the supremely confident faith displayed by Elijah as he faced the prophets of Baal on Mount Carmel.

Thus, American Christians who insist on voting their wallets election after election must be familiar with both the amazing grace and mighty economic works of the God of Elijah. Otherwise, we will continue to be tempted by false gods, false prophets and bad news.

Meditation Eight

Discerning Bad News from The Good News
(Part One)

"It's very interesting to me that the spread of communications has increased the misery of people. We're flooded with bad news. And this bad news is making people depressed at a time when prosperity is at its greatest ever."

Sir John M. Templeton

John Templeton refused to read, watch or listen to the mainstream media as he believed it was self-interested shadow-making at its finest. He even went so far as to predict decades ago that America's daily newspapers, with which I've had a love/hate relationship since I worked for one early in my career, would quickly lose readership as they were as enriching to Americans as Pravda was to Russians, to use his words. I have to read them as my clients do and I need to know with what irrational sentiments I have to deal today. I also understand the need to usually go the opposite direction of what most media is saying when determining reality and making investment suggestions.

John suggested ignoring the mainstream media out of experience,

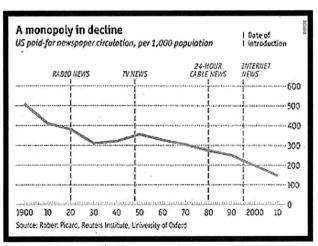

The Economist, 7-9-2011

not ego and believing he knew it all. One of his most favored principles reflected the biblical statement that Moses was the most humble man on earth. Though John invited Nobel laureates and professors from our leading universities to join the board of his foundation, he made the foundation's motto: "How little we know; how eager to learn." John believed all of reality reflects God but that none of us humans can grasp even 1% of God, or Ultimate Reality.

How little we humans know was an enriching point, which John made as often as possible. It is particularly spiritually enriching. For the past three decades, the perception that we do not have enough material wealth has been one thing about which progressives, conservatives, independents and the media, both Christian and secular, have seemed to agree. One candidate after another has promised that he or she can deliver additional prosperity. Consequently, most Americans have voted their wallets. Again and again, we have been disappointed as we wanted even more.

Neither candidates nor voters have seemed to understand the reality that GDP to a materialistic culture is like cocaine to a drug addict. The more you get, the more you want.

For much the same spiritual reason, John also had a point when he advised financial counselors to "under promise and over deliver." Politicians might heed that teaching as well. Yet one might think that if we're going to vote our wallets election after election, why don't we at least elect people who know something about economics, rather than lawyers, actors and such?

Even those economic advisors close to politicians are naturally reluctant to counter the campaign claims that got their bosses what they wanted most: power, the currency of politics. For example, I once chatted with Don Regan, who lived in my neighborhood. You may remember Don was the chairman of Merrill Lynch before becoming President Reagan's Secretary of the Treasury and Chief of Staff at the White House. I asked Don why he didn't just explain to the American people that they had simply increased the balance on the nation's credit card to spend the Soviet Union into oblivion. He replied: "Gary, you can't explain such matters to Americans."

Apparently, shadow-making is like sin; it can be of the commission or omission variety.

On another occasion, a retired chief of staff for the Speaker of the U.S. House of Representatives, who also lived just down the street, told me he didn't think there were a half dozen members of congress who truly understood the federal budget. I expect he was right. I've asked two congressmen I know if they'd ever once seen the size of America's assets compared to the size of the federal debt they cite constantly. They both said, "No." Ironically, both served on key financial committees in the House. Small wonder it's a House divided, reflecting our confused and divided republic.

Naturally, the root of such political evil is largely a fight over money. Many of those who don't have money want the traditional Golden Rule of Christianity legislated and enforced by government. Christ apparently had no interest in pursuing that, even if he went along with Moses on some "redistributionist policies," as we'll explore later. Yet Jesus also rejected the zealots and their demands for revolution.

Meanwhile, many of those who have money want the freedom to practice the new golden rule of capitalism: Those who have the gold make the rules. Christ was crucified by both the Church and the world for fighting that notion. Yes, there are probably a few "Christian libertarians" left in this country who would personally care for the poor more often if the government didn't. But the studies I've seen of money flowing through churches to the poor suggest most are kidding themselves.

Now that we've nuanced some political views, it might be a good time to nuance the media. The popular media tends to be quite pessimistic when it comes to economics. It can find a cloud in virtually every silver lining. For example, when there are plenty of people to work, we have an unemployment problem. When there isn't, we have a labor shortage rather than full employment. At the newspaper and radio network I worked for years ago, we followed the dictum: "If it bleeds, it leads." If nothing bled that day, you poured some ketchup on something to make the headline grab peoples' attentions.

We were also careful to never point out that tens of thousands of planes had actually arrived safely yesterday, though that was a much better depiction of reality than the occasional crash. Despite popular perceptions, air travel is now so safe you have a better chance of being hurt while the plane is on the ground than when in the air. Still, the perceptions created by the media encourage some to drive rather than fly, thereby subjecting themselves to greater danger. I see the same phenomenon at work each day as an investment advisor. The mainstream media covers crashes of the stock and real estate markets so fearful investors buy government bonds, which have never been as rewarding over the long-haul.

The popular financial media, like *Money* and *CNBC*, tends to be universally optimistic. A notable exception is at critical bottoms in the economy and markets when the best opportunities for investing abound. Then they're pessimistic as well. If making money was only as simple as this media usually suggests. Ironically, the easiest way to make money might be to buy when the media is most pessimistic. That sounds counter-intuitive, but it's reality for investors, as suggested by this chart comparing the University of Michigan's Consumer Confidence Index to the Dow Jones Industrial Index. While the past is never a guarantee of the future, notice that a conservative investor could have done quite nicely by simply buying stocks when consumer confidence was low.

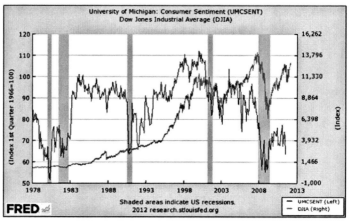

St. Louis Federal Reserve

That's precisely why both Sir John Templeton and Warren Buffett have suggested that if you must be swayed by emotion, you should be fearful when others are greedy, and be greedy when others are fearful. My experience is that very few investors can do so. In fact, most do the opposite. This is why academic study after study tells us the average investor makes about one-fourth of the returns the market produces.

That reality makes it quite like the paradoxical teachings of Jesus, which few people also understand, to "seek first" the spiritual kingdom and the material things we need will take care of themselves. As a minister has to convince parishioners to do the opposite of what popular culture encourages, I have to do the same with clients.

On behalf of our nation's true financial counselors, I'd ask you to always, always remember that popular culture usually encourages you to do something that is enriching to the shadow-makers, not to you. That's why I sent my son off to school for years with the question: "If everyone jumps off a bridge, will you?" He learned well. When he was eight, he left his sailing squadron during a storm and sailed straight for the dock all by himself. I was quite proud of him, and expect that independent and prudent spirit will serve him well in his career. Even the bravest sailor, which he normally was, needs to understand when it's time to seek shelter, as Sir John Templeton did in 2004 when he predicted "financial chaos."

That too is an interesting point for investors. John was so fond of stocks, even after he retired, that I discovered he didn't even know his own fund family had a bond fund, and a world-class one at that. So when he began telling us to buy bonds before the Great Recession, I paid particular attention. Had he been a bond fund manager who was always saying "buy bonds," I wouldn't have paid nearly the attention. Just a tip for when you're reading all those opinions from money managers in the popular media. As has been wisely said: "Never ask a barber if you need a haircut."

The more sophisticated economic media, like *The Economist, Financial Times* and *Wall Street Journal*, is reliable for good information. But you still want to think for yourself before coming to any conclusions. In a sense, reading *Christianity Today* or *Christian Century* for theology is comparable. They are simply more sophisticated than the typical televangelist.

Sir John Templeton also taught me that if I really want to know what is going on in America, I should read the European financial media, and vice versa.

John knew the American media doesn't like to irritate its readers, and particularly its advertisers, many of whom make their own shadows. The corollary is true of the European press. While reading both over the years, I've found that is generally true. You might notice when reading this book that many surprising statistics to Americans have been found in *The Economist* or *Financial Times*, both of which are British.

Sadly, when it comes to political economy, I've found the popular religious media, which is usually Christian radio and televangelists, just sticks a finger in the air to see which way culture is being blown by the secular media. That's not good news, for our economy or spirits.

Source Unknown

How pervasive the secular American media has become in political shadow-making was discussed in the December 12, 2011 issue of the *Financial Times*. Discussing our Republican primary in which one candidate after another has quickly soared only to go down in media-ignited flames, the sub-headline of the *Times* article read:

"Party's primaries have been dominated as never before by televised events."

The article detailed former Speaker of the House Newt Gingrich's considerable moral and political baggage. The article suggested that despite that baggage, Speaker Gingrich was likely resurrected by the secular media as other challengers to Governor Romney melted in the glare of media spotlights. The media always has a strong interest in controversies that will keep viewers glued to their advertisements, which pay their salaries of course. At root, that's the item that most concerns those who run the media. So when the media destroys one candidate, it must give rise to another. Such is the dichotomous nature of the media, as opposed to the unity of true faith.

To that point in the race, social conservatives of the religious right had placed their hopes in Michelle Bachmann, Rick Perry and Rick Santorum. Of course, none of those social conservatives inspired the economic wing of the party as much as Governor Romney. So the social wing defaulted to the Speaker. The Speaker had long espoused moderate views most libertarians question, such as praising Governor Romney's health care plan, which most impartial observers agree was pretty similar to President Obama's despite attempts at historic revisionism on the part of the Governor. In addition, the Speaker had converted to Catholicism, which many conservative Christians still consider a "cult." Apparently, more Iowans were looking at the political shadow-making of the media rather than the realities of the Speaker. Indeed, the *Times* added:

> "Dick Morris, the former Clinton adviser, last week underscored the changing political landscape when he said Mr. Gingrich did not have to go to Iowa to win its caucuses. **'You don't win Iowa in Iowa. You win it on this couch. You win it on Fox News. You win it in the debates,'** said Mr. Morris on the Fox & Friends morning show. Steve Doocy, one of the show's hosts, responded: 'That could make this the most powerful piece of furniture in America.'"

Notice that was in the European press. I don't remember anything similar in *The Wall Street Journal*. That might be because the *Journal*, as much as I love it, is now owned by the same foreign-based media conglomerate that owns *Fox News*. The point is that if you simply read the *Journal* and watch *Fox News*, you might indeed believe popular shadows like, "socialism has never worked anytime, anywhere in the world." Reality is more complicated.

It doesn't exactly break the hearts of the CEO's of giant media corporations when a nation cuts spending on public television.

Outlets like PBS just might inform us of the economic reality that Scandinavian countries take about half their citizens' incomes as taxes, but they are among the most happy, productive and affluent people in the world. Perhaps conservatives are correct in their speeches that a little competition is a good thing. If so, the pursuit of Truth might benefit from a little competition between the media of the private sector and the public sector.

This need for Americans to seek a more truly balanced perspective was clearly displayed when the Republicans in the House rejected a bipartisan tax measure crafted in the Senate. However, *Fox News* that night made it sound entirely like the Democrats' fault. But the following day, even the quite conservative editorial page of *The Wall Street Journal* strongly criticized the House Republicans. They did an embarrassed about-face the following day, providing tax relief to over one hundred million Americans. I have yet to read of any embarrassment or "mea culpa" on *Fox's* part. That was also the media's attitude when it drove many of us nearly insane over Y2K. If the media won't learn from such mistakes as it is so very short-sighted, we'd better.

I'm old enough to remember when President Kennedy, who was also a Catholic, was elected. We conservative Protestant Christians feared Fox's "powerful piece of furniture" would be the chair of St. Peter, but those fears were misplaced. As conservatives have warmed to the Catholic Speaker, they now apparently fear the Mormon leaders of Salt Lake City more than the Catholic leaders of Rome. Perhaps that's some form of progress. Jesus taught us to love even our enemies, which would surely include our own politicians of other parties and religions.

Yet it remains particularly ironic that many who advocate "America First," often fear foreign economic powers, but have no qualms about the Australian *Fox* in America's political henhouse. The *Financial Times* article added the Fox network:

> "...has strong ties to Republican politicians. Many of the current or possible candidates are paid contributors. Both Mr. Gingrich and rival Rick Santorum used to be on the payroll, while Mike Huckabee and Sarah Palin decided against running, partly so they could keep their lucrative Fox contracts."

That is another example of our ability to "compartmentalize," or fail to make connections between, our political and economic beliefs, not to mention our religious beliefs, or to selectively over-look our beliefs in the interests of political expediency.

"Anybody but Mitt...or Barack" is not a rational political approach. Sooner or later, our nation has to be for someone.

125

Most of my conservative friends believe PBS, and even mainstream media like The New York Times, has favored progressive candidates for years. They're probably correct. But I don't remember too many liberal politicians being on the payrolls of such media.

It's also futile for our nation's future when the GOP, or God's Own Party, suggests that it's morally superior when arguing two wrongs make a right as long as it wins. Ralph Reed once suggested on the editorial page of The Wall Street Journal that the conservative ends of limited government could be accomplished with the libertarian means of despising government. Jesus never taught the ends justify the means. His holistic mind knew the proper ends can only be accomplished with the proper means of love.

You don't have to be a cynic to wonder if the images projected on Fox News -- if you're a conservative or "faux news" if you're a progressive - have much to do with the real people behind the carefully crafted images. Even those grocery store tabloids often do us a favor by describing the differences in the public images and private realities of celebrities. Yet the stakes of such discernment are considerably higher in Washington than Hollywood.

The over-exposure of candidates is most likely destroying our confidence in government, and ironically killing both parties, and the media with them.

Again, maybe that's a case of God working in strange ways. As we will see later, God wasn't all that in favor of human kings when the Israelites wanted them. There's also a verse in the Bible where Jesus says to simply respond "yes or no" to a question as anything else comes from Satan. That's not a good slogan on which to build talk radio, or write a book I suppose. We all fall short. So as has been said, democracy is the worst system of government, except for all the rest.

Making laws in a democracy has long been compared to sausage making. You don't want to watch it done, but the final product tastes pretty good despite all that's gone into it. Still, reality is that most sausage contains ingredients you wouldn't normally consume, particularly if you're of the Jewish tradition. It's also usually less than healthy for anyone who consumes too much of it, as most Christians do political propaganda these days.

Meditation Nine

Discerning Bad News from The Good News
(Part Two)

*"There has always been something in human nature
which makes you buy a newspaper which has the most
horrible headline. Therefore, to be successful in the
publishing or television business, you have to feed the
public these catastrophes or the negative viewpoint.
Therefore the public is brainwashed."*

Sir John M. Templeton

After thirty years on Wall Street, I can assure you that trust is the lubricant of capitalism. It's always amazed me how retirees in Florida will invest major portions of their savings in projects all over the world simply as a rating agency or investment service has given that project a thumbs up. However, I can also assure you that the ancients were quite correct that no investment, not a single one, will ever provide the feeling of absolute security that so many investors seek from worldly investments.

Still, worldly investments are useful. When trust virtually disappeared during the financial crisis leading to the Great Recession, our economy nearly imploded, along with the economies of the world, causing considerable unemployment, pain to the working poor and the usual drop in charitable giving.

Cynicism is never enriching to an economy. Nor is it enriching to democracy.

Having a degree in political science, I can say confidently that prudent skepticism rather than cynicism has long made representative democracies function as smoothly as anything humanity has developed to date. But the media may have taken us beyond cynicism to paranoia about the people we elect to public office. If Jesus came back and walked on water, the media would probably tell us that he is incapable of swimming.

As noted earlier, Lincoln and Churchill suffered depression. Franklin Roosevelt accomplished a great deal, rightly or wrongly, but most Americans never knew he was in a wheelchair. The media of his day never showed it out of courtesy to him and respect for the office of the Presidency. Many thought John Kennedy was athletic as the media showed old photos of him playing football on his parents' lawn. Most Americans didn't know he could barely get out of the bathtub and walk around without serious medication.

But after Nixon's problems with Watergate were exposed, every reporter has seemed intent on making his or her mark on history, as Woodward and Bernstein did, by revealing that another politician is the crook that Nixon claimed he wasn't. So many Americans still remember Gerald Ford as uncoordinated simply because the media kept repeating his one slide down the steps of Air Force One. Reality was he had been an All-American football player and played golf nearly every day, albeit badly at times. But who doesn't?

I'm certainly not arguing the media should conceal the humanity of our leaders. I simply believe reporters might show the same grace they might desire. They might also remember that in reality, Watergate was a rather petty matter that the President could have nipped in the bud had he just humbly told the truth about the matter. It was the arrogance of the cover-up that disgraced him.

We all make mistakes. Not learning from them is the true problem, even if you're the President.

Yet the media doesn't seem to have gotten that reality as it's as mindlessly focused on negativity as ever. When crime was a major political concern in Great Britain a few years ago, *The Economist* published the following chart. It shows that crime had actually been in decline but reports of crime in newspapers had soared, thereby confusing perception and reality in the minds of the Brits.

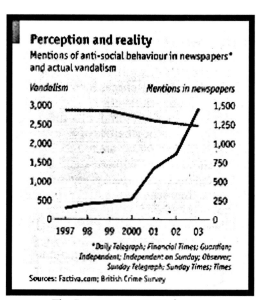

Perception and reality
Mentions of anti-social behaviour in newspapers* and actual vandalism

Vandalism		Mentions in newspapers
3,000		1,500
2,500		1,250
2,000		1,000
1,500		750
1,000		500
500		250
0	1997 98 99 2000 01 02 03	0

*Daily Telegraph; Financial Times; Guardian; Independent; Independent on Sunday; Observer; Sunday Telegraph; Sunday Times; Times
Sources: Factiva.com; British Crime Survey

The Economist, Date Unknown

Of course, that dichotomy could cause the wrongful allocation of the nation's resources by leaders, and that's a stewardship issue, as well as a moral issue.

Yet *The Economist* recently detailed a similar pattern in America. It noted conservative politicians, and therefore the media, have been rather focused on illegal immigration from Mexico. Yet such immigration has actually been in decline due to increased border security and the lack of lower-skilled jobs in America during the recession. That hasn't kept illegal immigration from being a campaign issue. Such disconnects from America's true problems might be major reasons so many have been disenchanted with the Republican field.

A NBC/WSJ poll announced on December 13, 2011 detailed that disenchantment. Fifty one percent described the field as "average." Twenty-seven percent described it as "weak." And only twenty-one percent, or one in five, described it as "strong." Of course, Republicans cite polls about how unfavorably Americans view President Obama's management of the economy. The Democrats retort that polls show the Republican House is held in even greater contempt than the President. It's dive toward the bottom of the spiritual reservoir. Is this a sane way to run our country, particularly when the media is held in as low regard as politicians? Apparently, a little good news might be enriching for everyone.

You simply can't imagine how difficult it is to get good news, or even realistic economic facts, out for the public to consider. Despite John Templeton's credentials in the field of economics, he had to start his own foundation press to publish his books. He kept counting America's blessings and the publishers wanted him to be negative. He refused. I've encountered similar problems. I once wrote an article about our nation's assets for my local paper. It deemed it of no interest, though I noticed it published a guest editorial of how to find a temporary home for your pet when you went out of town. I don't think it was coincidental that the senior editor has spilt a lot of ink deriding the federal debt the past few years.

As any experienced investment advisor knows, it's time to look in a different direction when everyone is looking at economics as our major problem. Or as a famous military leader, Patton as I remember, said: "If everyone's thinking the same thing, someone's not thinking."

It has been my contention since the early nineties that America's problems are spiritual and moral, rather than political and economic. Few, including many of the moral leaders of this country, but particularly conservative moral leaders, have wanted to believe that. I've grown to understand that's because most have an "early Old Testament" theology that God only rewards virtue. But the Book of Job nuances that theology. By the time Jesus came on the scene, he was telling us that God "makes it to rain on the just and the unjust." It was Satan, not God, who tempted Jesus with the world's wealth in the desert. I expect few leaders will still want to confess our past sins as that's never easy. But when seventy percent of Americans believe our country is going in the wrong direction, largely by focusing on obtaining more material wealth, it might be time to look in a new direction. Perhaps up.

I also know many Americans are hurting financially. But as I'll attempt to make clear, that has been because America's vast income and wealth has increasingly been concentrated in the public sector of governments, the independent sectors of foundations and such, and among the so-called "1%" of the private sector. Unlike others, I do not use that term in a negative sense. I know the vast majority of Americans are among the "1%" historically and globally. Still, joblessness has undoubtedly been made worse by our largest corporations, whose stock is held by a relatively few Americans, shedding jobs to produce record profits.

So America's problems of late have increasingly been inequality rather than wealth creation, which was our primary problem when President Reagan took office. That makes it quite difficult for conservative politicians who only understand material wealth creation. They must "change or die."

I believe our economic imbalances have resulted not so much from human nature, which is usually the case, but from the new moral philosophy of Ayn Rand that has so influenced our nation's elite. It essentially argues human nature should trump divine nature as there is no divine. When we get that morality wrong, it leads to wrong political decisions. Those lead to wrong policy decisions for our economy, particularly our poor. All that leads to financial harm for the so-called 99%, and spiritual harm for the 1%.

Fortunately, fewer Americans seem to be looking any longer for politicians to save our nation. More of us might be open to an alternative path to the future. I've learned my arguments will have no affect whatsoever on the most politicized minds. I'm writing for those who are increasingly questioning the way things are looking for the future due to the illusions of the past few decades. Obviously, different answers to those questions require a different way of looking at things. Not my way, but the way of Jesus, as best as I and others can discern it. So it's a "back to the future" movement that this book advocates.

A good place to begin on that way might be with Canon Anthony Deane, chaplain to King George V. He described the way in these insightful words in *The World Christ Knew*:

> "He would be no judge or divider. He was intensely anxious for the conversion of sinners, and not at all for the inversion of institutions

or the diversion of wealth. Indeed, the apparent aloofness of our Lord from those social and economic issues which seemed to them of primary importance must often have perplexed, and times provoked, the people among whom he lived. They had a similar effect upon some of his modern interpreters...He seldom glanced at them because his gaze was fixed steadily on something far more important. **The solution to economic and social problems would come in due time as a by-product of the work he planned to accomplish, but in themselves they were merely external and almost negligible symptoms; he had set himself to cure the disease."**

That way is never easy. Christ told us to expect considerable disagreement, even persecution, when we shared the good news that he was "the Way" out of the cave, "the Truth" rather than the shadows, and "the life" of enlightenment rather than darkness. We know he was rewarded for his trouble with the Cross. Similarly, Abraham Lincoln told us the Truth about slavery and how it was dividing our house as a nation. Few of us remember that he was one of the most unpopular presidents ever. Even he did not believe he could be re-elected. And contrary to prosperity preachers, Lincoln did not enjoy a long and prosperous life. More recently, Martin Luther King was murdered for reminding America of the Truth that all men are created equal.

That's a global reality. Gandhi told us the Truth about the power of non-violence. He died a violent death as a result. Lutheran pastor Dietrich Bonhoeffer told the German Church the Truth about Hitler and the Nazis. Most of the church rejected his perspective and he was executed by the Nazis for his efforts.

I have virtually nothing in common with those giants, much less Jesus. I'm too self-interested to risk martyrdom for my faith or those reading this book. I do not apologize for that. My father gave his life for his family and died before he could enjoy life. That taught me the true meaning of Jesus giving his life two millennia ago so each of us could "have life and have it more abundantly." So the best I promise is to write as truthfully as possible, with as little concern as humanly possible for book sales or encouraging people toward my family's business.

That's no small feat for a human. The past thirty years have taught me that very few of us want to, or even can, hear the Truth Jesus taught about one of our areas of faith, politics, economics and personal finance, much less four at one time. Despite what the prosperity preachers tell you, my net worth today is likely smaller than my annual bonus would have been had I been willing to sell my soul by continuing up Wall Street's ladder. I've still been financially blessed as few people in history have.

And like the Marine Corp looking for a few good men, I continue to look for a few good Christian friends, and particularly Christian leaders who are truly interested in "integrating" their worldviews. I've been most blessed to find a few over the years. The even better news is that Christ assured us only a few are enough to be "salt" that, while a tiny part of the whole, can still preserve culture. My friends are extraordinarily gifted. They are also an occasionally influential group, even though they too are always amazed at how immature Christians seem to flock to false prophets.

My friends also know that there are far more Americans today who believe it's correct to keep faith and business, faith and politics, and particularly faith and investing in water-tight compartments. In fact, when I was exploring attending seminary and was told the stress in my life was largely from keeping my faith and business in separate compartments, I replied, "That's terrible." The psychologist replied, "No, that makes you typical." He went on to explain that while atheism is living as if there is no God, secularism is living as if God doesn't matter from Monday to Saturday.

That's hard for ministers to grasp these days. Our culture is capitalistic and capitalism is primarily concerned with ever larger numbers in the here and now. So many pastors, particularly of non-traditional churches, simply seem obsessed with ever larger churches, ever larger audiences, ever larger sales of books and ever larger budgets which necessitate ever larger fundraising campaigns. Meanwhile, like their secular competitors, Christian financial advisors simply seek more and more money to manage.

The numbers simply attending church each Sunday, which has remained pretty flat, conceal the reality that our faith has lost more and more influence to our capitalistic culture. A money culture that compartmentalizes economic life from our faith that claims the love of money is the root of all evil, is bound to see our faith as irrelevant from Monday to Saturday, and hardly worth supporting on Sunday.

The irony is that Jesus only aspired to have twelve faithful disciples. As good as Jesus was as a teacher, one disciple betrayed Jesus for money. The other eleven abandoned him, also suggesting the power of self-interest over Truth. Jesus therefore taught that the way is narrow indeed. Garrison Keillor has famously added:

> *"If you think going to church makes you a Christian, sit in a garage and see if you become a car."*

If there is one moral principle on which a true church might help our growth-oriented capitalistic culture reflect, and thereby grow relevant to that culture once again, it might be: **Growth for its own sake is precisely the philosophy of the cancer cell.**

Meditation Ten

Salvation: Socialism? Capitalism? None of the Above?

"Only compassion can save - the wordless knowledge of my own responsibility to whatever is being done to the least of God's children. That is knowledge of the spirit."

Peter Drucker

During the presidential election of 2008, most of my conservative clients were concerned that then Senator Obama would try to "save" the world's economy with greatly increased government spending. The senator even joked during the Al Smith dinner that it was not true that he had been born in Bethlehem; that he had instead been born on Krypton, where Superman was born. Few clients thought even that more humanistic role would save them.

Yet no one seemed concerned when the cover of the November 8, 2008 *Forbes*, The Capitalist Tool, featured former presidential candidate Steve Forbes and the headline, "How Capitalism Will Save Us." But despite my working on Wall Street and never having had a real government job other than being an Army officer, it gave me pause. For both socialism and capitalism, as most understand them,

are humanistic. Socialism believes in the humans in government, while capitalism believes in the humans in markets.

During the mid-nineties, revered management consultant Peter Drucker, who once taught theology, wrote a prophetic book entitled *Post-Capitalist Society* precisely as he didn't think capitalism would save us. Peter, as he liked to be called, said repeatedly that executive compensation was "a disgusting spectacle" that reminded him of "pigs at the trough." He said there was no justification for any CEO to earn more than twenty times that of the average employee of the company that the CEO managed. Long before the Occupy Wall Street movement, Peter suggested there was anger brewing that would threaten our economic system. Though I was an advocate of moral markets and limited government, I had to sadly agree as I had also witnessed egregious compensation at Wall Street firms. In fact, it might surprise you to hear a survey cited by the *Financial Times* during December 2011 said 35% of U.S. millionaires support the Occupy movement. (I also happen to believe too much of the movement is currently based on envy and hate to accomplish anything enriching.)

The December 9, 2011 issue of *The Wall Street Journal* also said:

> *"The left-leaning Environment Working Group found that among the beneficiaries of various farm programs from 1995-2005 were David Rockefeller and Ted Turner, and companies that own farms such as John Hancock Life Insurance. Last month Sen. Tom Coburn (R., Okla.) put out a report, "Subsidies of the Rich and Famous," that indentified tens of billions of dollars of handouts to the wealthy. His report included programs to rock stars like Bruce Springsteen and former professional athletes like Scottie Pippen. Rather than stand up against all this, Republicans recently allowed the Federal Housing Administration to guarantee home loans of up to $750,000. Not many in the bottom 99% can afford such homes."*

The report went on to say the *Journal* had calculated that more than $200 billion is spent each year, not on millionaires, but those earning over one million dollars each year. Perhaps ironically, those are the same folks the *Journal* doesn't want to increase taxes on as it dubs President Obama's proposed tax increase on the very wealthy "the millionaire's tax," rather than correctly calling it the "tax on those making over a million dollars per year." There's a considerable difference.

For such reasons, it was about the time that Peter Drucker wrote his book that I coined the word "stewardism" to distinguish markets integrated with *The Puritan Gift*, a book by two friends, which means Calvinism, from the "free" markets of modern capitalism. As St. Paul explained the paradox, we must be "slaves" to that ethic so we can live in true freedom and prosper.

Contrary to what we often hear on Christian radio, it was actually the earning of interest (Exodus 22:25) and not debt itself (Luke 6:35) that was forbidden by the Bible. Yet Christianity has long grown alongside ideas that germinated in three cultures of the Middle East: Greek, Roman and Judaic. And the "classical philosophies" of Greece and Rome, and particularly Rome, sometimes disagreed with Judaism about that crucial dimension of economic life.

Many Greeks followed Plato, who was collectivist and became what we could now call communists, socialists, or progressives. Today, they'd favor governmental health care, Social Security, and so on.

The Romans, like Cicero, were "conservative" to "libertarian," wanting limited government or actually believing the only true role of government was to protect wealth with large armies. Today they might also favor the FDIC, Homeland Security, border fences, and so on. And like the Romans of biblical times, today's conservatives do not always want to pay for the security they desire through taxes.

But the economic thought of Israel transcended both humanistic approaches. It thought God owns all wealth. I generally find economists dismiss that paradigm as "unsophisticated" and "unrealistic." But it's most likely the most sophisticated and realistic of the options you have. One of the world's finest watch manufacturers is Patek Philippe. It regularly runs an ad in *The Economist* that shows a smiling father and son. The caption reads: "You never actually own a Patek Philippe. You merely take care of it for the next generation."

One would think that even intelligent deists, people like Thomas Jefferson, who view the universe as a clock its creator wound up and then ignored, might appreciate the fact our world has to be the most sophisticated and valuable watch ever made. And like the finest Patek Philippe, we aren't going to take this world with us one day. It will soon be stewarded by our children and grand-children. It changes everything, particularly spiritually, when we think that believing "what's mine is mine" and "you can't have it" can be a form of selfishness.

Since God owns it all, we stewards should therefore manage it within a Judeo-Christian moral framework. Very simply, that framework was built on human responsibility rather than human ownership. Since God owns it all, it cannot be considered "theft" of private property to pay taxes. It cannot even be theft for the poor to have what they need to survive, as the Bible explains time and again. Of course, it also balances those teachings by saying those who will not work shall not eat. Again, it's all about balance and discernment.

I therefore agree with those conservatives who argue balance, and particularly discernment, is difficult for government. Still, I also agree with progressives who argue that the Bible teaches the common good demands the selfish share God's bounty. I therefore wonder if we couldn't compromise by having a tax credit, which is a stronger incentive than the current tax deduction for a portion of our incomes that are given to more local humanitarian organizations that can use such discernment. In essence, this "third way" might mean government could encourage us to act virtuously, rather than force us to do so through taxation. That might broaden, not only care for the poor, but a greater character among our citizenry.

While Judaism did command "thou shalt not steal," it balanced that commandment with the principle that it is not stealing for the very needy to have access to God's resources they need to sustain life (Deuteronomy 23:24). Jesus and his disciples were exercising that privilege when they were plucking grain in fields that undoubtedly belonged to others and were challenged about working on the Sabbath by the Pharisees.

Moses balanced the conservative teaching about protecting private property by limiting the amount of security the nation could expect from the military by declaring, "the king is not to have many horses for his army" (Deuteronomy 17:16), a concept we rarely hear quoted by "Bible-believing" conservatives who want a strong defense, with all its attendant expenses.

Faith & Wealth by Justo Gonzalez explains the three ideas of Greece, Rome and Israel begat three different ways of thinking about the earning of interest, and therefore capitalism. He quotes Socrates as saying the wealthy "do not want to prohibit the extravagance of the young (as) their intention is to make loans to such imprudent people…The money makers continue to inject the toxic sting of their loans wherever they can, and to ask for high rates of interest." Apparently the Greeks allowed the earning of interest but considered it morally dubious. Yet Gonzales also wrote:

> *"All the great writers of Roman antiquity are conservative (and) since the earliest of times, the maximum rate had been fixed at 1% simple interest per month, and this was generally the legal limit throughout the history of Roman legislation."*

As the Bible attests, Romans were rather individualistic and weren't always known for loving their neighbors, or exercising social responsibilities. In that sense, C.S. Lewis confirmed Gonzalez's perspective when he wrote these words in *Mere Christianity*:

"There is one bit of advice to us by the ancient heathen Greeks, and by the Jews of the Old Testament and by the great Christian teachers of the Middle Ages, which the modern economic system has completely disobeyed. All these people told us not to lend money at interest; and lending at interest - what we call investment - is the basis of our whole system [capitalism]...It does not necessarily follow that we are wrong. That is where we need the Christian economist. But I should not have been honest if I had not told you that three civilizations had agreed in condemning the very thing on which we have based our whole life."

Notice three points: First, Lewis did not include the Romans as being concerned with charging interest. Second, he said the "great Christian teachers of the Middle Ages" had decreed earning interest to be immoral. The Roman Catholic Church forbade earning interest until around 1500 AD.

It was actually the Protestant Reformers who morally legitimated the earning of interest, if interest did not exceed 5% annually, the loan was for productive uses and not consumer purposes, and borrower and lender shared the risk equally. That essentially means we can be *traditionally* **Christian when earning interest on our investments, but not** *biblically* **Christian.**

That change in moral thought helped legitimate banking, and therefore capitalism. Yet the Reformers continued to insist on interest-free loans to the poor. Luther actually taught:

> *"Money lenders who do not want to put up with these terms are as pious as robbers and murderers."*

The Puritans brought that morality to America. *In God and Mammon in America*, Robert Wuthnow of Princeton tells the story of a Puritan merchant named Robert Keayne. In 1639, Keayne was ejected from the First Church of Boston and was tried by the Commonwealth for dishonoring the name of God. His sin? Greed. He was earning 6%, 2% too much, in his business! Prominent mutual fund manager John Bogle recently began his book *Enough* with this quote:

> *"The people who created this country built a moral structure around money. The Puritan legacy inhibited luxury and self-indulgence...Over the past thirty years, much of that has been shredded."*

Doug Meeks, who authored *God the Economist*, believes the church actually helped to shred that ethic with its sins of omission. He wrote:

"The way stewardship is practiced in North America often has little to do with the Bible. It stems primarily from the most influential American theologian, Andrew Carnegie."

Carnegie is famous for saying a man who dies rich dies disgraced. But during his time, he was considered a ruthless businessman. Teddy Roosevelt once said:

"I've tried hard to like Carnegie, but it is pretty difficult. There is no type of man for whom I feel a more contemptuous abhorrence than for one who makes a god of mere money-making."

It is no secret that some of the most notorious CEO's of recent years - such as Ken Lay of Enron with whom I served on a Christian board; Bernie Ebbers of Worldcom; and Richard Scrushy of Health South - were highly visible CEO's who also gave substantial monies to churches and ministries. Even B.C. Forbes, who founded the magazine that celebrates wealth creation, shared the reservations Jesus had when observing a Pharisee making a show of giving:

"Too few millionaires who aspire to win fame as philanthropists begin at home, among their own workers. To grind employees and then donate a million dollars to perpetuate his name is not a particularly laudable record for any man to live or to leave behind him. Of course, it is more spectacular, it makes more of a splash to do the grandiose act in sight of all men, where it will be read of and talked of. But it is rather a pitiable form of philanthropy."

The summer edition of the most conservative *Claremont Review of Books* confessed other conservatives have consciously worked to keep God out of American business:

"Many of the most visible capitalist intellectuals - giants like Milton Freidman, Fredrich Hayek, and Ludwig Von Mises - embraced a new moral case for capitalism that decisively rejected the old one based on the natural and divine significance of the individual. This new

LOOSE CHANGE

By Jim Warren

"Let's devote ourselves to something bigger than we are: money!"

The Wall Street Journal, Date Unknown

139

moral case was, either explicitly or implicitly, utilitarian and anti-metaphysical."

Freidman was the thinking man's economist. But some of us wondered about his heart and soul. He once said, "The church tends to believe it should exercise control not only over the spiritual realm but also over the material realm, and that's where all the difficulties arise." In *Post-Capitalist Society*, Drucker pointedly termed as "futile" Freidman's famous dictum that, "the only social responsibility of a business is to make money." Who among us would argue that the only social responsibility of government is to take care of government, or the only social responsibility of the clergy is to take care of church members? Politicians and the clergy may act that way too often but they would surely never articulate it as a moral philosophy. In essence, the irony is that it's better to be hypocritical and know right from wrong, than to be consistently wrong.

I once wrote *The Wall Street Journal* that Freidman's term for the Third World poor, "under-utilized labor units," did little to encourage ethics, much less compassion, in global markets. And our credit crisis and recession were caused largely by the new capitalism rejecting the Judeo-Christian ethic and foolishly believing lenders could charge even higher interest rates to sub-prime borrowers than to prime borrowers.

Yet the most secularizing of these capitalist philosophers has undoubtedly been Ayn Rand, mentor to Alan Greenspan, junk-bond king Michael Milken and tens of thousands on Wall Street and in corporate America. The Library of Congress has rated her book *Atlas Shrugged* the second most influential book in America after the Bible.

That's ironic as both evangelical apologist Chuck Colson and Lutheran historian Martin Marty agree those two books pretty much say the opposite, particularly about selfishness, which Rand deemed a "virtue." At the end of Atlas Shrugged, Rand's superhuman CEO-type savior, created in the image of Nietzsche, makes the sign of the dollar across the world. It symbolized the moral purpose of our lives is now to make money, rather than to love God and neighbor as much as self. Yet in 1994, *The Economist* said Rand's ideas were most popular with economic libertarians (who disdain government) and were instrumental in Reaganomics.

Yet Rand taught "every argument for God rests on a false metaphysical premise;" charity is "not a moral duty'" and most importantly, that capitalism and Christianity "cannot exist in the same man or in the same society." She also taught that "abortion is a moral right" and had a very public affair, with the full knowledge of her husband, who turned to drinking heavily. Not surprisingly, Rand died lonely and very depressed. Still, the retired CEO of BB&T bank, a Rand disciple, recently told The *New York Times* that her philosophy of selfishness will soon dominate America. I happen to believe it already does, at least from Monday to Saturday. While most church leaders ignore the root of all evil and/or promote it, most evangelical leaders really avoid Rand, most likely for politically expedient purposes rather than moral conviction.

So what do you do if you too are frustrated about choosing between Nancy Pelosi and AIG for your health care and/or Barney Frank and Wall Street for your retirement? Begin by understanding the *Claremont Review*'s statement:

> *"Nor did [these capitalist philosophers] have much to say to social conservatives, who are an indispensable element of the political coalition upon which capitalism's survival depends."*

It is a false political choice that we must become pagan Greeks if we're tired of the pagan Romans on Wall Street. On the other hand, it may also be conservatism's most prevalent form of moral relativism to say that capitalism, as it's been practiced lately, is at least better than the statism of socialism and communism. There has always been a third way alternative, which I call stewardism. It is a form of limited government with moral, rather than simply free, markets.

As Peter Drucker wisely counseled, it's a simple matter of accepting personal responsibility for what happens to neighbor, the least of these, the environment, and future generations...when making money as well as giving money. Wall Street calls that idea "socially responsible investing" (SRI) and "corporate social responsibility" (CSR). Drucker, who also taught theology, believed only that sort of love can save us.

Finally looking up after all these years of looking left and right while studying political science and working on a Wall Street that regularly threatened our futures with financial weapons of mass destruction, I can now see Drucker's point.

Meditation Eleven

It Truly Is Different this Time

*"The whole aim of practical politics is to keep the
populace alarmed — and hence clamorous to be led
to safety — by menacing it with an endless series of
hobgloblins, all of them imaginary."*

H.L. Mencken

Most Wall Street professionals know that Sir John Templeton famously said:
"'It's different this time' are the four most expensive words in the English
language." John knew that unredeemed human nature always fluctuates
between fear and greed in search of prudence. But there is good reason to
believe that the morality of America is truly different today than it was until
about three or four decades ago.

John Adams once wrote: "Our constitution was made only for a moral
and religious people. It is wholly inadequate to the government of any
other." Alexis de Tocqueville wrote in *Democracy in America* that if one is
to be dogmatic, he should be so in religion rather than politics, because
compromise is essential in a democracy. And the great theologian C.S.
Lewis said sick society would focus on politics as a sick man focuses on his
digestion.

After a momentous two weeks in 2009 during which the United States
tottered near default, brokered a weak compromise, saw the stock market
fluctuate wildly, and had a credit rating agency downgrade US debt for the
first time in seven decades, the economy certainly looked unhealthy. During
such times, it's easy to point fingers. Take your pick. Most Americans trusted
Washington as much as Wall Street, which ranked just above used car dealers
for ethics. But before we blame others, consider what those three great moral
thinkers are saying. Would they suggest in today's turmoil that we look to our
own moral character - take the log from our own eyes, as Christ Jesus put it –
before demonizing others?

I have a degree in political science, have spent three decades on Wall Street, and have written five books on the morality of political economy. So I am fascinated by the connections among the private, public, and independent sectors of our economy. Despite the cynicism toward Washington, I believe our true problem reflects the flawed thinking that has created the impasse between those who believe that government is the answer and those who have faith that "capitalism will save us," as Steve Forbes has written.

Strange as it may seem, the heart of this economic debate is moral, even religious. And it is particularly being debated among cultural leaders. For example, the current Republican primary has essentially turned into a battle for the soul of the party between the elitist Governor Romney, who can't connect with most conservatives as he's from the inner sanctums of Wall Street, and the more populist Senator Rick Santorum. As I send this manuscript to the publisher, the February 25, 2012 issue of the *Financial Times* has actually described this election as a major political realignment over economic differences, similar to the realignment that took place in 1968 over the Civil Rights bill.

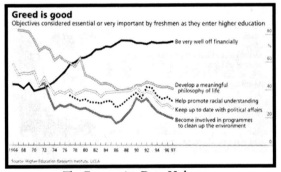

The Economist, Date Unknown

The article argues the Republican Party has lately become a party of working (and I might add religious) people rather than Wall Streeters who want government off their backs and out of their wallets. It concludes economic libertarians who are currently in the Republican Party will soon join the social libertarians of the Democratic Party. At the very least, that should make politics a bit clearer. Then those conservatives who want government to protect the unborn can also vote for a government that might better regulate Wall Street. And that could be crucial until we more selfish boomers die.

Each year, UCLA conducts a study of incoming freshmen. Before the late 1960s, when the influence of religion was stronger, most said they were attending college to master a meaningful way of life. Relatively few, the business students perhaps, said they were coming primarily to learn how to make money. The lines representing those percentages crossed during the early 1970s.

Today's baby boomer elites, who are now running our country, seem preoccupied with obtaining wealth regardless of profession. They read magazines like *Money* and *Self,* something inconceivable to their grandparents, who read newspapers with religion sections larger than today's business sections. This cultural shift in values is part of what sociologists term post-modernism. Broadly, the term means we no longer believe in a single Truth.

The Judeo-Christian ethic that virtue and altruism are to be valued more highly than material accumulation has largely been replaced by the post-modern belief that there are many truths. A Christian's idea of moderation in all things coexists with the $10-million-a-year athlete and the CEO's mantra that he too should be paid what the market will bear, as if he could hit a ninety mile an hour curveball! Famed management consultant Peter Drucker wrote that in the Judeo-Christian tradition:

> *"There is only one ethics, one set of rules of morality, one code, that of individual behavior in which the same rules apply to everyone alike. And this fundamental axiom business denies.... Business ethics assumes that for some reason the ordinary rules of ethics do not apply to business."*

Similarly, the Judeo-Christian ethic mandates the personal care of neighbors, which is in tension with the view of those elites who believe it's government's responsibility. These multiple truths complicate politics, to the point of paralysis. When held dogmatically, they make it nearly impossible to find common ground, which Tocqueville said is crucial to civility and prosperity in a democracy. As a result, politicians in a post-modern world spend a lot of time talking past each other.

What's different recently has been the rise of the Tea Party on the far right end of the spectrum (which may have given rise to the Occupy movement on the far left end, though that movement has yet to become political as I write). Libertarians at least say they want radically limited government. One extreme strand of this ideology, in particular, has been gaining influence: the notion that no one needs to care for the poor – and that government definitely shouldn't. This reflects the moral philosophy of Ayn Rand, a most dogmatic atheist who thought CEO-types would save us.

As a conservative at heart, I've supported Republican causes much of my life. But Ms. Rand was no conservative. In her words, she was a "radical for capitalism." After three decades on Wall Street, where this pernicious brand of corporate elitism ran amok before the Great Recession, I've grown increasingly worried for the health of our republic. I now believe her philosophy has been a major factor in America's tax policies, excessive

CEO compensation, and increasing concentration of wealth among the very affluent.

Very few Americans today know who Rand was, much less the sway her ideas now hold over today's tea party, and by extension the Republican Party, and by further extension, our economy. *The Economist* magazine has said her individualism and antigovernment philosophy shaped Reaganomics, primarily through former Fed Chairman Alan Greenspan, who literally sat at Rand's feet for years.

Rep. Paul Ryan (R) of Wisconsin, who has headed the GOP effort to cut entitlement spending, requires his staff to read *Atlas Shrugged*. Supreme Court Justice Clarence Thomas is a fan of Rand's thinking. Rush Limbaugh and Glenn Beck have preached her gospel on right-wing radio and television. Even many leaders of the religious right (Chuck Colson and Marvin Olasky excepted) have tried to integrate her thought with that of Christ, as diametrically opposed as they are. Theologians have long called that "syncretism" and it was that condition against which biblical prophets most railed.

The irony is that Rand wanted to be remembered as "the greatest enemy of religion ever," which may be why local tea party groups have disbanded rather than support the political goals of socially conservative Christians. Her ideas may have shaped Reaganomics, but she fought the Reagan candidacy because she rejected his Calvinistic vision of America being a "city on a hill." She also rejected Nobel laureate economist F.A. Hayek, a champion of even libertarians, simply because he argued that government might help stimulate an economy during a depression.

To be sure, all Republican leaders are not Randists. I was quite relieved when Peggy Noonan wrote these words in the January 7, 2012 issue of *The Wall Street Journal*:

> "Rick Santorum has a lot going for him, most especially a deep identification with and caring for the working class, for the displaced and un-empowered people who once worked in steel mills and factories and have seen it all go away. He is a Catholic who **sees society not as an agglomeration of random Randian individualists but as part of a community, part of a whole. He cares about the American family and walks the walk. All of this has such appeal!**"

The irony is that will likely be precisely the traits that repeal many individualists, including evangelicals. So today's impasse between the welfare-statists who think our government should maintain full care for the boomers, even if it bankrupts Washington, and the tea party activists who apparently think our needy and elderly should just get jobs, even while our largest companies are shedding workers while demanding more from those remaining, deepens as America sinks into European-style secularism, without Europe's commitment to social welfare.

In more religious times, the teachings of Christ Jesus helped unite most of us by providing a third way: each of us caring for our neighbors, particularly those in need, in a loving, voluntary manner. Yet should some decline that moral responsibility, as Rand did, Christ suggested the Law of Moses would remain a moral necessity, since the poor will be with us always. That law required the affluent to round the corners of square fields and leave the second picking of grapes for the poor, as well as the giving of tithes and offerings.

With the secularization of America, that moderate way - rendering "to Caesar the things that are Caesar's, and to God the things that are God's" - has nearly disappeared. True, Americans practice more charity than other nationalities. But studies by Empty Tomb, a Christian service and research group, and others indicate that most religious giving is simply tax-deductible contributions for the upkeep of our churches and other institutions. America's official foreign aid is among the very lowest as a percentage of income among the developed nations. So while the needy have a voice in the Democrats and the affluent have a voice in the Republicans, Christ's middle way has disappeared, perhaps causing the middle class to also disappear.

My hope is that public frustration with both parties will galvanize citizens to consider a third way movement based on a spirituality that transcends political labels and speaks truth to all power, not simply to the other side of the aisle. That's what Tocqueville observed when Americans were happier and had more confidence, even faith, in the future.

I don't pretend to know what God wants for America, and I definitely don't advocate a theocracy. But it might be time for us Christians to think about a return to an ethic where loving one's neighbors, even one's political enemies, is the norm. It is definitely time for many religious leaders to think in a more counter-cultural fashion about our political economy.

Meditation Twelve

Worldly & Divine Approaches to Money

*"Money in the modern era is a purely secular force,
reflecting the lower nature of man. Cut off from any
relation to spiritual aspiration, it has become the most
obvious example of a fire raging out of control...Very
little, if anything, is left of the absolute demand from
Above that is the essence of absolute ethics."*

Jacob Needleman
*Money and The
Meaning of Life*

*"History is a battle between creditors and debtors over the
nature of money. The former want sound money and the
later want easy money."*

The Financial Times

I respect syndicated columnist Dr. Paul Krugman's Nobel Prize in economics, but we often disagree. The primary reason is that his solution for most economic problems seems to be additional government spending.

I believe that has its place in certain times and places. For example, I live a mile off I-75 in a nice community with gas stations, restaurants, banks and so on. It wasn't even picturesque pasture land until Washington built the interstate a few years ago. Yet most of the time I'm skeptical of non-infrastructure spending.

However, Dr. Krugman and I do agree on this passage, which he wrote at the beginning of the election year of 2012 as I was putting the finishing touches on this book:

"In 2011, as in 2010, America was in technical recovery but continued to suffer from disastrously high unemployment. And through most

of 2011, as in 2010, almost all the talk in Washington was about something else: the allegedly urgent issue of reducing the budget deficit. This misplaced focus said a lot about our political culture, in particular about how disconnected Congress is from the suffering of ordinary Americans. But it also revealed something else: **When people in D.C. talk about deficits and debt, by and large, they have no idea what they're talking about - and the people who talk the most understand the least.***"*

Anytime someone who has won a Nobel Prize in economics agrees with what you've been preaching for years, you have to mention it. That may not particularly witness to Christian humility, but, like most Christians I know, I've always been quite proud of my humility. We humans are an interesting blend of angel and beast.

Of course, Dr. Krugman could have confessed that few mainstream economists know anything about theology, or even repairing a car, building a house, or raising children. He might then have helped Americans better understand that our real problem isn't simply politicians, but a key foundation of capitalism: the specialization of labor. Of course, it would have taken far more humility than economists are noted for in order to make that confession.

Yet when Dr. Krugman advocates increased government spending, it seems as one-dimensional as my friend and former vice-presidential candidate Jack Kemp calling again for more tax cuts. When listening to Krugman and Kemp over the years, I've often felt like I rotate churches whose pastors know only one sermon, each the opposite of the other. Each pastor is leading a choir that only knows one song. The Bible readings are always the same carefully selected passage.

That would be pure nonsense to most Christians. Yet if politicians and economists don't talk about issues in the same monotonous manner, we deem them "flip-floppers" and "wishy washy," or, even worse, "moderates." I'm not talking about such core beliefs as the right to life and marital fidelity, on which even family-oriented politicians have flip-flopped recently. You either know right and wrong in those areas, or you don't. I'm simply talking about, to put it in family terms, the occasional need, as when we lose our jobs, to spend some retirement funds on groceries. Normally, we wouldn't do that, but there are times when things aren't normal.

It makes me wish that progressives and conservatives alike understood the biblical reality that there's a time for every purpose under heaven. The only seemingly good thing about monotonous preaching, repetitious singing, and selective Bible quoting is that it appears to alleviate the need for us to think.

We can then just follow some human, or pretend to follow God on such mundane matters.

C.S. Lewis had it precisely correct when he said that God may have told us to feed the poor but God did not give us lessons in cooking. Instead, God gave us hearts, souls and minds, and the choice about how we'll respond to God's gracious gift of them.

Peter Drucker understood that reality. Peter taught the balanced approach that most government spending could produce little true growth; the exception being that government could develop infrastructure that would make it easier for the private sector to produce that real growth. That could be as obvious as interstate highways, or water lines and sewer plants. Yet it might also be the education and health of our workforce. It is such discernment and balanced moderation that our nation has lacked since politicians and the media have divided themselves into absolutist progressives and conservatives. That may hold our attention by making them more extreme and entertaining, but it does little to enrich our nation, particularly our spirits.

They need to get real. The word "entertaining" derives from two words meaning "between" periods of "attaining" reality. Whereas we used to get a measure of reality from newspapers and the evening news, while we got entertainment from our theatres and "I Love Lucy," we now get the convergence of "reality TV," as well as tabloid-style newspapers and gossip-style magazines. Sadly, those guide more than our selection of soap operas. They increasingly guide public policy.

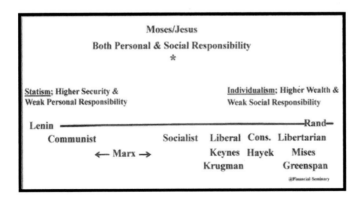

The chart might help you to better see through such distortions of holistic reality. The portion above the line shows the three primary ways of thinking about politics in the United States. The portion below the line shows their underlying economic philosophies. On the far "left" is the communist system, where government plays the dominant role in our well-being. The middle of the line represents what many of us call socialism, where government takes about half of people's incomes to provide for their health care, housing, retirement security, and so on. On the "right" is the conservative worldview where government gets "off our backs, out of our wallets, and out of our bedrooms."

Transcending those humanistic worldviews is the Judeo-Christian ethic where God, rather than government or individuals, owns the wealth. We "honor and respect" government, to use St. Paul's words in Romans 13, while making it ever less necessary by behaving virtuously and assuming responsibility for the well-being of ourselves and our neighbors, particularly those in need.

For every Pharaoh who wants to rule the world, there's an economic Joseph who wants to manage it for him.

So below those humanistic political worldviews are humanistic economic philosophers who offer support for the views of the politicians. On the left, Karl Marx might be the most deplored, but least understood, of the bunch in America. Most Americans associate Marx with communism as Lenin put *some* of Marx's ideas into action, but that's only partially correct. Marx did say that capitalism would dissolve into state-managed communism; but he added the state would eventually dissolve into a worker's paradise, where workers, who are supplying labor, rather than capitalists supplying money, would reap most of the material rewards.

Most Christians also remember Marx as an atheist. That was true during his adulthood. Yet Marx was both Jewish and Lutheran when maturing. This may have influenced his thinking about his workers' utopia looking rather similar to the economy described in the Book of Acts. My point is that conservatives may or may not be insulting progressives when we use the word "Marxist." We should also remember that while the state had been around since the days of Pharaoh, capitalism wouldn't be morally legitimated until considerably later, around the Protestant Reformation. If anyone is *economically* progressive, it might be political conservatives who place their faith in capitalism to "save" us.

Notice that despite political rhetoric, I don't believe there are any socialistic economic philosophers who significantly influence American politics today. I base that on my global worldview. The nationalistic worldview of most Americans is far more conservative. It would be political suicide today to advocate that America should more closely resemble the socialist nations of Sweden, Denmark, and France.

Presidential candidate Governor Mitt Romney insinuated during the New Hampshire presidential debate that President Obama has been a socialist as taxes now consume 37% of America's GDP. All the fact-checkers noted the Governor had confused many viewers, as I immediately suspected. Government at all levels has taken roughly 27% of GDP since I entered college in 1968 to study political science. America has long been, and I expect it will long remain, right-of-center in that regard.

Of course, today's libertarians want to get federal taxes down to 15% or lower, which is where *most* of Governor Romney's taxes have been. That's due to a loophole called the "carried interest" provision that was provided for managers of private equity funds and such. Yet much of Governor Romney's wealth is also in an IRA, which has the perverse effect of turning capital gains taxed at 15% into "unearned income" upon withdrawal. It is then taxed at much higher levels. I see many investors make the same silly mistake by putting long-term, growth-oriented investments in IRAs and earning interest and short-term gains outside qualified plans. Politically, I suppose one might hope our "economist in chief" would know better than to make such mistakes. But perhaps Governor Romney is planning on leaving his IRAs to his church, which would eliminate the taxes.

Anyway, the closest we probably have today to socialists are liberal, or progressive, economists. Those range from early twentieth century British economist John Maynard Keynes to present day *New York Times* columnist Paul Krugman. Generally referred to as "Keynesians," these economists wouldn't mind if more activist governments did take the 37% Governor Romney cited. Governments might then both police the world and our borders while providing income and health care during our retirement years.

If I had to hazard a guess, such economists have had the greatest influence on President Obama. That is debatable of course. Many conservatives, and virtually all libertarians, believe the President has been a socialist. But that's due to seeing things from a right-wing political perspective rather than objectively from the moral mountain-top. For example, because the President bailed-out General Motors but almost immediately re-privatized GM, *The Economist* magazine literally said the President was due an apology for people calling him a socialist, when in fact he's likely a pragmatist.

Most people don't know it, and libertarians would never admit it, but the facts show taxes have actually declined during the President's first term in office. I don't question that the President might take us in the direction of Denmark. But even the March 12, 2007 issue of *Forbes* thought Denmark might offer something from which our polarized politicians and economists, and voters I suppose, might learn, if we'd only be willing to see some shades of gray in our world. *Forbes* said:

"Is there a middle ground between Eurostagnation and cruel capitalism? One system that has grabbed lots of attention originates in tiny Denmark, which has managed to avoid the Continent's generally high levels of joblessness even as it maintains an open economy free of most onerous state intrusions into the labor market. The Danes credit a program called 'flexicurity,' which combines light regulation with a generous unemployment and adult education system for outsourced workers... Denmark has one of the world's highest levels of employee turnover, which at 30% a year puts it on par with the US. Denmark's 3% real GDP growth is the highest in Western Europe, and it recently surpassed the U.S. in the World Economic Forum's ranking of the world's most 'competitive' economies. Jobless rate: only 3.5%."

It is also noted elsewhere in this book that Denmark takes about 50% of its workers' incomes as taxes to pay for the "curity" part of "flexicurity." Still, I believe the President is much too pragmatic to attempt such enriching policies in today's political environment. There's also the small matter of constitutional checks and balances. If there's one irony about conservative candidates today who usually promise law and order, it's that many are promising to do things in Washington that the President has no authority to do.

Anyway, further to the right on our list of influential economists would be Fredrick Hayek, of the so-called "Austrian school" of economics. That school of thought has increasingly influenced conservatism during recent years. Hayek famously thought government taxation, spending and regulation were the "road to serfdom." Yet he acknowledged that government might play a role in stimulating an economy during times of serious weakness.

Even that minor exception did not sit well with the libertarian Ayn Rand, who famously mentored Alan Greenspan. Rand preferred the thought of Ludwig von Mises. He was also of the Austrian school, but more purist in getting government out of our lives. Presidential candidate Michelle Bachmann once said she takes a von Mises book with her to the beach. Presidential candidate Ron Paul would be another likely fan of von Mises. While conservative Christians often appreciate Congressman Paul's absolutist view of government, most also cannot understand his view on national defense, which seems more like the far left. Libertarians can actually be found on both ends of the political spectrum, but the most visible ones are usually on the far right end.

My mentor, Sir John Templeton, was also of the Austrian school. He was even a member of the Mont Pelerin Society, perhaps the most influential leaders of the school. Yet I believe John's faith made his thinking rather different.

John saw very limited government as the ideal. But having studied theology all his life and law at Oxford as a Rhodes Scholar, John was realistic enough to understand we humans are not angels. He knew a libertarian world was simply an idealistic aspiration of humankind, and most likely utopian in the mold of Marx and Rand's thinking.

John also thought any progress in that direction would be a result of spiritual progress, a notion with which most of the Austrian school, which tends to be quite humanistic, might disagree. As for me, I believe John was precisely correct. I'll gladly become a libertarian when the disciples of Ayn Rand, who are self-described "radicals for capitalism," bend a knee to Jesus Christ. Until then, I'll stand my ground as a conservative.

If you look to the right of the words "Ayn Rand," you will see the political line extends a tad further. That acknowledges the "anarchist" school of political thought. It wants to do entirely away with government. Even Rand thought the government played a legitimate role when it protected her private property. Ironically for a supposed champion of markets, Rand only invested in government-guaranteed bank deposits. But I've found that many Christians who supposedly hate government imitate Rand by insisting on having a strong military, border patrol, and FDIC insurance to protect their wealth.

Of course, they also don't want to pay for that protection in the form of taxes, which undoubtedly contributes to the federal deficit. That dichotomy in conservative thought is why anarchists don't even want government to protect wealth. I know of no economic philosopher who is influential in supporting the anarchist view. Ludwig von Mises is therefore most likely as anti-governmental as you'll run across in today's America.

Now you need to understand one more nuance in order to understand the basic political and economic philosophies of today's America. That would be between the "fiscalists" and "monetarists." Here you need to nuance between the Congress and the Federal Reserve. The fiscalists are so named as they believe the Congress should tweak the activities of the private sector, or stimulate or slow the economy, through fiscal policies, or by taxing and spending, which could mean running deficits or surpluses.

The "monetarists" on the other hand, with Nobel economist Milton Freidman of the so-called "Chicago school" being primary among them, believe the Federal Reserve should tweak the economy by putting more or less money in circulation. How they accomplish that is not that important for our purposes, though it is reflected by words we often read like "money supply" and "quantitative easing."

What is quite important to understand is the conflict between the fiscalists and monetarists in today's Washington. Wittingly or unwittingly, most of those young tea party congressmen in the House of Representatives have been highly influenced by the Austrian school of economics and the libertarian political ideas of Ayn Rand. For example, Congressman Paul Ryan, who is heading the Republican effort to scale back entitlement spending, requires his staffers to read Rand's books. Anti-taxer Grover Norquist, who encouraged most conservative members of the Congress to sign his "no new taxes" pledge, has famously said he'd like to reduce government until he could put it in his bathtub and drown it. Rand would gladly run the water, and make it very, very hot.

Yet the monetarists seem to have the most influence at the Federal Reserve. And that's very irritating to those in Congress, like Congressman Paul, who has written: "There is no greater threat to the security and prosperity of the United States today than the out-of-control, secretive Federal Reserve." As Mr. Paul is supposedly a Christian, one might assume that Paul believes those Americans at the Fed are Satan, as Christians believe the evil of Satan, rather than the Fed, is our greatest threat.

I rather expect Paul's view simply reflects the human will's need to control and create reality in its own image. Anyone who has ever lived in a gated golf course community in Florida knows those communities are as close to Rand's utopian, government-free communities as exist. We also know all too well that retired CEOs, who usually hate government interference and have too much time on their hands, are by far more dangerous to the spiritual well-being of their neighbors than are government officials. Those CEO types simply love making rules they like, which is why they so hate the rules made by others. It's not much different with the fiscalists and monetarists in Washington. We'd all be better off if both public and private tyrants learned to pray: "Not my will, but thine be done."

Since the depths of the Great Recession, the Fed has increased the money supply at an annual rate approximating 20% on occasion. We therefore have the Republicans in the House demanding austerity, but the Fed opting for stimulus. That's why Congressman Paul would like for the Fed to be run by the Congress. As an advocate of "hard" money, which usually implies going back on the gold standard, Paul often quotes that statistic about the dollar losing about 97% of its value over the last century. That statistic is true, and such "devaluation" has been happening with money since the ancient Romans shaved the edges of coins to pay the legions.

What Paul and his disciples don't always quote however is the increasing prosperity we've also seen during that time. On average, Americans lived on about $3,000, *adjusted for inflation,* in 1900. Today, they average about $50,000. That's where I believe leaders like Paul might be less dogmatic. As an investment advisor, I know that when investors, like Sir John Templeton, don't believe paper money will hold its value, and John certainly didn't, they will invest it in businesses, real estate and so on in order to protect their purchasing power. Mr. Paul on the other hand, invests his savings primarily in gold. As suggested by the biblical Parable of the Talents, businesses, useful real estate and such are far more productive than gold coins, or even dollars that can be converted into gold.

Even Aristotle understood gold is "impotent" to produce additional wealth, which is why he said it's immoral to charge interest when lending such assets. Martin Luther and John Calvin on the other hand understood businesses and farms are potent and that's why it's moral to share the wealth creation by charging and earning interest. I therefore wonder if self-protective investors like Mr. Paul could simply put their savings into gold coins, or dollars convertible into gold, that maintain their purchasing power, whether they would assume the risks of productive endeavors that enrich us all.

As an investment advisor, I routinely encounter very affluent people who almost pride themselves on their money being very lazy as long as they have enough for themselves. Many of them are Christians who supposedly believe in the Parable of the Talents, where Christ was quite harsh with the third steward who favored lazy money. Those clients have usually worked very hard and taken risks with capital to grow affluent; but once they are affluent, they don't mind lazy and safe. That is crucial to understand as capital is increasingly concentrated among the affluent. **That most unbiblical attitude that we don't need to be good stewards of God's resources as long as we're taken care of may be one of the very greatest threats to the economy our children and grand-children will inherit.**

I've also read enough about the Great Depression to know that Mr. Paul and his disciples sound remarkably similar to Andrew Mellon. If you're not familiar with Mellon's thinking about political economy and legacy before and during the Great Depression, you might Google his name.

Of course, there's another consideration just as important, if not more important, than how this debate affects affluent investors. That is how it affects the poor and middle class. There's no question in my mind that inflation hurts the poor more than anyone. Absent a more proactive government, and yes by that I mean one that transfers some income from the affluent to the needy, as Moses was quite willing to do, it seems logical that devaluing the dollar is quite harmful to those who live on fixed incomes, or a fixed number of those dollars that buy less each year.

That's why we "index" Social Security benefits and so on for inflation. And by the way, I do believe people will get their promised Social Security benefits. Voters may hate government in general, but they love those checks coming in. Even a majority of Tea Partiers don't want Social Security and Medicare cut. The financial importance of that political reality was illustrated by the November 2011 issue of *Smart Money*, the magazine of *The Wall Street Journal*. It estimated the typical Social Security recipient would need $280,000 to buy a comparable life-time income stream from a New York Life immediate annuity.

My investment firm is now considering that number when doing asset allocation for clients. Social Security is invested in a special form of U.S. Treasury bonds. So as the Smart Money article argued, most of us have far more bond-type investments than we think. Generally speaking, we begin asset allocation with a goal of investing one-third of a client's assets in bond-type holdings, one-third in stock-type holdings, and one-third into income-producing inflation hedges, usually conservative real estate. We then adjust it for the risks our clients are comfortable assuming as we don't think any investment is worth losing sleep over. We also adjust it to how various top investment professionals judge how over-valued or under-valued their various asset classes might be.

The reason for that approach is the policies of the Federal Reserve. One of the more reliable sayings on Wall Street is that you never want to "fight the Fed." Bulls make money, bears make money, but pigs get slaughtered. And there's no quicker way to the slaughter house than fighting the Fed.

Very simply, due to the Fed's influence, economics and personal investment planning is a bit like the story of the three bears. There are times the porridge, or economy, is too hot, or inflationary. That's when you need real estate and such. There are other times when the porridge is too cold, as during a recession. That's when you need bond type investments, so you can have dependable income. But most of the time, the porridge is just right. That's when you need stock-type investments, or equities.

That makes monetary policy crucial to the affluent. But the debate grows even more complicated when we consider the middle class. The reason is the middle class often has mortgages, education debt, business debt, and so on. That's why a prominent politician once said he'd never crucify the average American on a "cross of gold," by which he meant tying the value of the dollar to the gold standard. Odd as it might seem, devaluing the dollar might actually help the indebted middle class, hence the old saying that "inflation makes fools of prudent men and prudent men of fools." If you'll forgive another personal example, it might help you understand.

Before I was born, my father purchased a nice farm for $20,000, which was a lot of money in 1950. He borrowed $18,000 to do so and my grandfather told dad that he'd never pay the mortgage off. Yet inflation took the value of our farm to $200,000 by the time dad died many years ago. Even if dad had still owed the original $18,000, he could have paid it off and still had $182,000 remaining for my mother's golden years when he sold the farm to our neighbors before he died. Many Americans experienced the same good fortune with home mortgages and business loans before the dollar firmed during the Great Recession. That's essentially why a populist politician once said he would never crucify ordinary Americans on a "cross of gold" simply as the affluent wanted to protect the purchasing power of their money, presumably without taking the risks of true investment in productive endeavors.

Generally, I agree with most economists that inflation over a three percent annual rate is more harmful than good. Yet I also expect that too many rich Americans who resist the Fed's efforts to heat the economy out of recession would not mind buying our homes, stocks and so on at even deeper discounts. Hence the old Wall Street saying, "Bear markets are when stocks return to their rightful owners." No real steward can possibly believe that as those stocks belong to God, and the Catholics probably have it right that while God loves everyone, including the rich, God's love for the poor is "preferential." So the moral picture regarding Federal Reserve policies is mixed as, once again, we humans simply cannot judge what's in the hearts of other humans.

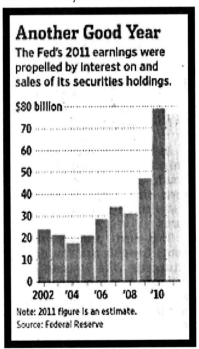

Another Good Year

The Fed's 2011 earnings were propelled by interest on and sales of its securities holdings.

Note: 2011 figure is an estimate.
Source: Federal Reserve

Wall Street Journal, 1-11-2012

Another complication for those hard money types who detest the Fed is that its profits go into the US Treasury to reduce our budget deficit. That has not been insignificant of late.

So which political philosophy and school of economic thought do I recommend? My answer is similar to the one I give when theologians ask if I'm pre-millennial or post-millennial, meaning do I believe Jesus will return to earth before or after the biblical thousand years of peace and prosperity. That is actually one of the first things any investment advisor should ask a Christian as the theology can greatly shape that person's economic worldview. If you believe humanity can usher in that thousand years without the physical return of Christ, you have a more hopeful worldview, or chance of believing we are making progress. If you believe Christ has to return for the thousand years to occur, you are likely more pessimistic about economics.

Anyway, I respond I'm "pan-millennial," meaning I believe things will pan out according to God's will regardless of what humanistic philosophers think. The important thing is for each of us to love God and neighbor as self in all we do. Then, we'll likely muddle through. Yes, we'll fluctuate between affluent creditors gaining the upper political hand and less-than-affluent debtors gaining it. But despite the short-term pain our human ideas will inflict, we won't violate God's economic laws too long before such matters will become self-correcting.

Greece and our sub-prime mortgage industry are currently demonstrating that truth all too clearly and dearly.

Part Two

Illusions of Cultural Religion

"It was the Church and not the world that crucified Christ."

Theologian Karl Barth

"I fear, wherever riches have increased, exceeding few are the exceptions, the essence of religion, the mind that was in Christ, has decreased in the same proportion. Therefore do I not see how it is possible, in the nature of things, for any revival of true religion to continue long. For religion must necessarily produce both industry and frugality; and these cannot but produce riches. But as riches increase, so will pride, and anger, and love of the world in all its branches."

John Wesley
Founder, The Methodist Church

Meditation Thirteen

Love & Money: The Eternal Feud that Makes Our World Go Round

"Nearly two billion people unblushingly call themselves Christian, happily breaking almost every commandment should the occasion arise, serving Mammon and goodness knows who else."

An Obituary for Jesus
The Economist
Easter 1999

To this point, I've been primarily preaching about culture. It's now time to meddle by getting closer to home by exploring more closely what I believe are economic misperceptions in the Church.

This section will be particularly unsettling for immature Christians as I will mention Christian leaders by name, but only when it serves a teaching purpose. I know evangelical Christians, and their leaders in particular, feel that's culturally taboo. I've learned I can make a lot of friends by openly discussing the sins of politicians and businesspeople, but lose a lot of friends by discussing the sins of religious leaders.

However, I believe the Judeo-Christian ethic demands it even more so if we are to discuss political and business leaders by name. There is no theological need to add hypocrisy to our public sins. The Bible counsels that "iron sharpens iron," even if sparks usually fly. Peter and Paul openly disagreed, as did Martin Luther and Pope Leo X. We protestant Gentiles in particular should be grateful that they were mature enough to discern the teachings of Jesus Christ from the teachings of Dale Carnegie about winning friends and influencing people.

There are probably three ancient claims about Truth from Judeo-Christianity that we should meditate upon in order to determine what kind of America we would like to leave to our children.

The first is whether the biblical "root of all evil" is still the love of money, verses all the other issues, mostly sexual, that we've politically focused on recently.

The second is whether judgment on our land - particularly its suspect financial institutions on Wall Street, media institutions on Main Street, academic institutions on College Street, and governmental institutions on Pennsylvania Avenue - still begins in the House of the Lord, or on the Church Streets of America.

Thus, the third is whether we can again stop wandering our spiritual desert to reassume the road to the Promised Land until we better understand the connections between the streets of our nation.

I believe Jesus and Martin Luther emphatically taught we simply *cannot reach that Promised Land until we deal with money* as its misuse remains the root of all evil.

Jesus made his first act during Holy Week the cleansing of the Temple of the money changers. Apparently, he thought that was the first step toward reforming a Judaism grown legalistic and financially corrupt. Though able to explain reality with parables, a whip was required to get his message across that day. The crucifixion quickly followed.

Of course, humans forget, and church leaders, even Popes, whose official pronouncements were supposedly infallible, are quite human. So fifteen hundred years after Christ, the medieval church that bore Christ's name was again legalistic and corrupted by the misuse of money. Thus, Martin Luther launched his Reformation by writing his Ninety Five Theses, which were largely about money. Pope Leo X called Luther the Antichrist.

Being an earthy, beer-drinking and stubborn German, Luther was even more graphic in response. Below is one of the woodcuts he used to communicate his perspective of church leaders. It depicts three devils excreting monks. Such was his devotion to the pursuit of Truth, as he perceived it. We should obviously aspire to a more gracious tone today, but I would argue the church could use far more of Luther's passion for Truth.

It's often said Luther "touched the crown of the pope and the bellies of the monks" with his stewardship theology that simply giving money to church would never save souls.

The Economist

Only a handful of the most insensitive televangelists would argue Luther was wrong. In essence, Luther said the notion that all we need for salvation is to give a few coins to the church is nonsense, likely closer to a Mafia protection scheme than Christian stewardship. Such schemes appear to protect *our* wealth *from* God while true stewardship surrenders everything *to* God. If God truly is the most omniscient and omnipotent force in the universe, it is quite irrational to forgo such counsel.

I believe most Christians, Catholic and Protestant, as well as the rest of the world, can be most thankful that Luther sought the applause of heaven rather than the approval of church leaders and members. Luther prompted the counter-reformation in the Catholic Church, which may be why Catholics are usually on the front lines today advocating ethical economics. If you're not familiar with their work, you should Google the Interfaith Center for Corporate Responsibility.

Luther's theology of the "priesthood of all believers" and "Protestant work ethic" enabled the laity to labor for God beyond the monastery. His legitimization of interest allowed money to move from under mattresses to banks in order to fund productive enterprises. Together, those teachings morally legitimated democratic capitalism, and therefore made our material standard of living more likely. Some historians argue his teachings were too worldly, resulting in our world being far more secular than divine. But we'll see that, as with most religious leaders, including Christ, Luther's followers simply remembered his teachings which they wanted to remember and forgot what they wanted to forget, usually due to financial self-interest.

Apparently, neither Jesus nor Luther were disciples of Dale Carnegie and his book about winning friends and influencing people. I've found that it is particularly difficult for conservative Christian financial leaders, who've seldom studied church fathers like Luther, to understand. They've essentially baptized President Reagan's famous eleventh commandment to never even speak constructive criticism of a fellow Republican.

Mark Galli, who is senior editor at *Christianity Today*, has seen the need to write for conservative Christians a book entitled *Jesus Mean and Wild*, which explains that dichotomy between Truth and popularity. My experience indicates few read it, so they will find this portion of this book particularly unsettling to read. But if I'm going to convey only a portion of how seriously both Jesus and Luther took stewardship and suggest it's time we better imitate them, I'm going to have to offend some church leaders, particularly of the financial variety. This always means confessing your personal sins first.

I've written extensively about my uncompleted journey toward the holistic stewardship of time, talent and treasure elsewhere. There's no reason to bore you by repeating that very long journey here. Suffice it to say I grew up in a devout Southern Baptist home outside Lexington, Kentucky. Reflecting our conflicted culture, our primary cash crop was tobacco. *The Wall Street Journal* has detailed the primary industries in Kentucky as marijuana, tobacco, bourbon, horse racing and religion, in that order. But what else would you expect from the land of the feuding Hatfields and McCoys? My friend Dave Miller of Princeton likes to remind me that America has had only two presidents who were born in Kentucky, and they presided over the Civil War!

I never realized our state was so conflicted until my pastor, who was the father of one of my best friends in high school, told me while grilling one afternoon that he could never grow tobacco if he wasn't a minister. I realized I had never heard that from the pulpit. I now understand that pastors need at least the choir to show up for church and even the choir wouldn't have been there had he moved from preaching to meddling by talking about tobacco. However, that was when I realized we'd light up at the mention of the Golden Rule, but dad would light me up if he caught me experimenting with the fruits of our labor. So naturally, I hid my bravest attempts at that particular sin. While sin is delightful to a teenager, I never could stand cigarettes. Anyone who's been in a barn of drying tobacco, as I was on many days, can understand. You simply can't breathe.

I've often taken Christian ethics far too lightly. Lutheran pastor and martyr Dietrich Bonheoffer called that "cheap grace." I spent too many years on Wall Street simply making investment decisions on the old "risk and return" formula. Then one day I recommended a municipal bond to a kindly but very intelligent Jewish widow. It was AAA-rated as it was guaranteed by the government, but paid 14% tax free. The bond was the best "risk/reward ratio" I'd come across. But she declined it. She simply couldn't get comfortable with the fact her money was to going to finance a nuclear power facility, which was a controversial matter back then, as it remains today.

I was startled she would reject such a financially rewarding investment. But as I grew to respect her thinking, we spent more and more time together. She eventually became a grandmother figure to my young son. Twenty years after her death, he still talks about her quite fondly and misses her. We both learned a lot from her. That's surely one dimension of eternal life.

Because of her selfless example, my investment formula is now more mature and rewarding, in the fullest sense of the word: "Prudence plus ethics equals return."

My growing understanding of my need for humility and grace prompted me a few years ago to leave the Episcopal Church I'd joined upon getting married.

I loved the intellectual approaches of the Episcopal Church but I joined the Evangelical Lutheran Church in America (ELCA). As I've reflected about why we moved, I've realized one major reason was that Episcopal priests kept calling us 'saints,' and I knew I wasn't one. The stained glass in our church showed Jesus being baptized in regal robes, and no one called our bishops by their first names, though no one called Jesus "Mr." or "Rev. Christ."

In essence, after un-intentionally climbing the social ladder as we prospered over the years, I grew to understand our world is growing flatter, and that just might be God's plan, which many religious leaders may have to adapt or "go out of business." The biblical prophet Isaiah shared these words in the fortieth chapter of the book named for him:

> *"Make straight in the desert a highway for our God. Every valley shall be lifted up, and every mountain and hill be made low. Then the glory of the Lord shall be revealed, and **all people shall see it together.**"*

There is nothing hierarchical in that vision of the future. Churches, as well as corporations and governments, might take note. A dear friend, who was a professor of political science in a Methodist-affiliated college and also an ordained minister in the Episcopal Church, took note of my populist tendencies. He wisely counseled me that Lutherans, often being Scandinavian, are just down-home Baptists who enjoy liturgy, or smells and bells. My wife likes those a lot. The other Lutherans are usually hard-headed Germans, as was my mother's family, so we seemed to be a true fit. So Sherry and I compromised by becoming Lutherans, but only after I'd seriously studied Luther's theology, and his disagreements with church leaders over financial teachings in particular.

The primary difference I've seen in these denominations is that Lutherans are more open about enjoying beer than are Baptists, whereas Episcopalians prefer wine and stronger spirits. It's often joked Episcopalians need those spirits as they are "God's frozen chosen." So perhaps you've heard that anytime you find four Episcopalians, you're sure to find a "fifth." As to Baptists, they probably like beer as much as Lutherans do; they just can't show it as they aspire to holiness rather than relying on Luther's amazing grace. So anytime you take a Baptist fishing, take two or the one will drink all your beer.

You should know I also worked with the Mennonites for a while. They may integrate their faith with economic life better than any people I know. Close your eyes and visualize the words Mennonite restaurant. Not exactly Hooters right? Now visualize the words Baptist restaurant or evangelical restaurant. Anything? That's as conservatives less routinely integrate economics and faith. On the other hand, even my Mennonite friends are the first to tell you that the theology cooked up by the Mennonites could often use a dash of Luther's grace. So their definition of a moral dilemma too often seems to be a free beer table, of which we Lutherans would definitely take advantage.

Funny as all that might be, it makes a very serious point about a major point of this book. Looking at today's church, one might never know that Jesus, who created wine with his first miracle and apparently enjoyed it himself, ever aspired for his church to "be of one mind." And if the Christian mind is conflicted over alcohol, it's more so over money.

Even though money was a favorite topic of Luther, even we Lutherans don't like to talk about using it responsibly any more than Baptists like to talk about drinking responsibly. When I was president of our church, I suggested we offer a popular money course for Christians. A member of the church council leaned back in his chair and proudly said: "I can tell you one thing. We need to keep all talk about money out of this church." A study by the Thrivent Mutual Funds, which are sold to Lutherans of all varieties, has said most Lutherans now believe it's wrong to talk about money in church, even though it was a favorite topic of Moses and Jesus.

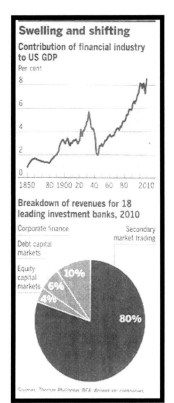

Swelling and shifting

Contribution of financial industry to US GDP
Per cent

Breakdown of revenues for 18 leading investment banks, 2010

Of course, that makes the church increasingly irrelevant, perhaps harmful, to our money culture, and those members in financial services in particular. The January 10, 2012 article on "Capitalism in Crisis" in the *Financial Times* was entitled: "Unless banks can better demonstrate their usefulness to society, they face a debilitating battle against new regulation." The chart below showed that while banking has been growing by leaps and bounds, much of that growth has been from trading in the secondary markets, rather than raising capital for industry. Some of that trading serves a socially useful purpose, but too much of it is simply selfish speculation.

There are huge spiritual dimensions to our insensitivities to money. There was literally a picture of Jesus whipping the money changers in the Temple at the opposite end of the council table from where I served as president of our church. We were spending so much money on our church facilities and so little on true benevolence; I literally had to leave during one meeting after our council approved another major expenditure on ourselves.

I even noticed we called our tithe to the synod a "benevolence." I was happy we were funding denominational over-head, but calling it a "benevolence" seemed to this businessman quite similar to a franchisee calling his franchise fee "charity." As an independent investment advisor, I pay such a fee to a national company to deal with regulators, custody securities, and so on. I can't imagine my church wanting me to call that charity simply as it goes outside my family.

Then I was told that even though I was president, I couldn't be informed about the rate of return on the church's foundation. And no one could, or would, tell me what the rate of return on our investments had been in recent years. But I was supposed to promote the foundation anyway. That kind of accounting and accountability in corporate America caused Sarbanes-Oxley.

I'm even *persona non grata* at Thrivent. *Smart Money*, the magazine from The *Wall Street Journal*, once asked me why Thrivent has no particular ethic while every other religious mutual fund does. I had to honestly reply I had no idea but thought there were "secular" mutual funds with sound ethics that might be just as appropriate for Lutherans. I didn't say anything about devils excreting church leaders. But I could have added that a group of Lutheran pastors once sued their pension fund for having basically the same investment ethics employed by my mentor, Sir John Templeton, who was a legendary mutual fund manager. That's rather ironic as ELCA leadership has written and published a statement of ethics that clearly encourages the Christian ethic be applied to every dimension of life.

That suit by Lutheran pastors was also very well documented in the financial press, which is always looking for moral justification to ignore ethics. Again, that's not a promising way to evangelize our money culture.

That problem goes far beyond my ELCA. One minister friend who taught financial ethics for another major denomination years ago sadly confided that his denomination's pension fund was the most unwelcoming place he'd ever attempted to enter. We just don't seem to understand that the rich young ruler who encountered *Jesus had obeyed all the Mosaic laws, which included tithing*, but still went away sad as he didn't want God touching the money that actually belonged to God. Therefore, God couldn't really help the young ruler with his greatest love. Notice the Scriptures do not say the ruler went away unredeemed or such, only sad. That could be a good description of most dispirited church leaders I know today.

Interestingly, that reluctance to integrate faith and finance may go to the very top of American religion. Even Billy Graham once confessed the worst sermon he ever preached was about why there would be a pink Cadillac convertible in heaven for each of us! Further, the presiding bishop of the

ELCA, who has been the leader of the world-wide Lutheran community, is one of the most Godly men I've had the pleasure of meeting, but he always cringes when he sees me coming.

Like me, the bishop is a product of the sixties so he's quite attuned to political issues, but ethical economics just isn't his cup of tea. And if money doesn't trickle down, influence does. So he's quite representative of even Lutheran clergy, which is surely ironic considering Jesus' and Luther's interest in the matter. Yet virtually every denominational stewardship leader I've known during the past twenty years has told me that the "spiritual" leaders of their churches just don't understand money. In fact, I've often observed the irony that when money gets tight, the spiritual leaders often fire the financial leaders, showing short-term thinking is prevalent beyond Wall Street. Over the decades of talking with clergy friends, I've grown to understand only the best of our clergy have dealt with the spiritual issue of whether they are serving God and neighbor or simply holding down a job. That creates enormous anxieties in their souls, and probably keeps them from dealing with our similar anxieties.

This lack of spiritual discernment could result because most seminaries no longer teach the biblical and historical reality that the potential misuse of money is the most dangerous matter on earth for the spiritual. When I explored going to an Episcopal seminary years ago, I told the board I wanted to study the moral and spiritual foundations of political economy and personal finance. That is what church leaders used to know as holistic stewardship. The board members' eyes simply glazed over. They explained that none of their seminaries offered even a sub-course in the subject. I asked if they knew it was a favorite topic of Moses and Jesus. They replied, "Yes, we just don't teach it."

When historians try to explain the moral crisis resulting in the Great Recession that would be a great place to begin.

The second place would be a December 29, 2011 *Financial Times* article. It said that a major commission in Great Britain concluded that the Great Recession was made worse as financial professionals are not required to study any financial history whatsoever. The same occurs in the United States. Still, we often say those who don't remember the past are doomed to repeat its worst mistakes. If so, you should expect further volatility in the markets. That should keep politics volatile. As the Bible cautions, "When a nation sins, it will have one ruler after another" (Proverbs 28:2).

The good news is that I've been working with Luther Seminary lately. Its bookstore stocks my previous book, *Faithful Finances 101*, which John Templeton wanted me to write for seminaries and colleges. The bookstore even sells a few copies as the seminary makes my area an elective. Still, the work they're pioneering will take years to reach fruition. In the meanwhile, my informal survey of the ELCA pastors I love indicates even they no longer remember Luther's theses were actually entitled: "Ninety Five Theses on the Power and Efficacy of Indulgences." Google them and you'll understand Luther had to deal with pragmatic, but theologically challenged, teachings by the church of his day. One of the most interesting is his thesis that Christians should be taught it is better to give to the poor than to the building of churches because by works of love people grow more Christ-like.

Of course, Luther's nemesis, Pope Leo X, had good intentions when teaching otherwise. He simply wanted to glorify God by constructing St. Peter's basilica in Rome, and he needed money. Lots of it. Who has visited that magnificent building could object?

So the pope tolerated, perhaps encouraged, some less than biblical teachings about money. In that, Leo was quite like the Pharisees, who were actually devout believers, but also had to fund the expensive operations of our faith's first "mega-church," the Temple in Jerusalem. So it's ironic that Leo had forgotten that Jesus assured us even the most magnificent religious structures would crumble, while the Truth would endure forever.

We seem to have forgotten that once again as churches only seem out-numbered by banks in our increasingly secularized America.

Meditation Fourteen

Pursuing Ponzi Protection From Financial Wolves in Sheep's Clothing

"I've seen more money stolen in the name of God than any other way. Seven out of ten of our cases involve affinity fraud, and in the South, probably 40 to 50% have a religious angle."

Joseph Borg
Alabama Securities Regulator

(This article was first published by MSCI on January 26, 2009, and reprinted by the Associated Press after the Bernie Madoff scandal. It has been updated to reflect recent activities in the religious marketplace.)

The October 20, 2011 issue of *The Wall Street Journal* contained yet another story about Ponzi-operators impoverishing church members though "affinity marketing." Perhaps reflecting the reality that few seminaries still teach anything about holistic stewardship, which was a favorite topic of Moses and Jesus, a prominent bishop of a mega-church allegedly recommended those offering the investments even though none had securities licenses. Investors were to receive 20% returns from "guaranteed" and "socially conscious" short-term time deposits.

The January 28, 2012 issue of *The Economist* contained a two page article entitled "Fleecing the Flock." The article said Ponzi-scheme operators have stolen more than $23 billion from investors over the past decade. It estimated total affinity fraud, or fraud tied to religious and civic groups, has likely approximated $50 billion. It added the problem is getting worse. The typical scammer has offered 38% average annual returns. Obviously, there is a very gullible, and apparently very greedy, public that believes such returns are possible, even though Sir John Templeton became an investing legend for producing less than 15% annually.

Perhaps most sadly, the article added: "Religious fraud is particularly common, because people find it hard to imagine that the pastor is a perp."

I would simply affirm that if one group of Americans can be "perps" when it comes to money, it might be pastors, though most doctors run a close second. Ironically, that means they badly need the laity in order to relate to our money culture. Yet such fraud makes that risky. It's a vicious circle that is marginalizing the Church.

Both articles reminded me that Bernie Madoff perpetrated a fifty billion dollar Ponzi scheme that devastated investor confidence, as well as several charities in Palm Beach. A hedge fund operator in my hometown of Sarasota perpetrated another swindle of three hundred and fifty million dollars. It too has affected hundreds of investors, including the foundation of the Y on whose board I serve and several other charities. The more things change...

I trained at Merrill Lynch with a broker who, after leaving Merrill, perpetrated what was likely the largest Ponzi scheme in the history of Florida until Madoff. We attended church together and played tennis at his country club. Later, I served on the board of an international ministry affected by the New Era funding scandal, probably the largest Ponzi scheme to hit our nation's charities.

I then served on another major Christian board with Ken Lay of Enron, who was considered a most gracious and generous man.

It's inevitable that you will lose some money during thirty years of investing. But I've thus far avoided the worst Ponzi schemes and scandals, largely by understanding these realities:

1) My thirty years of studying such things tell me that investments offered by Christians, or investments that support Christian causes, neither helps nor hinders risk-adjusted returns. The higher the return, the higher the risk. Expecting a "guaranteed" investment to earn ten to twenty times what banks are paying on their federally insured deposits is to expect a miracle that only the worst preachers of the prosperity gospel offer.

2) Financial con men never look and act like con men. (And they are usually men, though they usually have gracious and sociable wives.) Their schemes depend on confidence, so they go to great lengths to look and act impeccably respectable.

3) So with the possible exception of heavily regulated trust companies, never, ever entrust one person or organization with all your investments. If you do use one financial advisor, consider having that person or institution diversify among non-affiliated investments.

4) Ponzi-scheme operators always insist on secrecy and total control, so always separate the manager and the custodian of investments. The custodian

can therefore provide a valuation of your holdings that is independent of your manager's assurances.

5) Never believe it won't happen again or to you. After New Era, I attended a meeting of Christian foundations and heard it expressed that "at least it's over." I replied that like the poor, Ponzi schemes would be with us forever. And note I said I've avoided such scandals "thus far." I know all too well we live in an age of synthetics, when wolf fur can be made to look remarkably similar to the wool of sheep.

Meditation Fifteen

Judgment Begins In the House of the Lord

"Stewardship must not be reduced to a fund raising campaign on behalf of institutions, religious or otherwise. It is a way of life and not mere rhetoric for motivating charitable contributions. God has a prior claim on everything and not just that which we label as tithe."

Bishop Ken Carder
United Methodist Church

I recently attended another "stewardship" conference. I was surprised when someone asked if we should even use that word anymore. Some, myself included, volunteered that we rarely use it as the church has basically reduced it to financing our institutional needs. I even prefer the term "spiritual investing," which is appropriate for both giving and investing with a Christian ethic.

A conversation ensued about the definition of stewardship. Some thought stewardship should be purely about raising money to pay the church's bills. Conference organizers seemed to agree. Virtually every break out group, regardless of subject, led directly or indirectly to funding our churches and ministries. Some said it was about the proverbial "time, talent and treasure," without being very clear about what that meant. Several shared the belief that "it's all God's," again without being clear on how to put that theology into practice. Even Wall Street knows the word stewardship really means empowering the poor, caring for the environment, acting in a responsible manner when managing wealth, and so on. In addition, the federal budget actually uses the word to describe our government's management of our nation's wealth.

It was only the latest evidence that the Church, and many stewardship leaders in particular, may be even more confused over money than is our culture. It was times like these when Luther suggested we go back to the financial teachings of the Bible.

Thirty years ago, stewardship to me simply meant that dreaded time of the year when we had to appeal to my Episcopal church to get the bills paid.

Our efforts were exclusively about buying a juvenile pledge card program and going to creative lengths to get people excited about it. Truth be told, people hated it. And the only person who hated it worse than I did as church president was our pastor. After all, his talk usually began with the "theological distortion" that we were giving to God, which is impossible if God really owns it all.

What we were really giving to was God's work on earth. That included the pastor's salary, which the most honest pastors I know acknowledge creates dissonance for them on stewardship Sunday. As to the laity, they surely wondered how much faith we church leaders had if we had to ask donors

Source Unknown

to estimate the church's revenue before we could prepare a simple budget. Just imagine what you would think if a businessperson sent a card asking how much business you would do next year as he couldn't prepare a budget without it! Most stewardship leaders would be thrilled if they could increase giving from 2% of our incomes to 4% by teaching we should give 10%. But that still leaves us 90% short of holistic stewardship.

All that is a good example of how the Church aspires to mediocrity in financial matters, and usually settles for incompetence.

Those experiences and my financial background resulted in my helping one hundred and twenty churches on the west coast of Florida as a volunteer planned giving officer. I did my best to get people to come hear about wills, trusts, and so on; but it was futile. People viewed the sessions as just another fundraising effort on the part of an increasingly irrelevant church. Oddly, when I did seminars about the same techniques as an investment executive trying to save taxes and increase incomes, attendees thought I was some kind of whiz kid.

My planned giving work, which in Florida was actually "barely deferred giving," caused me to attend several of my denomination's annual stewardship gatherings. They too were exclusively about funding the church. Yet that led to my writing a financial book for the national stewardship department. It was picked up for publication by an evangelical publisher. It did cover all the "stewardship" topics I'd been trained in by the church. But my research into how money managers like Sir John Templeton managed our denominations' endowments and pension funds caused me to include a chapter on the embryonic "socially responsible investing" movement. *Christianity Today* said it was the first book that explained the biblical roots of the exploding movement to create wealth ethically, as well as give it generously.

At the end of our next annual stewardship gathering, our leader acknowledged the meetings were getting boring and asked what would interest us. The number one reply was "socially responsible investing." He quipped that I would have to speak at the next meeting. But of course, when we got there the church's financial needs trumped the interests of attendees and we talked about the same old techniques for funding the church. By now I had noticed a pattern, so I essentially made a deal with the church that I would talk and write about everything but giving. While I try to acknowledge the importance of giving, we seem to have adequate people covering that topic and including it in my seminars wasn't helping attendance.

Writing the book seemed to make me some sort of expert. So I was invited to speak to ecumenical groups. I quickly noticed two completely different approaches. The mainline churches of Canada and the United States meet annually for the North American Conference on Christian Philanthropy. Oddly, it went far beyond philanthropy into issues of social justice, environmentalism, and so on. I realized this was residue from the so-called "social gospel" of early last century.

On the other hand, evangelical stewardship leaders met annually as the Christian Stewardship Association. Oddly, despite it using the holistic word "stewardship," I spoke there several years and never observed any interest in anything but Christian philanthropy. I was beginning to understand why religious sociologists increasingly say there is little connection between what most Christians say and what they do.

I spoke about the growing disparities in wealth, which contribute to unwanted pregnancies and other social pathologies, the anti-Christian ethics of Wall Street, the misperceptions about the American economy which greatly reduce giving, and other challenges that true and holistic stewardship might help solve. But while my evaluations were solid, they routinely indicated few understood what any of that had to do with stewardship. Basically, evangelicalism is so new on the church scene it simply doesn't have the historically deeper perspectives of the subject. It's simply funding the Great Commission, which too often means simply talking our faith rather than walking it.

As the following chart shows, the more we've made the past century, the lower the percentage we have given, which is the most basic of stewardship requirements. Jesus strongly cautioned the Pharisees about tithing even the mint, dill and cumin from the garden while forgetting the more important teachings of the law. We might therefore wonder if our inability, or unwillingness, to fund our bills isn't because all of us, including our pastors, have totally forgotten the more important concepts.

So how do we understand stewardship in its holistic and biblical sense? First of all, it's not fundraising, or even tithing and giving. Fundraising begins, and usually ends, with the financial needs of our institutions. It's not unlike the ancients paying Temple taxes to keep the fires burning. Tithing also usually begins with a legalistic understanding of your finances. It's a standard that the church still teaches despite having forgotten most other dimensions of stewardship. It's safe to say that institutional self-interest, which is legitimate but theologically limited, has a lot to do with that concept's survival.

As important as survival might be, our example is unlikely to save our increasingly selfish society.

We need a more holistic approach. I believe that would surely include the responsibility to manage wealth in a socially responsible fashion. More importantly, Moses did too. In Exodus 21:28, Moses said the habitual failure to manage your bull in a socially responsible fashion was a capital offense. Now that's important! There are two reasons I believe that is a crucial passage at this time: 1) you didn't have to directly and meaningfully harm someone in order to be guilty. You simply had to ignore your responsibilities, and 2) the bull is the symbol of Wall Street, where most investors do not watch over how their assets are affecting their neighbors.

Even soulful giving hardly satisfies our responsibilities as stewards. Jesus clearly knew the difference between giving and stewarding treasure. He taught that if we are about to "give" at the altar and remember a neighbor has something against us, we should go away and make peace with that neighbor before coming back to give. No, we don't hear that too often these days. But like the prophets, Jesus knew the sacrifice of selfishness in our daily lives was the sacrifice God preferred, not simply cash in the Temple.

Jesus also said our hearts will always be where the "treasure" we steward for ourselves is, not where the money we gave went too. As one corporate leader has said, tithing is simply about what we give away; stewardship is also about what we keep. Try this: Give to Focus on the Family to stop the spread of casino gambling, but invest your IRA into casino stocks. Open the paper the next morning and see if your heart is sad or glad that your casino company is prospering. In short, if our treasure is invested in our culture, our hearts will be that of cultural Christians. This is also why Billy Graham has said that if we get our money right, the rest of our lives just fall in place. He too understands that money is the last area of our lives we'll submit to God, even if it's the most important, as the root of all evil hasn't changed over the millennia.

That's why I specialize in stewarding all the financial resources that belong to God. That even includes areas like trying to pay the full amount of taxes I owe each year without being a grump, as Paul commanded in Romans 13. Yes, I'm still working on that one. But I know that managing money is only one dimension of stewardship, and far from the most important one at that. Watching Sir John Templeton grow old, as my father never had the chance to do, convinced me that time is far, far more valuable than money. In fact, the less time we have left, the more money we usually have. If possible, we would gladly trade it for more time. So once again, contrary to common wisdom, money is far more than money.

So I decided twenty-five years ago to imitate John and use one-half of my time for ministry and one-half for business. But I found "the hound of heaven," to use C.S. Lewis' term, to be a jealous God. The more time and talent I gave, the more God wanted. So I soon realized that God wanted all my time, as well as all my talent. So my investment practice and my ministry were soon "integrated." That causes both "worlds" enormous indigestion. I lose a lot of business and ministry opportunities as Americans, and probably pastors most of all, are skeptical of people who actually mix faith and life. Wall Street thinks I'm totally nuts.

Yet many tradition-challenged ministries, and conservative ministries in particular, believe capitalism and Christianity are synonymous.

For reasons we will explore in the next meditation, Tony Perkins of the Family Research Council has even written an article for CNN entitled "Jesus was a free market capitalist." Just as Bruce Wilkinson created a materialistic theology for conservative Christians by extracting The *Prayer of Jabez* from the rest of the Bible, and particularly the Lord's Prayer which simply asks for daily bread, Tony focused exclusively on the Parable of the Talents, which even I have long termed the great parable of capitalism. Taken out of the context of those passages where Jesus said to sell what we own and give it to the poor, and all those passages about the spiritual difficulties with which the rich are burdened, the Parable of the Talents does make Jesus seem more like a capitalist Scrooge than the loving Christ.

As has been well said, even Satan can quote scripture for his own purposes. And with that particular article, I believe Tony better presented Satan's case than Christ's. For it was Satan who offered Christ all the kingdoms of the world, or "enlarged territories," as Wilkinson put it, which Christ unhesitatingly declined. That's not to imply Christ wanted each of us to don sack cloth and ashes. It's simply an appeal for conservative Christian leaders to teach the world the balanced Christian perspective.

Such unbalanced teachings are likely why, despite all the moral problems documented by even the headlines of the secular media, the December 9, 2011 issue of *The Wall Street Journal* said this in "God and the Economy in Iowa" just before its caucus to elect a president in 2012:

> *"Evangelicals make up between 50% and 60% of the conservative primary electorate. Yet a recent Washington Post/ABC poll found that some 70% of likely caucus-goers list the economy as their top issue; 14% listed social issues. Or how about this: A recent Public Policy polling survey found more voters (42%) had 'major concerns' with a candidate who supported an individual health mandate than they did (34%) a candidate who had cheated on a spouse...**As much as participants in***

a recent focus group talked about their faith, the conversation was overwhelmingly dominated by their concerns about the economy."

My experiences on Wall Street suggest most of Wall Street's elite believe Ayn Rand's teaching that Christianity and capitalism cannot co-exist. Over the past twenty years, I've asked several investment firms and mutual fund companies to develop funds for what I believe is the largest, most underserved market in the world: affluent Christianity. None have seen any reason to do so. That's a shame on our part as I can assure you that Wall Street, like Washington, usually gives us what we want.

If we want an economy, and particularly a financial system, that more resembles the prudent, ethical, and even compassionate economy of God, we'll have to demand it. No one is going to volunteer it.

That was affirmed to me when a mid-west based investment firm wanted to hire me on a friend's recommendation. It actually confessed that it wouldn't hire anyone who was openly Christian. The manager, who was a Christian, sadly confessed to having asked if he could hire me if I had legal baggage, obtained speculative clients in bars at night, and so on. He was told that would be fine; but the firm couldn't risk my being a Christian who publicly witnessed to his faith. I realized that when I produced the same business decades ago as a closet Christian, the same firm would have actively recruited me and paid me a bonus of a hundred thousand dollars or more. As a visible Christian, I was unemployable. That's a perfect example of the secular nature of America's financial services industry these days.

(I am very pleased to report however that since I wrote those words, my national firm has developed and introduced a series of funds for religious investors. They generally reflect the Catholic ethic. That is quite similar to what evangelicals desire when they think about ethics as both groups are particularly concerned with life issues. Yet I'm also talking to company management about appealing to broader Christian markets. So things may be about to improve for Christians, at long last.)

In fairness, I understand investment firms have to be wary as "affinity fraud," primarily by those professing religion, has been quite rampant in recent years. In my way of thinking, that's just another reason real Christians on Wall Street should witness to their faith. No one else is going to talk about the people who are trying their human best to do what is right in perhaps the most difficult corner of our world, particularly when success may be quite dependent on all participants being counter-intuitive and counter-cultural.

One of my oldest and wisest counselors tells me I've forgone considerable business over the years by being public about my faith. I don't identify myself as a "Christian financial planner," or put a fish on my business cards. I just try to be the best "counselor to ethical and spiritual investors" possible. That doesn't say anything about me, other than I only want to work with ethical and prudent investors. Apparently, even that is too much for many Christians to handle. If so, we should *never* criticize Wall Street.

I still believe I've been blessed to do what I've done the way I've done it. When I was exploring seminary about the time my son was born, the psychologist sensed that I had a very distant relationship with my father. Without my having told the psychologist so, he knew from his ink blots that dad was an entrepreneur who was loving but always working. Turns out, that is a cultural characteristic that has afflicted men since we left our family farms and began working in factories and offices.

The psychologist also sensed dad had died young of cancer without my receiving "the blessing" of biblical times. Both caused a sense of loneliness deep in my soul, even if they drove me at work. Not wanting my son to grow up with that spiritual poverty, I moved my office into my home. An unintentional by-product is that I greatly reduced what we now call my "carbon footprint" by no longer driving to work each day. Sherry, who had worked in the marketplace to that point, did the same by coming home to school Garrett.

As I have less and less time on earth, I realize the blessings of those days could never be matched by the corner offices, titles, and pension plans that I "gave up." Sure there were financial costs, assuming I could have remained sane while living in two worlds and thinking with two minds. Stewards should never fail to estimate those. My best friend in management training school, who was a Christian, ran the huge Wall Street firm last year, as I predicted he would. His annual bonus was probably more than my accumulated net worth. Having read about our old firm's problems in the headlines, I don't envy him a bit.

Even in my far lower orbit, I produced one-half the commissions last year that I did when I left the major firm twenty-five years ago. Adjusted for inflation, they were probably one-fourth. Yet by any standard other than Wall Street's, I was still blessed beyond my wildest expectations as a youth. My wife has now put up with me for thirty years. My son and I are close, to the point he's joined me in my practice. I have time to write, speak and serve African orphans and on boards. On one of those, I served with Ken Lay, the disgraced chairman of Enron. Ken gave lots of money to ministry, but will never be remembered as a great Christian steward.

So God hounds me for even more. The more I've seen and church history I've studied, the more I've realized we are all called to steward the life-enhancing teachings and traditions of the church. Those are under assault from secular humanism on both left and right so we have forgotten many of them. Knowing what had once made the church so relevant to economic life, I also realized the church is in dire need of a Second Reformation. So on counsel of an ordained friend, Sherry and I became Lutherans. My friend knew the Evangelical Lutheran Church in America is both evangelical and socially responsible and would meet this old Baptist's needs for down-home people and polity, as well as my wife's need for higher liturgy and sacrament, or smells and bells.

Lutherans tend to be as ecumenical and public-relations oriented as the Amish and Mennonites, which means barely at all. We could probably learn from more media-savvy evangelicals in that regard. We have a good story to tell. Few know that *Forbes* has estimated Lutheran Social Services is substantially larger than the YMCA, Red Cross and the Salvation Army, America's second, third and fourth largest charities. It is four times Habitat for Humanity. I attribute that to Luther teaching there's nothing more holy about a priest tending a church than a person plowing a field or tending a home. That theology is known as "the priesthood of all believers" and is another idea we desperately need to resurrect, even in the ELCA at times.

Yet Luther soon discovered even his own parishioners liked the idea that simply giving a few coins is all it takes to get into heaven. Luther also discovered church leaders' financial self-interest caused them to like the theology even more. But it's my guess that he was blessed by Christ.

When Jesus also essentially reformed God's wayward church, he whipped Pharisees and cleansed the Temple of money changers. The examples of both Christ and Luther might suggest the modern church will never be relevant until it deals with money. That, in turn, might free all our time and talents for God's work.

Ironically, our Jewish and Catholic friends seem to have learned. During the eighties, the only person who asked me about investment ethics was a Jewish lady who became a dear friend. The U.S. Catholic Conference of Bishops has confessed this in a pastoral letter:

> *"Concentrating on one specific obligation of stewardship, even one as important as church support, could make it harder - even impossible - for people to grasp the vision. It could imply that when the bishops get serious about stewardship, what they really mean is simply giving money."*

Before he died, John Paul said:

"The decision to invest in one place rather than another, in one productive sector rather than another, is always a moral and cultural choice."

So the challenge we face today may not be the ones that Jesus and Luther faced. The real challenge may be with the newer branches of Christianity. I believe they too are quite popular today largely as they demand so little in the way of stewardship. The November 2009 issue of *Christianity Today* contained an article about J. Lee Grady, editor of *Charisma* magazine, who has long battled "prosperity theology." In it, he says:

"Martin Luther had to say something, or they were going to keep selling indulgences. Now we have that going on in our midst. If someone says 'Send your $100 to be saved,' that is selling indulgences, and there are people doing that on Trinity Broadcasting Network."

If we realize that's essentially, if unwittingly, also going on in most conservative churches and many mainline churches as well, we just might ignite that reformation, of the Church and then culture.

Meditation Sixteen

Is Jesus a Free Market Capitalist?

"Jesus was a free marketer, not an Occupier."

Tony Perkins
President
Family Research Council
Editorial to CNN

*"The Judeo-Christian ethos...provides a ringing
endorsement of capitalism as a moral endeavor."*

Rabbi Aryeh Spero
"What the Bible Teaches About Capitalism"
Editorial to The Wall Street Journal

I virtually ignored the editorial by Tony Perkins. After twenty years of teaching stewardship, I'm accustomed to conservative Christians arguing God is a capitalist, by which they actually mean a free marketer who wants limited government. I'm just as accustomed to progressive Christians arguing God is a socialist, by which they actually mean a "statist" who wants the government to redistribute wealth. In my view, neither group truly understands the historical teachings of the faith.

However, upon reading the second editorial by a religious leader who apparently thinks God agrees with his views, I just had to write a letter to the editor of The *Wall Street Journal*. It basically argued our omniscient, omnipotent, transcendent Mind of the universe has not come back to earth to advocate quite cultural ways of thinking about political economy and personal finance. I have no reason to believe the *Journal* will take my letter seriously, so I may as well share it shortly.

The reason I do is that while many American religious leaders were arguing that American capitalism has been Godly, the greatly respected money manager Jeremy Grantham of GMO was writing these words in his quarterly letter to shareholders:

*"To move from the problem of long time horizons to the short-term common good, **it is quickly apparent that capitalism in general has no sense of ethics or conscience.** Whatever the Supreme Court may think, it is not a person. Why would a company give up a penny for the common good if it is not required to by enforced regulation <u>or</u> unless it looked like that penny might be returned with profit in the future because having a good image might be good for business? Ethical CEOs can drag a company along for a while, but this is an undependable and temporary fix. Ethical humans can also impose their will on corporations singly or en masse by withholding purchases or bestowing them, and companies can anticipate this and even influence it through clever brand advertising, 'clean coal' being my favorite. But that is quite different from corporate altruism. Thus, we can roast our planet and firms may offer marvelous and profitable energy-saving equipment, but it will be for profit today, not planet saving tomorrow.*

It gets worse, for what capitalism has always had is money with which to try to buy influence. Today's version of U.S. capitalism has died and gone to heaven on this issue. A company is now free to spend money to influence political outcomes and need tell no one, least of all its own shareholders, the technical owners. So, rich industries can exert so much political influence that they now have a dangerous degree of influence over Congress."

Even the *Financial Times* of Great Britain is running a series, which I've quoted often in this book, about the "Crisis in Capitalism." So it's surely ironic that religious leaders who have been assured that people perish for lack of a better vision, seen to believe that God has nothing better in mind for humanity than what we've seen from Wall Street and corporate America lately. Neither will ever change if those religious leaders keep baptizing fear and greed by writing editorials that God is as well pleased with CEOs as with Jesus upon his baptism.

I might add that I found it interesting that the *Journal*, which published some truly sound theology over the years under Robert Bartley, chose to print the last editorial implying God approves of casino capitalism. The *Journal* is now owned by Rupert Murdoch's News Corp. My mentor Sir John Templeton was a major stockholder in Mr. Murdoch's company decades ago and knew Mr. Murdoch fairly well. But late in life, Sir John seemed to have concerns about having financed Mr. Murdoch's enterprises so heavily.

Mr. Murdoch's company also owns the Christian publisher that published my first book about John. Upon giving John a copy and telling him that one of Mr. Murdoch's companies had published it, John remarked, "You know,

Rupert says he's a Christian." I replied that I knew that, but I also knew Mr. Murdoch published some less-than-biblical tabloids as well. John replied, "Well, I guess we'll just have to give him one of your books."

I rather doubt John did so, for there's certainly little evidence that Mr. Murdoch read it. Mr. Murdoch was the focus of an article in the July 23, 2011 issue of *The Economist* entitled, "Great bad men as bosses." It essentially said it's still quite difficult for a rich person to achieve the holistic mind of Christ:

> *"With the world debating, in the wake of Mr. Murdoch's appearance in the House of Commons, whether he is an evil genius who is showing his years or an evil genius who is pulling the wool over everybody's eyes, it is important to remember his greatness as a businessman...Balzac supposedly wrote that 'behind every great fortune lies a great crime.'* **It would be truer to say that behind every great fortune there is a psychological aberration."**

As you may have read elsewhere, after buying *The Wall Street Journal*, Mr. Murdoch's company came under some considerable heat by the British government over some less-than-biblically recommended journalistic ethics. My point again is that there's a huge difference in allowing your religious ethic to shape your business philosophy and allowing your business philosophy to shape your religious ethic. That's also true of political ethics, which was actually the case with the editorial in the *Journal*. It was suggesting God approves of Governor Romney's activities at Bain Capital, to which I made this response:

> *"Twenty-five years ago, I thought of leaving my position as a senior vice president of Paine Webber in order to attend seminary. I discovered few seminaries any longer taught anything about the moral foundations of political economy and personal finance. I'm afraid Rabbi Spero must have attended one such seminary if he believes the Bible teaches the individualistic, Ayn Rand style of capitalism he described. What he says is fairly accurate, but the Rabbi commits far too many sins of omission for any but the most cultural of believers to take seriously.*

> *Jesus was Jewish and fairly knowledgeable of the Law of Moses. Jesus summarized that Law for his followers with his Great Commandment to "love God and neighbor as self," or virtuously accept social responsibility, which the Rabbi failed to mention, as readily as one accepts personal responsibility, or taking care of number one, of which the Rabbi myopically focused. Hopefully, the Rabbi has read Exodus 21:28, in which Moses teaches the failure to prevent one's bull, ironically the symbol of capitalism, from harming others is actually a capital*

offense. There are similar economic justice teachings about putting rails on roofs, forgiving debts each seventh year, and so on.

I'm not aware that Moses ever taught the penalty for envy, which the Rabbi seems to believe is the root of all evil, is capital punishment. [Note: At this point, I was tempted to remind the Journal that envy is the basis of considerable advertising that keeps the media in business, but I somehow held my tongue.] My guess is that if those teachings make Moses and Jesus "socialists," they would happily plead guilty, as evidenced by the communitarians in the Book of Acts, even if Jesus didn't advocate statism. I expect Moses and Jesus would suggest that what they had in mind for us moderns is a church pension or endowment fund that voluntarily, even lovingly, invests in socially responsible ways.

I founded The Financial Seminary to better explain that "spiritual third way" alternative to selfish capitalism and statist socialism. In political spheres, we may indeed err toward statism. But in the marketplace, I've found the greatest threat to the teachings of Moses and Jesus is the assumption that the only consideration for investors is the risk/return to the individual. I've therefore written several books about the financial theology of my friend Sir John Templeton, the mutual fund legend who long avoided the stocks of alcohol, tobacco and gambling companies due to his Calvinistic beliefs, which are more heavily influenced by the laws of Moses. I believe Sir John would emphatically suggest the Bible advocates moral markets, not free markets or capitalism.

John Bogle, another Calvinist of note and the founder of the Vanguard mutual funds, advocates the same. To claim otherwise is to create God in our own image, a major concern of Moses and Calvinism but apparently fairly rampant in religious circles today. A major evangelical leader committed the same sin recently when also writing that God is a "free market capitalist, not an Occupier." Now why would any religious leader possibly believe Jesus might be particularly compassionate toward the down and out rather than those who constitute the 1%?!

*During my seminars, I often say that when one can't quote God, one does well to quote C.S. Lewis. In Mere Christianity, Lewis challenged the notion that capitalism is biblical. I included his words, along with these other quotes from economic historians, in a chapter I've just written for the forth-coming book entitled **Becoming a Stewardship Leader**, being published by the Christian Leadership Alliance, the largest group of conservative Christian leaders in America.*

185

I had hoped these perspectives might help Wall Street and the church to humbly reflect on **The Financial Times**' series entitled "The Crisis in Capitalism." Those of us who belong to Christian denominations with European traditions can remember when German Christians baptized another humanistic "ism" regarding political economy. This was under Adolf Hitler. Similarly, the Times seems more careful than the Journal in claiming "God is on our side."

The Times most likely understands that simply saying capitalism with all its recent faults is still better than socialism at its best, may be the greatest form of collective moral relativism of our age, especially as even Forbes has written admiringly about the economy of Denmark, whose government takes half of its citizens' incomes as taxes. Humbly understanding those facts might prompt us to consider repenting of our sins. Deluding ourselves with editorials about why God approves of all of our politicians' and capitalism's recent activities probably won't do so.

My chapter for the CLA's stewardship book includes this passage, beginning with this quote from Lewis regarding capitalism:

"There is one bit of advice to us by the ancient heathen Greeks, and by the Jews of the Old Testament and by the great Christian teachers of the Middle Ages, which the modern economic system has completely disobeyed. All these people told us not to lend money at interest; and lending at interest - what we call investment - is the basis of our whole system... It does not necessarily follow that we are wrong. That is where we need the Christian economist. But I should not have been honest if I had not told you that three great civilizations had agreed in condemning the very thing on which we have based our whole life."

Perhaps you noticed that Lewis did not say the conservative Romans objected to interest. That may be why, despite all the "Bible-based" teachings about debt today, I've never heard a conservative financial ministry question the earning of interest. Paying interest yes; earning it no. Yet there are still a few Old Order Amish in Pennsylvania who still refuse to earn interest on bank deposits, as do most Muslims. This is how Justo Gonzalez explained the ancient conservative view in Faith & Wealth: "All the great writers of Roman antiquity are conservative... Since the earliest of times, the maximum rate had been fixed at 1% simple interest per month, and this was generally the legal limit throughout the history of Roman legislation."

Professor Niall Ferguson confirmed Lewis' perspective of Christian history by writing these words in *The Ascent of Money*: "**For Christians, lending money at interest was a sin. Usurers, people who lent money at interest, had been excommunicated by the Third Lateran Council in 1179**. *Even arguing that usury is not a sin had been condemned as heresy by the Council of Vienna in 1311-12. Christian usurers had to make restitution to the Church before they could be buried on hallowed ground.*"

*It was actually the Protestant Reformers who, correctly in my view, formally legitimated the earning of interest within moral boundaries. As Paul Schervish states in **Wealth and the Will of God**: "Prior to Calvin, the Roman Church and most secular authorities banned usury on two grounds. Philosophically, usury violates Aristotelian precepts, which held that making money on money is a base and unnatural form of profit. Scripturally, many interpreters read Luke 6:35 ('Lend, hoping for nothing again') as outlawing usury...In his own legislation, Calvin outlawed charging interest to the poor; but he allowed interest to be charged in other transactions."*

*That moral change went a long way in making banking, and therefore modern capitalism, possible. Yet the Reformers always placed moral constraints around such activities. For example, Martin Luther wrote, in his typically blunt manner: "**If, after diligent work, his efforts fail, he who has borrowed money should and may say to him from whom he has borrowed it: This year I owe you nothing**...If you want to have a share in winning, you must also have a share in losing. The money lenders who do not want to put up with these terms are as pious as robbers and murderers."*

*That moral framework apparently influenced our economic activities until the founding of America. Princeton sociologist Robert Wuthnow provided this example in **God and Mammon in America**: "In 1639, the elders of the First Church of Boston brought charges against a Puritan merchant named Robert Keayne for dishonoring the name of God. Soon after, he was tried and found guilty by the Commonwealth as well. Writing his memoirs some sixteen years later, he was still stung by the disgrace of the event. **His sin was greed. He had sold his wares at a six percent profit, two percent above the maximum allowed**."*

Somehow, none of that reminds me of junk bonds, proprietary traders in investment firms taking risks with taxpayer money, private equity funds making over 100% annual returns while laying off workers, sub-prime mortgages made to those who can't afford them, high frequency trading by young parasites of Wall Street, and so on.

We might therefore consider repenting, for the end of Rand-style, individualistic capitalism that ignores neighbor might indeed be near, as well it should be!

(End of letter to the Journal.*)*

When conservative religious leaders have deemed to teach anything about capitalism, they've usually taught that government borrowing would "crowd out" the ability of businesses on Main Street to borrow, which is a bit ironic as most also teach those of us on Main Street shouldn't be borrowing anyway! But the following chart from the *Financial Times* shows that any crowding out before the Great Recession was probably more due to Wall Street than Washington. Some major Wall Street firms were leveraged 33 to one, meaning they only had 3% equity in the firms. They used much of their borrowed money to manufacture sub-prime mortgage bonds. When they couldn't sell the worst of those bonds, they suffered losses that wiped out the small amount of equity they had, which meant they were technically, or actually, bankrupt. Hence the financial panic leading to the Great Recession. The ultimate irony is the US Government had to borrow quite a bit of money to keep those Wall Street firms in business.

I certainly have nothing against true financial professionals making a better than average living by financing our nation's needs, even wants. Ours is a tough business that, much like being a pastor, requires being nearly super human due to human nature being what it is. But too many within large Wall Street institutions have simply desired to

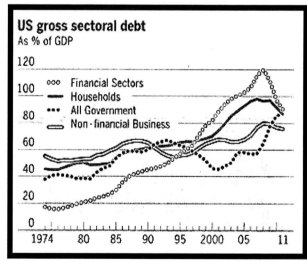

borrow money and trade money against true investors. And unlike fulfilling needs and wants, trying to fulfill desires usually causes pain, spiritual and/or financial. This time it caused both, at least to Main Street.

The January 21, 2012 edition of *The Economist* explored the question "Who exactly are the 1%?" and concluded: "The most striking shift has been the growth of financial occupations, from just under 8% of the wealthy in 1979 to 13.9% in 2005. Their representation within the top 0.1% is even more pronounced: 18%, up from 11% in 1979," the year before President Reagan took office.

Meditation Seventeen

The Spiritual State of Our Church & Therefore Union

*"This framework of separated areas of life is deeply
embedded in the Christian Church, in its theology and in
the daily life of its people. On Sunday morning or during
our devotional or prayer life, we operate in the spiritual
realm. The rest of the week, and in our professional lives,
we operate in the physical realm and, hence, unwittingly
act like functional atheists."*

Bryant Myers, Ph.D.
WorldVision

There was a time I considered my lack of a formal business education to be
a disadvantage. But in recent years, I've learned that business academia's
complex theories have impoverished so many that my ignorance may be a
distinct advantage in writing a book about ethical economics. I've also grown
to understand more generally that people with advanced degrees, which
largely means our leaders, too often know more and more about less and less
until they know almost everything about almost nothing.

Capitalism depends on the "specialization of labor," in which we know quite
a bit about our relatively narrow sphere of endeavor. This presents particular
problems for those few Christians who prefer to think in a biblically holistic
manner, as Richard J. Foster explained in his classic *Freedom of Simplicity*:

> *"It is not wrong for us to isolate some aspect of the spiritual walk for the
> sake of study, as long as we understand the artificiality of the isolation.
> And we must always come back to the whole. **Perhaps the technical
> sciences can ignore the whole for the part, but in the spiritual walk
> it is ruinous. The life with God, hid in Christ, is a unity, a seamless
> robe.**"*

The artificial divisions in our thinking impoverish us, spiritually at first and
then financially. Irving Kristol put it this way in *The Wall Street Journal*:

"Religion is not some kind of psychic exercise that occasionally offers a transcendent experience. It either shapes one's life - all of one's life - or it vanishes, leaving behind anxious, empty souls that no psychotherapy can reach."

This relatively uneducated fellow has finally learned the hard way to focus on the big picture and count his blessings. I therefore aspire to help you do the same, albeit with less spiritual cost than I've paid. Yet I've also sought to spare you simply dwelling on my own thoughts and feelings about these matters. I usually find financial books of that nature are from egomaniacs. While they are usually extreme, and therefore entertaining and popular, they are also evidence of why the word "entertainment" derives from two words meaning "between" and periods of "attaining" reality.

The Economist, Date Unknown

Popular authors often profit nicely from such entertainment, yet impoverishment lies ahead for the reader. Think of all those best-sellers from the early nineties where authors with no training in economics predicted economic doom. Then there were those in the late nineties from non-computer experts who predicted Y2K would end western civilization. We are so besieged by real and imaginary problems, studies tell us there has been no increase in people's confidence about the future despite the fact our GDP and wealth has soared.

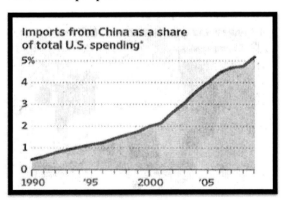

The Wall Street Journal, 9-27-2011

Whereas we worried during the seventies and eighties that OPEC and Japan would buy us, we now worry the Chinese will. When I ask my clients how much of our goods we buy from China, I get answers ranging from twenty-five percent to as much as eighty percent. In reality, the above graph suggests we spend five percent of our income annually on imports from China. This is about the same percentage that we have historically spent in Canada, which until very recently was actually our largest trading partner.

Most of us also aren't aware, as detailed in the November 2, 2011 issue of *The Wall Street Journal,* that over one-half of China's rich are either leaving China or considering it. Forty percent of those are considering moving to America, while another 37% are considering Canada for their home country. Apparently, the grass remains greener on the other side of the fence, no matter where you live.

Extreme half-truths seem to have altered reality for us baby boomers who matured during the political excesses of the sixties and seventies and the economic excesses of the eighties and nineties. Like most boomers, I am approaching my retirement years. I also expect those years will be less materialistic. But unlike most boomers, and perhaps our younger neighbors, I think life might actually be considerably richer from a greater balance of material and spiritual wealth. In anticipation of those years, many lives might be enriched by Forster's *Freedom of Simplicity,* in which he writes these words about moderation:

> *"Christian simplicity lives in harmony with the ordered complexity of life. It repudiates easy, dogmatic answers to tough, intricate problems. In fact, it is this grace that frees us sufficiently to appreciate and respond to the complex issues of contemporary society...**To deny the goodness of the created order is to be an ascetic. To deny the limitation of the created order is to be a materialist.***"*

After sixty years on this planet, I finally understand that a gentle breeze is most welcomed on a hot August evening, but even then, too much is called a tornado or hurricane. Water is a key biblical metaphor for helping us understand the needs of body and soul. Even Noah, though, knew too much could destroy human life. So the author of the Bible's Wisdom Literature prayed for "neither too much nor too little." St. Paul later counseled us to seek moderation in all things except love. Later, St. Benedict taught us that the place of perfect spiritual peace is precisely between the pull of differing poles. Such is the nature of reality. Being in touch with that Reality is a moment of pure bliss.

Unfortunately, I believe many of us miss that bliss by pretending to embrace Christian spirituality while acting quite differently, particularly about economics. In fact, there are reasons to believe such pretension actually causes many of us to be *even more miserable, anxious and angry* than our society in general. The June 26, 2010 issue of *The Economist* shared this reality:

> *"Those who buy counterfeit designer goods project a fashionable image at a fraction of the price of the real thing. You might think that would make them feel rather smug about themselves. But an intriguing piece of research published in* **Psychological Science** *suggests the opposite: wearing fake goods makes you feel a fake yourself, and causes you to be more dishonest in other matters than you would otherwise be."*

The principle of moderation applies to political economy as well. We need government, but too much stifles the human spirit and creativity. We need strong leaders, but we chaff under dictators. We need freedom, but too much is anarchy. We need markets, even if they too often become mobs.

For such reasons, our Founding Fathers established a republic with three branches of government held in tension, rather than a direct vote of the mob, as Pilate conducted. The Founding Fathers didn't actually want all of us voting on every matter of importance to the republic. They wanted each of us attending to our own business. So they established a republic where we elect leaders to make collective decisions for us. Moses and Jesus did much the same when choosing judges and disciples respectively.

March 2009

Yet the democratizing influences of our pervasive media, which encourage us to think we know more than we actually might, have radicalized our perceptions of the Founders' intentions. Everyone, but particularly the Tea Party and Occupy Wall Street movement, seems to believe he or she better knows how to run our nation than do our democratically-elected leaders. Perhaps. There is great value in collective wisdom, but wisdom is quite different from information and particularly perception. As you're now familiar with Plato's Cave, you know he thought most of us confuse perceptions shaped by others who have their own agendas with reality.

Our polarized and polarizing popular media makes the tensions in our political life far worse. As recently detailed in a cover story of *The Economist* entitled, "The Missing Middle: The Woeful Gap in American Politics," this politicized democratization, perhaps balkanization, is not enriching us economically, or spiritually. It has coincided with our global economy growing incredibly complex; to the point that former Fed chairman Alan Greenspan, who was a numbers guy if there's ever been one, told Congress he had missed some important realities about human nature by deregulating Wall Street CEOs before the Great Recession.

Trust me, I am not advocating for the status quo. I've advocated peaceful and gradual change on Wall Street and in Washington for nearly twenty years. There's considerable evidence that it might now be necessary for that change to become more urgent. However, there's a right way and a wrong way to do everything. We simply must do the right things and make the right changes. Any true change must begin with us. Most objective evidence suggests our hearts, minds, and particularly our souls, are quite confused these days. Most Christian leaders seem to simply claim that, "God is on our side." We may be quite wrong.

November 5, 2011

By labeling ourselves "conservative Christians" or "progressive Christians," we may simply be dooming ourselves by that ancient habit the biblical prophets railed against of mixing our faith with pagan ideas. Theologians call that "syncretism." Yes, there is over-lap between the ideas of Judeo-Christianity and classical, or Greco-Roman thought. Yet there are also crucial differences, particularly in the area of managing the political economy.

For Truth to have a capital "T," it must be true for all people at all times. I believe Truth is only found in the teachings of Moses and the personhood of Jesus. Both taught us to love our neighbors as ourselves in all that we do, rather than simply our charitable activities. That is what we truly seek for our political economy. I have long called that "stewardism" to acknowledge its biblical roots and differentiate it from statism on the left and selfish forms of capitalism on the right.

I also believe the negativity of the media and the Good News of God's unconditional and graceful love for us are incompatible. The negativity of the media, particularly when regurgitating partisan politics, is making us quite despondent and cynical. Few of us have read a headline about ten thousand planes arriving safely yesterday. Thus, many people feel planes only crash and burn. They don't know flying is much safer than driving per mile traveled. They therefore drive and unwittingly expose themselves to more risk due to their misperceptions.

The same is true regarding markets. Markets function on confidence and trust, as well as efficiencies. So Peggy Noonan, perhaps the most spiritually discerning of *The Wall Street Journal* writers, recently wrote:

> *"The biggest threat to America right now is not government spending, huge deficits, foreign ownership of our debt, world terrorism, two wars, potential epidemics or nuts with nukes. The biggest long-term threat is that people are becoming and have become disheartened, that this condition is reaching critical mass."*

Jesus would likely sympathize with both OWS and the Tea Party. Both have very legitimate concerns. I believe I understand the concerns of the average supporter of the Tea Party, though I'm not convinced they are always based on reality. I am only beginning to understand the objectives of OWS as it has only very recently sprung into the American conscious. But after twenty-five years on Wall Street, I expect my local paper was pretty accurate when it stated:

> *"The Occupy Wall Street movement was sparked by all-too-justifiable anger over what passes for capitalism these days - a rigged system in which taxpayers bail out profligate risk-takers; pillagers and incompetents are rewarded with golden parachutes; and ever greater wealth accrues to just 1 percent of citizens. Such a system insults the American ideal of 'liberty and justice for all.' The occupiers' outrage is not far removed from the sentiments of most Americans."*

I expect God is even more disappointed.

Meditation Eighteen

Moral Man; Immoral Society

*"Wealth and enterprise have so woven themselves around
the message of Jesus that popular models of Christianity
appear as nothing more than self and greed at the center,
with strands of Christian thought at the periphery."*

Ravi Zacharias
Jesus Among Other Gods

*"Most evangelicals simply don't think. And it's always
been a sin not to love the Lord our God with our minds as
well as our hearts and souls. Evangelicals need to repent
and develop the mind of Christ."*

Os Guinness

Most pastors confess that we live in a "post-Christian culture," where many
confess and preach the principles of our faith, but few live them. But if you
ask those same pastors what sort of culture we do live in, most can't make a
guess. A few of the more sophisticated say "post-modern," which essentially
means people believe there are many truths, but no Truth.

That's a very convenient way of thinking for an anxious and confused
culture that's fallen in love with money rather than God and neighbor. For
example, a political truth lets you believe we need to get government out
of our lives, while another financial truth lets you believe you should only
invest in government-guaranteed securities. We were actually taught this
by televangelist Pat Robertson on two consecutive pages of one of his books
years ago. To make matters worse, just before advising readers to invest
only in government securities, Pat said the federal government was likely to
default on the federal debt. As government securities are the federal debt that
suggests Pat actually had three conflicting truths in mind.

The mind of Christ, as explained by St. Paul in Romans 13, also suggests
Pat may be conflicted in yet another way. It explains we should "honor and

respect" government as it was created by God. It may be somewhat forgivable for pastors to not understand such economic and political realities, but it would seem a former presidential candidate might understand them, as should all those teaching Christian approaches to finance. Teaching political economy and personal finance before learning about them, as many evangelical leaders do as readily as politicians do, is quite similar to "ready, fire, aim." We often shoot ourselves, and our faith, in the foot. At least most pastors don't commit sins of commission with their silence.

The irony of many pastors' response about the nature of our culture being post-modern is that it contains several truths but no Truth. So in the pursuit of Truth, I'd suggest the big picture is that since most Americans stopped thinking about loving God and neighbor, they think mostly about making, spending and investing money. Studies actually suggest we men think more about money than sex, or even sports, much less religion. Ironically, if there's a subject more taboo in church than sex, its money. So most men find the church as relevant as the Chinese would find a Christian missionary who can't speak Chinese.

Of course, it's possible my perspective is slanted as I've long lived in the world of money. But I think most of us do today. And like many businesspeople working for large corporations, I learned years ago in the big Wall Street firms that my total value to them was how much revenue I produced. In fact, I've never seen anyone on Wall Street given an award for helping clients be prudent and ethical. How much revenue you produce for the firms is all that matters. Stop producing revenue for them and you go from MVP status to persona non grata very quickly. Even today as I work "off Wall Street," my value to many clients, and most of them are Christian, is simply how much money I make for them.

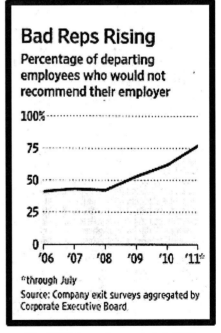

The Wall Street Journal, 8-8-2011

It's long pained me that many wonderful Christians I have known, seem to assume a less-than-Christian mentality when engaged with markets and politics. Of course, even St. Peter denied Christ when confronted by the mob. But it often seems that when markets are rising and people are making money, I'm "loved." But when the markets are in turmoil, often due to politics, and my clients are experiencing only a few months of those lean years our world has experienced since Joseph was in Egypt, my value as a fellow Christian seems to decline rather sharply.

I only wish they understood why even Sir John Templeton's Growth Fund under-performed the markets rather substantially during its first five years, only to go on to greatly superior performance in coming decades. That reality meant only one of John's clients, a Canadian, was actually rewarded by the returns that John produced ethically and prudently over those decades. I expect that dichotomy between what our culture encourages and our faith aspires to is also hurting our faith as much as my feelings. Many other professionals confide that Christian love too often disappears with the phrase "nothing personal, it's just business." Yet Jesus taught us that everything, absolutely everything, is personal and therefore subject to the rule of love.

That never means you shouldn't fire an incompetent or unethical advisor. It simply means you should do so with grace and after exhibiting the Christian ethics of patience and considering the advisor's well-being as your own. Trust me, experienced advisors are quick to discern those investors who determine relationships by whether the first trade is profitable and those who are only interested in their well-being. Neither encourages the advisor to take a long-term approach or care for such investor's well-being.

Sadly, our ability to compartmentalize our faith and business is just as true, and perhaps more true, when investing money for churches. A major reason for that is simply that church leaders change quite often. So no matter to which investment strategies leaders and I agree, there are constantly new faces who have no idea what we discussed earlier.

A related problem with churches is that you inevitably have to deal with committees or boards. If I had room on my desk, I'd put one of those paper weights that says: "For God so loved the world, he didn't send a committee." Even politicians know that if you want to look like you're doing something without actually doing it, you appoint a committee. It's a perfect way for everyone to avoid responsibility. And this book argues that if there's one concept that will put our faith and this country back on course, it is responsibility, both personal and social. That's quite different than the legalistic obligation that so many financial teachers espouse. Responsibility, as I understand and teach it, is about making a loving "response" with our God-given "abilities." That has nothing to do with the obligation to tithe.

My experience is that such dysfunction worsens as the church grows larger. Perhaps you noticed that I served on the board of The Crystal Cathedral during its better times. The church has since gone bankrupt after being one of the most recognized churches on the planet. But there have been even worse experiences that have shaped my perspective.

During the early nineties, I spoke at a well-known church on biblical financial principles. I didn't know at the time that its leadership had bought into radio commentator and financial author Larry Burkett's best-selling book entitled *The Coming Economic Earthquake.* So ignoring the Parable of the Talents, church leaders had buried its retirement plan of several million dollars for hundreds of employees into a money market fund. Worse, it was within a high cost variable annuity. So they may as well have buried the money in the ground, as the unfaithful steward of the biblical parable did.

I was invited back the next year and chose to speak about John Templeton's hopeful economic perspective. I'll never forget the people in the aisles crying after hearing the possibility they might have a future after all. But the board stayed put...until John's funds had their best year in history in 1993. So *after* the funds had gone up, the church board finally asked me about putting its employees' money into John's mutual funds. I simply explained there were no guarantees but John's flagship fund, which most employees should utilize, had averaged fifteen percent annually for decades with prudence and ethics. John held his stocks five times longer than the typical fund manager and avoided the "sin stocks" of alcohol, tobacco, gambling and adult literature companies. I also explained that because they had over a million dollars to invest, there would be no sales charge but they could utilize my services at no additional expense.

(Those watching over endowments and such who are unaccustomed to managing larger sums should underline that last sentence. Few advisors will tell you about the feature as it's a very low-cost way of managing money. And most so-called "load funds" have that provision. When the commission is waived, they can be as inexpensive, or more inexpensive, than many "no-load" funds, yet you still get an investment counselor. Hopefully, that counselor, whether Christian or not, will discourage your thinking that you are Joseph and can predict fat years and lean years. John Templeton looked for that person for fifty years and never found him or her.)

So the board *then* decided it was time to move the money to John. Of course, most employees ignored my counsel and invested heavily in John's developing markets fund as it had just increased the most. Of course, that meant it was also his riskiest fund. That's why I often time my own investments by doing the opposite of what church employees do. You try to help them, but it's usually as futile in changing behavior as the minister's sermon on Sunday morning. Still, things went pretty well for years. But then the technology and Internet stock manias took hold in 1999.

The church had hired John and me as we were prudent enough to avoid stocks at unbelievably high price/earnings ratios. But they left us for Fidelity and its funds that had loaded up on tech stocks. Ironically, as I explained to the board, Fidelity was also the one major fund company that refused to consider ethics when investing money. Fidelity had publicly stated that its objective was simply to pursue as much money as possible. But of course, as tech fever had infected the mob, that was what the board wanted. As the board was comprised largely of aggressive financial types, I never felt John's developed sense of ethics had impressed it anyway.

More sadly, the board and church administration actually misled the stewardship officer of the church. He had become a dear friend and was most concerned about the direction they were heading. In essence, the board and employees were doing the opposite of what he was teaching at the church. I've learned that is fairly typical if churches actually have a knowledgeable stewardship minister rather than a simple fundraiser. The board told my friend for months that I had been advised of their concerns. I was startled when they moved to Fidelity as John's flagship fund had averaged the 15% the previous board had said would be heroic. My friend was even more startled.

The irony, and perhaps justice, though not for the employees, is that tech stocks imploded almost immediately while foreign markets, in which John specialized, soared during the coming decade. Worse, when I wrote the well-known pastor that all this appeared less than Christian, not to mention an embarrassment to Christian stewardship, I received no response. Such are large churches, as well as many large mutual fund companies, large investment firms, large governments, large banks and so on.

Theologians therefore discuss moral man but immoral society. As evidenced by Peter's denial of Jesus to the mob, something about being in large groups makes our personal morality seem dispensable. *Sound Mind Investing*, one of the country's most read Christian investment newsletters, has even confused Christians for years by arguing that no reason exists for mutual fund investors to worry about ethics as one investor is nothing in the scheme of things. Of course, when everyone believes that, you have a financial crisis. Morally, it's not unlike one young girl believing a single abortion doesn't matter in the scheme of things.

As has been very wisely said, the things that are wrong with our nation today are only the sum total of the things wrong with us as individuals.

Yet we never seem to learn. Over the objections of my stewardship friend, the church has since featured Dave Ramsey, the latest radio financial celebrity and author. He too seemed intent on saving the world from evil credit card merchants, while also discouraging ethics when investing. I expect the pastor has spoken about greed and how it has devastated our economy, particularly for the least of these. Maybe not come to think of it.

I expect many members still make their livings, and make their donations to the church, by aggressively trading the markets. As with most pastors in one way or another, it's in this pastor's financial interests not to understand why famed mutual fund manager Peter Lynch compared such speculators to gamblers in the world's largest casino. Yet I do expect the pastor has lamented the drop in charitable giving that accompanied the Great Recession. And that drop resulted largely from financial speculation. So it goes in America and its cultural churches. We just don't make those connections.

I also noticed the last time my friend asked me to speak at this church, none of its many pastors saw any reason to attend. I spoke primarily about economic philosopher Ayn Rand, a woman who literally aspired to be the anti-Christ predicted by her mentor Nietzsche, who proclaimed the death of God. Though virtually unknown in religious circles, particularly conservative Christian circles, I've written and spoken about her while conservative Christian leaders were demonizing the federal debt, Y2K and so on.

The former head of BB&T bank recently told *The New York Times* that Rand's atheistic philosophy would be the predominant philosophy in America within twenty years. I believe he is wrong as it's been our Monday to Saturday morality for years. Now why would any pastor want to hear about that when they can hear a radio celebrity demonize credit cards, which Christians increasingly use to make donations for emergency aid and such? Why care if Jesus chastised the Pharisees for straining gnats and swallowing camels? Judgment still begins...

The good news, however, is also worth pondering at length. I have far more often thought about it than the poor stewardship of the church. After many years, I still consider the stewardship officer to be a true and cherished brother in Christ. So the spiritual reward to me was worth the pain. That may be why God lets such apparent nonsense happen to us, if only we're wise enough to see it. If we never taste sour, we never know how sweet most of life can be. So while I still believe true heaven is beyond my leaving this old world, I also know I've glimpsed it in our relationship.

So I beg all Christians, and those leaders aspiring to evangelize the world in particular, to remember that non-Christians' views of our faith are shaped far more in the marketplace from Monday to Saturday than from our radio, which rarely appeals to non-believers, and/or in church on Sunday. We desperately need to confess that capitalism may know the broadest way to worldly wealth, while also witnessing to the narrow Truth that "man does not live by bread alone."

On the other hand, "spiritual" leaders of the church might also confess, primarily to the businesspeople of their congregations who need validation of their own ministries, that bread is so important to life that the Body of Christ will forever come to us during communion in the form of bread. The church has no more right to the moral leadership of our nation than it has the right to its members' donations. We leaders must earn both by being most faithful and relevant to believers and non-believers alike, both spiritually and materially.

Sadly, cultural Christianity has bowed down to the false gods of Marxist statism on the left and capitalistic consumerism on the right. In turn, that has led to the false perceptions that church is a Sunday morning concern only; that economics and morality are diametrically opposed; that economics must therefore be a hopelessly "dismal science;" that politics must be paranoid and partisan; and that our future must therefore be as dark as Plato's Cave.

Pepper ...
And Salt

THE WALL STREET JOURNAL

"The hard part will be the marketing."

So I might conclude this sermonizing, particularly to pastors who usually detest being sermonized, with a most appropriate, if irreverent, joke that I often tell at the beginning of my seminars. It suggests the need for humor and humility as I tell you things that you may not want to hear.

An elderly couple was sitting in a Florida church one Sunday morning. As the pastor was hitting the high note of his sermon, the lady takes a pen out of her purse. She makes a note and passes it to her husband. He opens it to read, "I just let a silent one; what should I do?" He makes a note on it and passes it back. She opens it to read: "Change the battery in your hearing aid."

That joke always embarrasses my wife, but it's a favorite among my audiences. Apparently, the way people hear things is far more important than what is actually said. I pray that pre-dispositions, such as we adequately understand the holistic nature of Christian stewardship, did not keep pastors and development officers from tuning out this meditation.

Meditation Nineteen

Are Social & Political Conservatives Economic Liberals?

"Our personal and professional financial habits are, in a word, liberal...John warns us, we delude ourselves. We are wrapping our sin in the disguise of darkness and pretending that our finances are in faultlessly good order."

Christianity Today

"It is possible to envision a time when evangelicals have the 'consistent Christian perspective tools,' [or holistic worldview], they require in this area of life. But it is probably best to expect Christian theology for life under modern high-tech capitalism to come mainly from where it now does - from Jewish, Catholic, Reformed, and Lutheran sources, in which traditions exist for relating doctrines of creation to matters of redemption in a modern economic context."

Professor John R. Schneider
Calvin College

When I was young, my mother made sure that I attended a conservative Southern Baptist Church most faithfully. At home, I slept beneath a poster of the Capitol Dome with Thomas Jefferson›s quote: "Here, sir, the people govern." While others were protesting the Vietnam War and President Nixon during the sixties, I pursued a degree in political science and became a Distinguished Military Graduate. My family was economically pragmatic. We may have lit up at the mention of the Golden Rule but we grew tobacco for the use of others and had no qualms about price supports. Some thought us hypocritical. But we had simply learned to keep our politics, faith and economics in separate compartments.

That was perfect training for Wall Street and conservative politics during the eighties. I once received a gold card from the Republican National Committee that was preaching fiscal conservatism. Then President Reagan "proved deficits don't matter," to use the words of Vice-President Cheney. During the nineties, I served on the board of advisors of vice-presidential nominee Jack Kemp's Empower America. Jack was a fellow Christian who thought tax cuts could cure cancer.

The past decade, I watched as President "W" waged two wars while cutting taxes, a radical economic approach never before attempted in America. While it surprises most of my clients and friends, particularly those who have been taught "neither a borrower nor lender be" is biblical rather than Shakespeare, true economists can actually estimate the amount of debt that is actually beneficial to our culture, regardless of what politicians might say. And some can actually be beneficial. Think about it this way. Suppose you have an apple tree in your backyard. You pick the lower fruit but can't reach the higher fruit. So you borrow your neighbor's ladder. You pick the higher fruit and share some apples (or interest, if you will) with him when you return his ladder. You are both better off, so it's a very moral endeavor.

That's essentially what the Protestant Reformers, particularly John Calvin, the founder of the Presbyterian Church, realized when they legitimated some forms of interest on some loans. No longer did people have to keep their financial savings tucked under their mattresses. They could make their savings productive by lending it, even earning interest. While capitalism wasn't around at the time, Jesus hinted in the Parable of the Talents that lending was far more moral than hoarding. He told the lazy third servant that he could have "at least" put the money with the bankers and earned some interest.

While I believe that Parable of the Talents is about far more than money, there's no reason to exclude money. Yet there's a caution about capitalism in Jesus' statement in that he knew the bankers might not do what a truly faithful steward would do with the money. If we have had a financial problem in America lately, it has been that too many of us haven't

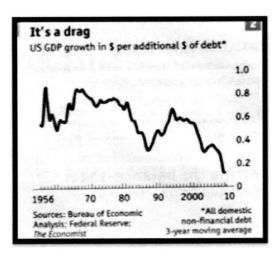

The Economist, Date Unknown

cared about the "how" but only about the "how much" when putting out money with bankers.

It doesn't do you or your Apple tree (the economy and the environment) any good if you decide one ladder is so enriching that borrowing a dozen ladders must be better. You'll only break the tree down and/or work yourself to death. It's the same way with debt. And America has reached the point that additional debt will add little to our nation's growth. Yet as economic growth is not the only consideration for the steward, there may still be good reasons to borrow. For example, if a depression threatens, we may want to borrow simply to avoid having the economy decline too far. That's where we need wise leaders who know what they are doing at best, or will humbly listen to others at worst. But there is no need to be cynical simply as past leaders have chosen to borrow. Skeptical, yes. Cynical, no.

We might also remember that when President George W. Bush took office, official projections were that we would run so many budget surpluses into the future that America's federal debt would be nearly paid off by now. Wall Street was actually concerned about there not being enough Treasury securities around for conservative savers. That turned out to be another quite unnecessary worry. That may be one reason Jesus suggested we not worry about tomorrow, as "the pagans" do, as tomorrow will have enough worries of its own.

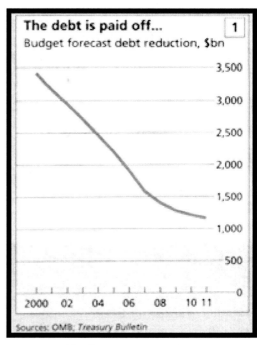

The Economist, 3-17-2001

While I have never worried about the federal debt as much as my conservative friends I have recently re-registered as an independent. Why now? The "big tent" revival within the GOP, or God's Own Party, organized by President Reagan insists on singing the praises of both Ayn Rand and Jesus Christ. To be sure, Rand's philosophy of individualism had something right when encouraging "personal responsibility." All heresies must contain some truth or people would not be deceived by them. But Jesus taught personal responsibility is actually "loving neighbor as self," rather than "instead of self."

Rand pales in comparison to Jesus in the area of social responsibility, and would do so proudly. In her book *The Virtue of Selfishness*, Rand wrote that we can rescue our fellow passengers in a shipwreck as long as it doesn't endanger us. Even conservatives reject that notion when we admire our soldiers, police officers, and the firemen who entered the burning World Trade Center. We admire such selflessness.

Yet Rand also goes on to say that just because we save drowning victims does not mean we have any responsibility for them when we get back to shore. Then it's every man or woman for himself or herself again, except of course, you should be nice to those "worthy" elites who can help you fulfill your selfish desires. That's precisely why junk bond king Michael Milken re-read Rand's philosophies in prison. He had taken care of his firm's few clients who wanted to sell junk bonds. He had just forgotten about all those who bought them, or his social responsibilities.

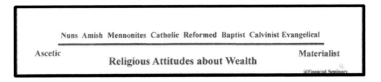

Alan Greenspan was part of Rand's inner circle during the sixties. That was a major reason *The Economist* said that Rand's ideas were influential in shaping Reaganomics. Mr. Greenspan confessed before Congress that his thinking about deregulating our S&L's in previous decades, and then Wall Street's sub-prime mortgage originators, had been "flawed." Most would say "tragic." But Greenspan simply cited one of Rand's radical and utopian ideas, i.e., that self-interest, and it alone, should regulate business, even the world. A soon to be released documentary entitled *The Flaw* is about that very tragic and, oh, so costly idea.

I wrote a book in the mid-nineties about my mentor, the legendary mutual fund manager Sir John Templeton. I contrasted his real world ideas, shaped as a Rhodes Scholar and by decades as the "dean of global investing," with those of Ayn Rand, who only worked in Hollywood and at writing fiction. Neither occupation suggests that Rand, who also abused drugs, was in touch with reality, particularly economic reality.

Templeton, however, advocated that our economic activities be guided by the Golden Rule. For example, he never invested in cigarette manufacturers, which humbled me. Rand taught traditional religion is an "evil," only of benefit for the weak-minded, and that humility is no virtue. She despised human emotion, hence her disdain for charity and welfare. Neither kept her from being financially supported by relatives for years or her husband from filing for Social Security.

She worshipped human reason to the point of teaching it is humanity's *only* way of understanding Reality, to the exclusion of Revelation and tradition. Ironically, she also excommunicated any disciple who did not reason as she did. In effect, she taught her disciples "the mind of Rand" rather than "the mind of Christ." Yet she hypocritically taught Christianity is irrational without acknowledging that Jesus taught us to love God and our neighbor with heart, *mind* and soul, and without acknowledging that virtually all Christians believe things not taught by the Bible, particularly in the area of economics, but affirmed by centuries of collective wisdom.

Rand's philosophy was particularly embraced by increasingly-depersonalized capital markets. Most in those markets suffered as Rand's great commandment was essentially "take care of number one; let your neighbor take care of number two." As number one barely understood what was going on in those days on Wall Street, number two certainly didn't. In effect, a few evil geniuses on Wall Street created in the mold of Rand ignored centuries of moral economic thought. That's why John Templeton's real world experiences caused him to teach us that capital markets are lubricated by trust, which depends on true ethics. When that trust in Wall Street evaporated in 2008, capitalism nearly died.

The poverty of Rand's teachings is not simply relational and spiritual. Rand's teachings about selfishness have brought considerable economic pain to millions. That was the subject of a feature article I wrote for the September 2010 issue of *Christianity Today*. Since then, several progressive and conservative Christian leaders have written about the irreconcilable differences between Rand's and Christ's teachings. (Google "Ayn Rand and Jesus Christ.")

Conservatives seek to "conserve" the traditions that shaped our nation. Rand wanted her disciples to be "radicals for capitalism." Her teachings therefore contradict the teachings of Jesus about "render unto Caesar," as well as those of St. Paul in Romans 13 that we "honor and respect" government.

Conservatives should never forget our personal or social responsibility, whether exercised through the state, through mediating institutions like the Church, or personally. While Americans tend to individualize most biblical teachings, those three sectors of our economy might actually be the three stewards Jesus referenced in his Parable of the Talents. He assured us the most effective, which is quite different from simply efficient, steward would be rewarded while the least effective would wither. That morality strikes me as a more likely road to the Promised Land than politics has been recently.

So I believe it is crucial in these troubled times that we reason with heart and soul as well as mind. We might remember that the biblical prophets railed about mixing Jehovah with pagan gods, but rarely against atheism. As John Calvin taught, people will always worship. If not God as Christ taught, or the state as Marx taught, they'll worship money and human reason, as Rand taught. Modern theologians term such mixing "syncretism." Yet conservative Christian sociologist George Barna has termed syncretism "America's favored religion."

Economic syncretism is why confessing Christian businesspeople, like Ken Lay of Enron think like Christ on Sunday but like Rand from Monday through Saturday. That pervasive mental illness has been well documented by sociologist Laura Nash of Harvard. I'd particularly recommend her marvelous books *Church on Sunday; Work on Monday* and *Believers in Business* if that idea resonates. Both are similar to my friend David Miller's book *God at Work*. All describe what is often called "the Sunday/Monday divide." All explain why businesspeople often feel like simple spectators at religious events on Sunday morning, which, of course, we usually are. That's usually as most pastors teach us they're the ministers, whose ministry we should simply fund, rather than that they are simply pastors who should be turning each of us into the "priesthood of all believers" that Luther imagined.

The ability of evangelicals in particular to compartmentalize economic life, which causes us to be quite liberal in matters of economics, was unwittingly documented in the Winter 2012 issue of *Philanthropy* magazine. Attempting to be complimentary, it discussed various evangelical efforts to integrate poverty-reducing efforts of the private sector, or the business sector, with similar efforts in the independent sector, or non-profit sector. It concluded: "The concept of combing investing and doing good, however, is off to a promising start."

It made those efforts sound so revolutionary that readers probably wondered if we've ever heard of the biblical Boaz using his fields for the good of Ruth and her contemporaries. It's much the same story with socially responsible investing, community development banking, microenterprise in the Third World, and so on. The good news is that some do seem to be indeed going back to such conservative ideas now that our faith in free, rather than moral, markets has proven quite disappointing.

Many evangelicals aspire to transition from "success to significance." In a way, that could be a step forward. But Mother Teresa might tell us that it's a tiny one. She said, "We cannot do anything significant for God; we can only do small things with great love." After her death was eclipsed by the death of Princess Diana, I expect Mother Teresa would tell us that if we think our activities are significant in the scope of Reality; our ego is bigger than our concept of God. Such is the influence of humanism.

Dietrich Bonhoeffer, a Lutheran minister who was martyred by the Nazis, also wrote:

> *"God is not interested in success but in obedience [not significance].*
> *If one obeyed God and was willing to suffer defeat and whatever else*
> *came one's way, God would show a kind of success [and significance]*
> *that the world couldn't imagine."*

Philanthropy interviewed a socially responsible businessman who is now doing work in African banking for the poor. He also advocated more humble and holistic thinking by saying:

> *"Sometimes Christian friends tell me they want to spend the first half*
> *of their life making money and then the later portion 'giving back.' I*
> *ask them:* **What are you going to 'take' that you feel you have to give**
> **back later?** *People needn't feel there is a contradiction between making*
> *a financial return and having a positive impact on society. Successful*
> *enterprises do both."*

I wanted to cheer at that encouragement for Christians to live a more integrated life. My father also compartmentalized life into the first half of his life and the second half. He thought he would work the first half and enjoy life after retirement. When he was within a few months of retirement, we discovered he had prostate cancer that had spread to his bones. After a few gruesome months, he died, creating definite spiritual poverty among those who loved him. That is precisely why the Gospel, if not modern authors, tells us to avoid putting off until tomorrow what we should be doing today.

In conclusion, when our modern Pilates ask if we want Rand or Christ, which they do during every election day and work day, most conservative Christians may be tempted to rationalize they can vote, or opt, for "all the above." Yet the question to ponder before answering is: Was the Great Recession the end of the Puritan ethic that enriched America before the sixties and we've now placed too much faith in the new Rand-style capitalism?

My most fervent political prayer for our grandchildren's futures is for all Americans to again respect those nearly extinct politicians who are faithful to

St. Paul's admonition for "moderation in all things," rather than willingness to experiment with radical, utopian philosophies, on either end of the political spectrum.

Meditation Twenty

Christians Exiled in the Shadowlands Of Capitalism

"It's almost a shame to say but evangelicalism doesn't have that rich a tradition, and so you look for other sources that represent an authentic Christian witness in society."

Michael Gerson
Chief White House Speechwriter
George W. Bush Administration

I often quip in my seminars that when I cannot quote God, I quote C.S. Lewis. He said two things in particular that I believe we might remember during this time of confusion and turmoil. First, he said: "Christianity, if false, is of no importance, and if true, of infinite importance. The only thing it cannot be is moderately important." He also said that when God told us to feed the poor, God did not give us lessons in cooking, by which Lewis meant God gave us minds rather than recipes.

In other words, Lewis suggested that Christians must be very serious about, for example, God telling us to feed the poor. Yet he also suggested that we be quite humble about the extent to which God has told us how to run our world. While most immature Christians would like to have an easy recipe for life, particularly political economy, there would actually be no possibility of virtue in such a world. As has been wisely said, there's no virtue in avoiding the temptation to play golf in a land with no golf courses.

Like many academics in particular, Lewis also had to learn a more Christian humility. That is essentially the theme of the movie "Shadowlands," which is about Lewis' life. I won't ruin a wonderful movie for you if I tell you the great scholar and apologist, like many academics, was rather know-it-all during the first portion of his life. That is portrayed during the first portion of the movie. He grew far more humble near the end of the movie upon losing Joy, the great love of his life. So while I've hopefully helped you better understand the illusions surrounding us, I also hope you walk humbly with your God and neighbor.

Furthermore, image making, even political shadow-making, is not inherently evil, or even patently false. For example, most historians believe the story about a young George Washington chopping down the cherry tree was likely myth. However, the story still contains an inspiring truth about the character of our first president. It's often said most saints were hell to live with on earth as few could live up to their examples. Still, their legends inspire the best in us today. My animal loving wife even has statues of St. Francis all around our home.

But the evidence remains that shadow-making has increasingly played a more impoverishing role in shaping Christian conservatives' worldview, particularly over political-economy and their roles in it. In my view, that began in earnest when President Nixon, who was narrowly defeated by President Kennedy during the first campaign shaped by television, said:

"People are motivated by fear, not love. They don't teach you that in Sunday School but it's true."

Being a Sunday School teacher for high school students, I can affirm we do acknowledge this old world works that way. But unlike cynical politicians since Nixon, we also teach it shouldn't work that way. Yet for some time now, politicians and the popular media have cynically encouraged Americans to fear the giants in our Promised Land, regardless of the realities about our milk and honey.

Ironically, that's one thing about which both parties seem to agree. In 1992, then-Governor Bill Clinton told us America's problem was "the economy stupid." Yet Sir John Templeton, a Rhodes Scholar in economics before being termed "the dean of global investing," was on record predicting a strong economy and soaring stock market for the nineties due to the collapse of the Soviet Union and the resulting "peace dividend." Few paid any attention to John as the media joined the politicians in their fearful negativity.

There was too often very little difference in the secular and religious media in that regard. I often say I spend half my time wishing the old, established but declining churches with traditions of teaching economic morality would talk more about money. I spend the other half wishing the new, growing evangelical churches that often have to make stewardship theology up as they go along, wouldn't talk about money. I've found they usually believe they are growing as they hold the line on biblical social teachings. I believe they are growing as they talk about money as if there were no biblical or traditional teachings about the subject.

There are more people in America who want to be "Christian" but also free of moral constraints over money than over sexuality. That's a very old story. Jesus had to remind the money-loving Pharisees that only those without sin could cast the first stone at the prostitute. Martin Luther was stunned to discover his members actually preferred teachings from Rome about salvation being available for a few donated coins to true Christian stewardship theology. When you don't know such history, you are doomed to repeat its worst problems.

The book-of-the-year in conservative Christianity in 1992 was about an inevitable "economic earthquake" occurring during coming months, primarily due to the federal debt. It was written by Larry Burkett, a one-time friend who endorsed my first book and referred people to my investment practice. At one time, Larry taught personal finances, primarily debt management, and supposed economics on over a thousand evangelical radio stations. However, Larry was actually an engineer. Like accountants, engineers tend to think one plus one always equals two. Unfortunately, in political economy it often equals three or one, sometimes nothing, as we too often see by adding the two chambers of Congress!

I've written at length about our differing worldviews and I hope I don't appear to be holding any form of a grudge, particularly now that Larry has passed on. Like the Pharisees, Larry was a devout and well-intentioned Christian. However, we know where good intentions often lead. I find many of my conservative Christian clients, who usually believe the Pharisees were historical rather than living, still believe a lot of what Larry taught during the eighties and nineties, particularly his nearly paranoid perspective of the federal debt.

That perspective has done much to divide our nation, both politically and theologically. Neither has it enriched our spirits and finances. Like those predicting the end of the world year after year, Larry often re-set his economic doomsday clock. Yet his 1993 newsletter entitled "A Nation under Siege by Its Government," stated:

> "I don't believe an economic collapse will occur in 1995 as Harry Figgie projects in his book [The Great Depression of 1990], although that is always a possibility; I believe it will be more in the era of 1998-1999. But I do believe at this point the die is cast and cannot be altered."

My friend Sir John Templeton was saying the exact opposite, but I've found most conservative Christians only read those financial books recommended on evangelical radio. Since John and I disagreed with most of the economic perspectives of evangelical radio for two decades, which I believe were actually political perspectives, very few have heard of my books and therefore our views. I expect that will remain true with this book, although many evangelicals tell me they are now as cynical of Christian economic gurus as politicians and the secular media.

It's as dangerous to look around for human Christian financial advisors as to look right and left for politicians and economists. We need to look up for transcendent counsel. Sadly, too many evangelicals seem to worship Christian media celebrities, which may be the most dangerous form of idolatry as it's so subtle.

Most evangelicals have not been exposed to the full economic and political perspectives of Moses and Jesus, and particularly the protestant reformers who more than tweaked biblical teachings, particularly concerning borrowing and lending. Nor have most even heard from modern economists such as Professor Bruce Howard. Bruce chaired the economics department at solidly evangelical Wheaton College but wrote a book that refuted most of Larry's teachings about debt.

Most people who are interested and experienced in finance and economics do not typically go into the media, much less the religious media. While being a media celebrity can be ego-gratifying, the pay and actual influence on Americans' finances are considerably less than on Wall Street if you really know what you're doing. As John Templeton used to say, the church turned the economic realm over to politicians and economists decades ago. I sometimes quip the major difference in working for Wall Street and teaching for the Church is the Church always asks you to stay in those hotels that do not furnish the little bottles of shampoo. In fact, the more you teach, the more you save those little bottles.

It's also been said that those who can do, while those who can't teach. I'm praying that isn't why I'm writing this book. When I thought about attending seminary to bring the various dimensions of my life together, their evaluations told me I'm a teacher rather than preacher. That is, I'm more cerebral than emotional. I may have fooled the psychologists on that one as investing greatly depends on discerning the emotional from the rational and soulful. But should I retire, which is coming soon, I plan to spend my time doing irrational acts of kindness, for kids in particular, as well as the hurting, depressed and so on.

Larry had a big heart too. Back then, he often seemed the only person even trying to integrate faith and finance. So his influence went well beyond the evangelical sub-culture into mainline, Baptist and Catholic Christianity. A feature article in *Christianity Today* therefore called him a "one-eyed king in the land of the blind." It was a good description of his economic perspective as Larry, and the princes surrounding him, could usually only see one side of America's balance sheet: the negative side describing our debts. I tried at length but could never get Larry to understand why the two-eyed biblical prophet Isaiah had a more balanced perspective, saying:

> "As with the lender, so with the borrower; as with the taker of usury, so with the giver of usury to him, a debtor for every creditor."

If you can see beyond the political illusions over the federal debt and demonization of credit cards in our culture, economic reality is that for every dollar borrowed, there has been a dollar saved and loaned. For every dollar of interest paid, there must be a saver earning that interest.

As indicated by the following chart, when Larry wrote his best-seller during the early nineties, Americans on average were not having any more problems servicing their debts than they did when President Reagan took office. Even today, the chart shows Americans aren't paying any more of their after-tax income to service their debts than they were three decades ago. Basically, while the nominal size of our debts has indeed increased, which is all the pessimists talk about, our assets and incomes have also increased, contrary to popular perception. The cost of money, or our interest rates, is also determined by supply and demand like any commodity. So increased savings has meant interest rates have dropped, keeping our ability to service our debts fairly constant over the decades.

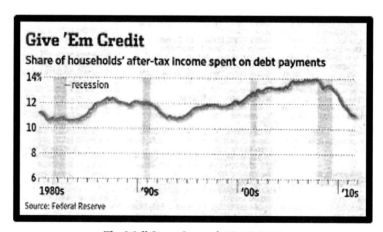

The Wall Street Journal, 12-19-2011

If Larry ever looked at those positives, he didn't focus on them when teaching. I therefore grew interested in helping the partially blind and dispirited to see our true economic circumstances, or count our blessings, as the Bible actually suggests. I had little idea the challenge I had assumed.

I had wandered into the land of the blind when an evangelical publisher elected to publish my first book, which I'd written for the Episcopal Church's stewardship department. No matter their other challenges, Episcopalians know a few things about money. I'd also learned something about the Bible while growing up as a Southern Baptist. So I felt like the proverbial shoe salesman in the shoeless kingdom when offering Christian economics to evangelicals. Unfortunately, most evangelicals had been taught they didn't want to buy shoes, particularly from anyone who knew anything about shoes.

Larry and his one-eyed princes who could only see the faults in others, taught cynicism, rather than appropriate skepticism, toward anyone who worked on Wall Street or for the government departments tracking our nation's economy. Larry and the princes were even cynical toward those Christian academics who taught economics in Christian colleges. Professor Bruce Howard's book entitled *Safe and Sound* was truly balanced and hopeful. And it soundly refuted Larry's fearful best-seller. Yet few evangelicals read Bruce's book either. It wouldn't have been as thrilling as Larry's; but it would have been far more enriching, to both finances and spirit, if not the author.

A good way to understand that dilemma is to always remember that many bored people pay to ride roller coasters to be entertained; few pay to pray in order to get in touch with Reality. I hate to confess it but after I shared my economic perspective on an evangelical television station during the mid-nineties and we went to break, the host said my perspective would enrich viewers' spirits and finances but it would never get them off their couches to buy books and get involved in politics. A lot of light entered my cave at that moment.

Larry often gave investment advice, though he wisely swore off it several times. That's not to say evangelicals were encouraged to seek wise counsel in that area. I was once startled when Ron Blue, an accountant who had founded an investment firm with Larry's encouragement, began his talk by saying he didn't know anything about investing or economics, but was going to raise a billion dollars for evangelical ministries. The audience applauded. I just wondered why Ron hadn't founded a fund-raising company. Even most evangelical ministries teach our interests and abilities must align in order for us to succeed.

As years passed, there were persistent rumors that Ron's focus on fundraising wasn't doing much for his investment firm's clients. There were persistent rumors that Ron was eventually asked to leave his firm as it had never proven as rewarding to shareholders as to management. That's also been a very common complaint about the major firms of Wall Street, again suggesting judgment begins in the house of the Lord.

It's ironic, but hardly surprising, and quite illuminating, that *The Wall Street Journal* once looked at Ron's firm and told the financial world there was virtually no difference in what it counseled and what secular investment firms counseled. I couldn't disagree. While the firm noted it encouraged people to give to ministry, financial professionals know there is nothing particularly Christian about the Fidelity mutual fund group, but its Gift-trust account is one of the largest charities in the world.

Then *Christianity Today* reported Ron's firm actually *discouraged* investors from considering ethics when investing. That didn't surprise me as I'd earlier

'Christian' Planners Appear Worldly to Secular Rivals

The Wall Street Journal, Date Unknown

discovered it had adopted the most controversial compensation plan in our industry. It's called "fee-based" planning. It sounds good, but it actually means the firm can charge both fees for the planning and then commissions for the products recommended. Sometimes clients don't understand the last part as they assume the initial fee is all they pay. I assumed the same when interviewing Ron's firm for financial planning as before my son joined our firm and studied to be a Certified Financial Planner, we only invested for our clients. I was startled when the firm's legal officer sent a letter that explained their business plan much clearer than the firm's brochures had. So note this: If you simply want to pay once, even at Christian financial planning firms, you actually need a "fee-only" planner, rather than a "fee-based" planner.

All this occurred after Ron had written these words in his best-selling book *Master Your Money*...

> *"Worldly advice may be logical, but it is not necessarily right. Many Christians fall into the trap of listening to non-Christian counselors and expect the non-Christian counselor to give them godly advice. The advice may sound good and may even be good, but unless it is advice that comes from God, it is wrong."*

I expect that kind of illogical thinking, which is actually the feeling of religious superiority that characterized the Pharisees, brought a lot of unsophisticated money into Ron's investment firm. But I don't know too many humans who really know who's Christian and who is not. The best insight we have is to consider an individual's "fruit," which is obviously scarce in Ron's investment philosophy.

I therefore countered in one of my books that Christians do not need a Christian financial planner as much as they need a Christian financial plan. There is a considerable difference in an age when evangelical sociologist George Barna has said only one in ten "born again" Christians have integrated faith into their lifestyles, which would include businesses. Sadly, by all accounts, Ron Blue & Co continues to shun ethics.

I have no idea if it has ever changed its business plan. Contrary to the teachings of cultural Christianity, St. Paul actually told us we have to associate with "pagans" in this old world but we should at least avoid associating with suspect members of the Body (1 Corinthians 5--13). I'd therefore conclude that **if you want a financial advisor who practices a Christian ethic toward you, you might look for one that wants you to practice a Christian ethic towards our neighbors and future generations**. There are many of those, both Christian and non-Christian, associated with the Social Investment Forum, which you can Google.

Even Merrill Lynch has concluded that could be in your financial interests. It published a major study in the summer of 2011 entitled, "Values Based Investing Comes of Age," which said:

> *"After enduring years of skepticism and a worldwide financial crisis, this global phenomenon has fully emerged as a way to align personal financial goals and performance with the prospect of a better world."*

The cover of that report showed the following chart, with this caption: "For the past decade, the leading VBI Index has generally outperformed the major broad market measure:"

There is a very important reason I share this information about Christian financial advisors, even though I know it will be soundly dismissed as simple criticism from a supposed competitor, even though I don't serve Christians who dismiss ethics. After separating from his firm for whatever reason, Ron decided to teach those once suspect Christians in Wall Street firms how to do what he had done. After all these years and the Great Recession, no one is still sure where he stands on ethics. He seems to favor them one day and seems opposed to them the next.

So when one of his board members called recently to ask me to join their organization, I replied I wasn't his best prospect. He asked me why. I began to explain but he quickly shut me off and said he had no interest in talking

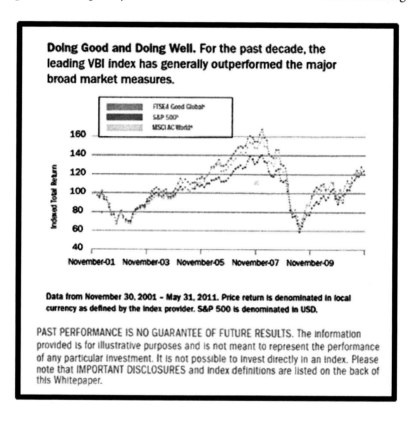

Doing Good and Doing Well. For the past decade, the leading VBI index has generally outperformed the major broad market measures.

FTSE4 Good Global*
S&P 500*
MSCI AC World*

Data from November 30, 2001 – May 31, 2011. Price return is denominated in local currency as defined by the index provider. S&P 500 is denominated in USD.

PAST PERFORMANCE IS NO GUARANTEE OF FUTURE RESULTS. The information provided is for illustrative purposes and is not meant to represent the performance of any particular investment. It is not possible to invest directly in an index. Please note that IMPORTANT DISCLOSURES and index definitions are listed on the back of this Whitepaper.

to any Christian who offered constructive criticism of another Christian. I later learned he was new to integrating faith and finance and knew little of this history. Thus is accountability in the church today, while we constantly remove the specs from the eyes of others.

Of course, I do know the Bible says we are to hold each other accountable privately before going public to the church. Just as I'd tried to work with Larry for years, I had flown to Ron's office at my expense to talk about ethics and investing. I explained why I thought the movement would continue to grow due to Wall Street's ethical blind spots. Ron responded his firm was in a bind. He explained he had lost some clients who had looked at what their investment dollars, as opposed to their philanthropic dollars, were financing. He added that if the movement was going to grow, they wanted an option for clients. But if the movement wasn't going to grow, they didn't want clients thinking about ethics. I literally about fell out of my chair.

I've since grown to believe that no one knows if Ron is for ethics or opposed to them as his organization is financed by Wall Street firms offering both kinds of investment products. There are times he seems to favor both philosophies. That is rather similar to his approach to charitable giving instruments. When raising current funds for ministries, he seems opposed to charitable remainder trusts, foundations, and so on, arguing you should "do your giving while you're living, so you're knowing where it's going." Again, control is a big issue with the spiritually immature who have little faith in God or their fellow mankind. But he's also been instrumental in establishing a national Christian foundation to capture assets the affluent aren't quite ready to give yet.

Again, it appears the views of too many Christian leaders are still determined by money, rather than Christian ethics. Obviously, that appeals to a lot of cultural Christians. I therefore believe his Kingdom Advisors organization has the potential to complete the job of turning the monastery into the world, or secularizing Christianity for Rand's money culture. I risk the bluntness of Luther in saying that. But I hope this book might challenge the organization to turn itself and then the world into a monastery, or re-moralize and re-spiritualize the economies of the world. That's worth bluntness.

Many historians believe monasteries were Christianity's last true economic witness to the world. You can glimpse a truly biblical economy, if that's your interest, and it honestly isn't mine, by Googling the words "Mount Athos." Even that monastic community enjoys a medieval rather than biblical economy.

If there's a parallel to monasticism and its example to the world how we can love others as ourselves in the economic arena, it might be the socially responsible investing movement. While ignored or dismissed by many conservative Christian financial leaders, the movement has long had both secular and religious practitioners who prudently seek to do their neighbors no harm, or even enrich those neighbors, while enriching themselves. We will provide some guidance on that area near the end of this book.

Meditation Twenty-One

Quoting Scripture for Our Own Financial Purposes?

"Obviously, we live in a post-biblical era where general knowledge of the Bible cannot be assumed...We may lament the neglect of the Bible in popular culture and secular education, but we can understand it. But what about the church? What about the evangelical church? If it is true that biblical illiteracy is commonplace in secular culture at large, there is ample evidence that points to similar trends in our churches...The Bible has become a springboard for personal piety and meditation, not a book to be read...Few genuinely know its stories."

Christianity Today
The Greatest Story Never Read

After televangelist Jim Bakker went to prison for financial misdeeds, he had time to actually read the Bible. He wrote a most interesting book afterward in which he said that while he was on television, he had little idea what was actually in the Bible and had simply taught what other ministers of the prosperity gospel had written in their books. He confessed he had become an "unwitting false prophet."

Similarly, despite the occasional good that fearful and/or greedy evangelical financial celebrities have done for some burdened by credit card debt, those celebrities have most likely created far more problems for many more Christians. Yet they often seem to have a cult-like following. I believe that is largely as they quote Scripture. Yet it's often and wisely said that even Satan can quote Scripture for his own purposes. Satan did precisely that when tempting Jesus in the desert with earthly wealth.

I purposefully use the word "cult," albeit in its theological rather than cultural sense, to make another point about how we unwittingly divide the Body of Christ by playing God and judging who is and who isn't a "real Christian." In his book entitled *The Kingdom of The Cults*, Walter Martin began with this quote from Dr. Charles Braden, professor of History and Religion at Northwestern University:

> *"By the term 'cult,' I mean nothing derogatory to any group so classified. A cult, as I define it, is any religious group which differs significantly in some one or more respects as to belief or practice, from those religious groups which are regarded as the normative expressions of religion in our total culture."*

Note that culture defines what is or is not a cult. Yet true Christianity very definitely asks us to be non-cultural, even counter-cultural, particularly when we live in a culture that worships wealth and power. Still, many cultural Christians seem to believe that anyone who doesn't believe what they believe, about most anything, must be a cult member. I've even heard very conservative evangelical leaders apply the word to my mentor Sir John Templeton.

John once graced a poster for a Bible society that attributed any success he experienced to the Bible rather than his study as a Rhodes Scholar. John taught we never question or change biblical morality. Yet he also taught *the practice* of the biblical ethic for stewarding sheep and goats in a faithful and loving fashion must be updated for the bank deposits and mutual funds we steward today. If that makes John a cult member, I suppose he was, as am I.

The Pharisees also saw Jesus as a strong leader who was tampering with their traditional religious practices, which were often quite financially rewarding to the Pharisees, if impoverishing to believers in general. As the Bible is a living Word rather than religious history, we might remember that Jesus was baptized by John in the river as Jesus apparently appreciated John not charging the poor for doing so. The Pharisees did charge when they allowed the poor to bathe in the Temple pools. Jesus clearly understood that any religion that doesn't question cultural religion, particularly in the area of money, is simply irrelevant ecclesiastical history rather than living faith.

The irony is that Larry Burkett and his princes were also strong leaders who taught less than orthodox approaches to Christian economics and personal finance. They just haven't known it as they didn't know, and continue to not know in most cases, those orthodox Christian teachings and traditions about political economy. I strongly believe that's often encouraged them to deepen America's cultural Christianity while seeing more orthodox Christians as cultish.

For example, the stewardship leader of one of the country's largest conservative denominations once asked me to review a financial study guide Larry had prepared for the denomination. I showed the leader where

Larry's teachings about debt were diametrically opposed to Moses and Jesus. In essence, Larry's approach to debt was to simply avoid it. That sounds practical, but Moses and Jesus knew that wouldn't always serve the needs of the poorest when the kids are missing a meal, sleeping in a car, and so on. So both Moses and Jesus, on the Mount no less, said the affluent simply must lend generously anytime someone is in true need. That meant they wanted quite a bit of borrowing as Jesus promised the poor would be with us always.

Larry and his princes also taught we absolutely have to repay any borrowing "no matter what," to use the words of one prince, even if we've been granted bankruptcy protection. Sounds moral enough, especially to capitalists who want their loans back. But God usually looked at things from the perspective of the borrower rather than the lender. Catholic theologians have long called that God's "preferential option for the poor." That concept was captured in Mary's *Magnificat* where the young virgin praised God for sending "the rich away empty-handed."

For that reason, Moses had actually taught *unconditional* seventh year debt forgiveness. He also taught the concept of Jubilee. That was when debts were canceled each fiftieth year and property returned to anyone who had lost it. As Richard Forster wrote in *Freedom of Simplicity*:

> *"There was an important social principle in the Jubilee. If faithfully executed (which it was not), it would have utterly eliminated the age-old problem of the rich becoming richer and the poor becoming poorer. It was, in effect, legislative justice on behalf of the poor; an institutionalized legal mechanism for solving a social and spiritual problem."*

As God has graciously provided all we need for the abundant life, one might well wonder if a major contributing factor to America's concentration of wealth today, alongside growing numbers in poverty, hasn't been the reversal of biblical financial teachings by popular, but non-theologically trained, financial advisors. While recent capitalism has too often depended on "trickle down," God's economy is always built on solid foundations.

That simple biblical concept of the affluent freely lending to those in true need and then acting graciously toward them until, and if, the needy could get back on their feet could have saved a lot of Americans from the burdens of high cost consumer debt during recent years. It could have also softened a lot of the paranoia over the federal debt in the conservative Christian community. Unfortunately, the stewardship leader of the denomination shocked me by responding, "Yes, but Larry says..." It was then I learned to pray like Jesus: "Father forgive them, they know not what they do."

The irony of our selectively using Scripture for our financial and political needs is that it often comes from our desire for Scripture to be a simple recipe for life. We might reflect on these words from *Political Engagement as Biblical Mandate* by my friend Paul Hanson. Paul is a fellow Evangelical Lutheran who was professor of divinity at Harvard before turning his attentions to politics. His book argues our faith operated in at least six different political economies during biblical times, from the benevolent theocracy of David to the exile in Babylon to occupation by Rome. Paul therefore stresses:

> *"In our political engagement, we are deployed not with a time-less blueprint in hand, but with the examples of ancestors in the faith who responded to the call to covenant partnership in an ever changing world. Inspired by Abraham, we dare to move beyond comfortable boundaries, with Moses we dare speak God's word of truth to tyrannical power, and like Amos we embrace as our strategy doing justice, loving kindness and walking humbly with our God."*

Too often, we also seem to reverse the simple counsel of Jesus to sell what we have and give it to the poor. It too often seems affluent Christians will create all sorts of complex charitable trusts, foundations and so on in order to simply avoid turning loose of money they can't take with them. Again, contrary to some advisors, there's nothing wrong with those instruments *per se*. Even Jesus commended the Good Samaritan for leaving money behind with the inn-keeper to care for the needy man in the future. But as a financial advisor, I often have to question the *motivation* behind people's desires to complicate matters. That is particularly true of those "Christian attorneys" in Florida who help affluent Christians appear bankrupt so their tax-paying neighbors have to pay for their medical expenses.

Such complications are too often encouraged by financial advisors who also do not want to turn loose of the money. The typical Christian buys into their counsel as survey after survey tells us Americans know very little about economics and personal finance. But at the time I grew to know Larry, I was still hoping it might be different in "Bible-believing" Christianity. After all, the biblical "root of all evil" resides in the financial area, rather than the political or sexual areas. I quickly learned the way cultural Christianity actually deals with such tensions is to ignore or refute them. Larry even authored another book lamenting the end of the American dream. It often seems the American dream has become the kingdom of heaven for many evangelical Christians.

We could learn a great deal about biblical economics by occasionally breaking free of our "holy huddle" and observing Catholic nuns, the Amish, Mennonites and even Muslims. As much as we might hate to confess it, Muslims actually practice a far more biblical ethic than most

Christians as they usually eschew earning interest, which means they missed the losses of the financial crisis, as well as alcohol, tobacco, gambling and speculation, which are particularly impoverishing to the poor and unsophisticated.

If the past thirty years have proven anything, it's that cultural Christianity has done little to put our country in the right direction. Yes, Larry's ministry did accomplish a measure of good for those struggling with credit card debt. But as we'll see later, such spendthrifts are far fewer in American society than we're often told. We should understand that debt counseling ministries often exaggerate the need for their services, just as politicians and corporations do. Reality is that we've had far more serious financial problems, such as the concentration of wealth and huge lay-offs in a time of record corporate profit margins. Those may better explain many Christians' dependency on credit cards and consumer debt.

Studies also tell us a high percentage of credit card delinquencies and personal bankruptcies are actually due to medical emergencies. Yet many conservative Christians still resist any form of health care reform, even though both Governor Romney and Speaker Gingrich thought the universal insurance most countries have was an excellent idea until President Obama made it law. But politics aside, as we chant "What would Jesus do?" perhaps we might ask ourselves if Jesus ever charged for healing the needy who were also sick, lame or possessed. In short, it's unfortunate that Christian radio the past three decades has focused on our supposed economic symptoms rather than the actual diseases.

In fact, we probably helped to spread some of those diseases. When we aren't grateful for what we have, we usually support public policies that encourage economic growth. Those often lead to greater inequality, which means more Christians on Main Street must max out credit cards for health care, and so on. America has certainly had enough wealth for some time. Enough just hasn't been available to the less fortunate American.

Larry never understood such economic realities, but his worldview has too often been passed down and never questioned. So in a rather non-biblical fashion, one of the leaders of the ministry Larry founded called me "a tool of Satan" after Larry had passed on. My unforgiveable sin? I had explained God's economic blessings on America at a church growth conference. Independent Sector had just identified economic pessimism as a major deterrent to charitable giving.

Two major centers for philanthropy have recently quantified that reality. They estimated that, regardless of a person's *actual* financial situation,

when that person's economic anxieties over the future rise *just one level* on a scale from one to five due to economic *perceptions,* charitable giving *drops by over 30%.* (Google "Feeling Poor, Acting Stingy.") We might therefore wonder why economic pessimism seems a staple of the evangelical media.

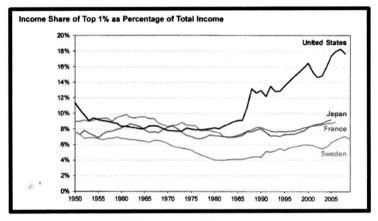

GMO Investment Management

That seemed an appropriate topic if we truly wanted our churches to grow as quickly as credit counseling ministries have been growing. I had not known Larry's disciple was scheduled to speak just before me so I couldn't change my Power Point presentation. But I thought I was still gracious toward his quite differing perspective.

We were in a large Lutheran church at the time. So it was relatively easy for this Lutheran who knew Luther had been called "the Anti-Christ" to take his over-stated judgment of my sinful nature as a compliment. He actually blessed me more than he could imagine. It was at that time I truly realized the division that was judging our nation had roots in our churches. I gave *precisely* the same presentation to eight hundred Lutheran development officers the next week and got a standing ovation with whistling and clapping. Apparently, they understood all too well what scarcity theology does to our churches, colleges and social ministries, even if it sells books and tapes for those preaching it.

Larry always claimed he taught biblical principles of finance. And in some ways, he succeeded. But I've also learned the more people talk about the Bible, the less they usually know what is truly in it. Indeed, Larry wrote a book on what the Bible says about managing money. While he included verses that were clearly out of context, Larry completely ignored absolutely crucial passages about the social responsibilities of the affluent, other than giving to ministries of course.

For example, in Exodus 21:28 Moses actually says it is a *capital offense* to habitually ignore your investments causing harm to others. You didn't even have to do anything harmful yourself. All you had to do was *allow the wealth you steward* to cause harm to others. I can't imagine any biblical financial concept more serious than that, meaning one Jesus would tell us is a "more important teaching" than the one about tithing mint, dill and cumin.

I grew up in the tobacco business. Many of my friends and relatives remain in it. I have also watched Christian investors finance cigarette companies decade after decade. Some even rationalize they can cure the cancer they cause by giving to the American Cancer Society. That nonsense from the perspective of those who have cancer, as my deceased father and mother-in-law suffered, is why I featured the concept of socially responsible investing in my first book, which Larry endorsed.

Christianity Today said it was the first book to explain the biblical roots of the socially responsible investing movement. But perhaps as Larry didn't include such verses in his book and virtually never spoke about the concept on his shows, his one-eyed princes could only see the personal financial rewards of investing. So they have often cynically argued socially responsible investing is a new age concept dreamed up by modern liberals. In fact, it is a deeply biblical concept that has become an explosive, counter-cultural movement to the sins of Wall Street, for very good reason. Even *The Economist* magazine, no foe of capitalism and bankers, forthrightly discussed the ways in which Wall Street had lost its moral bearings with a 2002 cover story entitled, "The Wickedness of Wall Street." Unfortunately, I've found few Christian leaders read *The Economist*.

I did economic commentary on Christian radio for UPI during the nineties and Skylight around the time of Y2K. I grew to understand Larry was just typical in letting his insecurities and/or celebrity status blind him to biblical teachings about our need for humility. Larry often taught businesspeople to form an accountability group that might keep us on the right path when our thinking fails us. Yet Larry's best-seller began by saying he ignored his group and wrote the book anyway. That's a perfect example of evangelical sociologist George Barna saying there's nothing wrong with the teachings of our faith, we simply fail to live them.

Even the secular Peter Principle says we too often grow to our point of incompetence. It might have reminded Larry that it's one thing to counsel spendthrifts about consumer debt but an entirely different matter to essentially teach that no one in Office of Management and Budget knows as much about our nation's finances as Larry did. Many conservative Christians therefore believe the same, though they usually know quite little. That's simply un-Christian hubris.

Larry also didn't do the spirits or finances of Christians any good with his counsel about Y2K. I still have no idea why he, evangelical financial guru Ron Blue, Jim Dobson of Focus on the Family and other evangelical leaders decided to talk at length about that technological issue. Even *The Wall Street Journal* devoted a page one, column one article to the nonsense Focus preached over that supposedly very real but actually imagined giant in our Promised Land.

It's surely ironic, and certainly unbiblical, when evangelical ministries embarrass our faith and drive the thoughtful from it, often in the pursuit of money. The Focus program did at least include one computer expert who said Y2K was hype. But the child psychologist, accountant and book publisher who also participated derided the computer expert's most realistic view. Sadly, an employee of Focus later told me the tape of the program was the ministry's best-seller in history. *The Economist* has detailed how a similar video kept Jerry Falwell's ministry afloat as it struggled with a mountain of debt. Fear, though not of God apparently, seems to move money in cultural Christianity as surely as it did in the days of the Pharisees, and as surely as greed does on Wall Street today.

There was a reason Numbers 12:3 describes Moses, who never got to experience the Promised Land of milk and honey, as "the most humble man on earth." Having moved among Christian media celebrities for a while, I can assure you that many would do well to remember that particular verse. Though I've never heard that biblical concept mentioned by Christian celebrities, it's likely why famed management consultant Peter Drucker, who insisted on being called Peter, once told *Forbes* magazine: "I have no interest in celebrities."

It now seems to me that finding a humble Christian celebrity who enjoys wealth and influence over tens of thousands, is as likely as finding a poor and humble presidential candidate. Abraham Lincoln suggests it can be done, but there have been few Lincolns in the White House. In fact, I'm not sure cultural Christians would vote for such a candidate today. We seem to want leaders who have been more "successful," or "significant" than faithful.

Yet Deuteronomy 17:14-17 tells us that is exactly the kind of leader *we do not* want for our nation. It suggests we consider poor leaders so

they'll never believe they are better than the average person. The day our Christian leaders remember that teaching might be the day we no longer believe our political leaders are out of touch with the average person's circumstances.

The ability of the leaders of cultural Christianity to entertain us with extreme illusions is why the January 2010 issue of *Christianity Today* contained a story entitled, "Chicken Little Was Wrong." It began by cautioning cave dwellers that: "The statistics we most love to repeat may be leading us to make bad choices about the church." It then quotes a leading religious sociologist as saying:

> *"Why do evangelicals recurrently abuse statistics? My observation is that they are usually trying desperately to attract attention and raise people's concern in order to mobilize resources [increase donations] and action for some cause….Evangelical leaders and organizations routinely use descriptive statistics in sloppy, unwarranted, misrepresenting, and sometimes absolutely preposterous ways."*

Unfortunately, we don't seem to have learned that either. Becoming a celebrity on Christian radio still apparently requires the experience and abilities that Paris Hilton displays in the secular world. Dave Ramsey, the most popular financial celebrity on evangelical radio today, rose to fame as he went bankrupt and wrote a book about it. I know this sounds harsh as we Christians believe in redemption. But we also supposedly believe in discernment. And just like Larry, Dave seems to think he's saving the world from evil credit card merchants. Demagogues always need a highly visible, but actually small, enemy, or need imaginary windmills against which to tilt.

Like Larry, Dave articulates an absolute faith in free markets, which is a requirement on conservative Christian radio. **But freedom is simply a political value, not a moral value. True Christians are to live as if "slaves to Christ." That means any faith we have in markets must be in *moral markets* rather than *free markets*.** Yet Dave also discourages ethical and responsible investing, despite my spending considerable time with one of his leaders disproving Dave's claim that ethics must cost us financially. Again, as the old root of all evil hasn't changed, that's probably as he is compensated by brokers who don't care to deal with ethics. Dave's cultural perceptions and teachings may be further impoverishing us as investors, as well as our grandchildren. A *Morningstar* report dated March 12, 2012 that was entitled "Social Responsibility and Fund Performance," discussed several academic studies about screening harmful activities from mutual fund portfolios and concluded: "There's no need to worry that screening itself will hurt your performance." Now if we could only get Christian financial teachers to understand that right and wrong does not depend on whether it makes us money or not, perhaps secular Wall Street might understand.

Ironically, the fearful false perceptions Dave spreads about credit card debt likely provides substantial political coverage for progressives advocating the new consumer financial protection agency, which conservatives detest in theory. I happen to believe that is a definite case of God working in strange ways as even Bloomberg recently estimated the huge expense of fine print, of which credit card issuers are masters. But if even the best known Christian financial celebrities are going to discourage financial ethics, perhaps Moses would tell us that we do indeed need another government agency.

Again, we might know better had we learned from past mistakes. The cover of the second edition of Larry's earthquake book said it was "revised and expanded for the Clinton agenda." The book began by saying:

> "I completed work on **The Coming Economic Earthquake** in March of 1991. It was the first of many books on the critical status of the U.S. economy that have hit the book stores around the country since that time. These books, along with Ross Perot, helped to focus the election of 1992 around the economy and, because of it, President Bush lost his job."

In other words, Larry began by taking credit for sending the first President Bush packing. Indeed, Larry and the secular media often made the case that President Bush was "out of touch" with the economy. Larry didn't make the connection, or think before writing and speaking, but that also meant his negative economic perceptions helped to elect President Clinton, who Larry railed against the rest of his life. And had Larry been sufficiently humble, he might have acknowledged the earthquake book was basically controversial Professor Ravi Batra's Great Depression of 1990 with a few Bible verses added for the Christian market. Such is political and economic life in the land of the blind.

I can see the possibility that Larry and his followers helping to elect President Clinton was a case of God working in strange ways. Even Peggy Noonan, who was President Reagan's favorite speech writer, wrote in *The Wall Street Journal* that the first Bush White House probably didn't deserve re-election. But I can't imagine we want to make a habit of not seeing the connections between our economic thinking, fundraising, and the political reality we help to construct. **The most reliable way to predict the future is still to create it, for better or worse**.

Reality is that Larry's fearful perspective likely caused a hundred times more damage to the finances of millions of Christians who manage credit cards prudently than it did good for those few thousand of his followers who couldn't, or wouldn't, manage credit prudently. What Larry's one eyed perspective of our negatives never allowed him, and millions of others, to see is that he essentially railed against the increasing prosperity that allowed additional savings to occur. Such savings can be invested in equities, like stocks and real estate, loaned to others as CD's, bonds, and so on, or hoarded in gold coins and cash. By definition, as the loan portion of our savings increased, so has our debts. If I had the money that Larry's book cost American Christianity during the bull market of the nineties, I could likely evangelize China. It was the same with Y2K. Such are the individualistic approaches to faith for which conservatives are famous. Yet having a "personal relationship with Jesus Christ" does not always mean we understand how our good intentions for ourselves and our own ministries hurt so many others, and thereby pave the road to hell for our world as we marginalize our faith. Spiritually, the damage was even worse.

Fear closes the hand around our money. So spendthrifts can be helped on occasion. But it also closes the hand around money that could have been invested, which affects what can be given. A closed hand also cannot be productive.

I still have a client who went to one of Larry's seminars during the early nineties and came back in a panic to move her investments into a money market fund. Her money is still there and she's still anxiously anticipating the earthquake. Like the end-times, the earthquake just seems to be on a clock that needs to be regularly reset. Like St. Paul, Luther also thought he lived in the end-times. But the world didn't end once again so my client called recently to say she's now old and doesn't have enough money to live on.

I didn't have the heart to tell her the U.S. market soared during the nineties while foreign markets soared during the past decade, as John Templeton predicted. Yet as Wall Street had its earthquake in 2008 and Europe is having one now, she's like many anxiety-prone Christians in still thinking Larry was prophetic and the sky is indeed falling. They just never understand **earthquakes have always been one of those giants in the Promised Land that God deemed wise to make part of reality**, perhaps to build character for heaven. Our secular concerns should not blind us to that reality.

We all should therefore understand that there's a branch of Christianity called the "prophecy" movement. It basically teaches that Jesus was suspect in teaching we humans will never *know* the end of this old world. Prophecy is therefore of particular interest to those who *feel* Chicken Little was right. I'll leave the legitimacy of that theology to the theologians, though this old fundamentalist still sees little need for supposedly "Bible-believing" conservative Christians to dispute a fundamental teaching of Christ just for a little more certainty about life on this planet. As a Lutheran now totally dependent on grace rather than being in control of my future, I can live with the mystery of when the world will end.

I would simply say again that St. Paul and Martin Luther also feared this old world wouldn't last much longer. Some theological historians believe St. Paul may have caused an economic depression among early believers by suggesting there was no need to plan for the future. I've heard it speculated that Paul may have taken up the "Great Collection" for Jerusalem for that very reason. This is also likely why Martin Luther supposedly said he'd plant a tree today even if he was quite certain the world would end tomorrow. In short, I've seen a lot of money lost due to false prophecy.

So while that movement isn't my particular cup of tea, I do read a financial newsletter that I'd suggest for any Christian inclined toward prophecy teachings. It's called the *Eternal Value Review* and is written by a quite thoughtful prophecy expert named Wilfred Hahn. You can visit his website at www.eternalvalue.com. Wilfred often puts false prophets in their proper places, and there's as many today as there were when the ancient Didache said Christians should stone anyone who made a false prophecy in the name of God, which is increasingly important in our media-saturated world. For example, Wilfred recently wrote:

> "It is interesting to reflect on the significance of the fact that of all the countries in the European Union today, Greece could be the catalyst for the possible dissolution of a unified Europe. After all, back in 1981, Greece was the 10th nation to join the EU, which at the time drove prophecy observers into a tizzy. Understandably, many were absolutely sure that the 10-nation revival of the Roman Empire was at hand. As it turned out, only five years later both Portugal and Spain joined, pushing ECM membership to 12. Membership has since expanded to 27 nations."

Wilfred could just as easily have reminded stewards that Hal Lindsey predicted the end of the "late great planet earth" decades ago, but had reportedly invested in zero-coupon bonds that would pay nothing until after the world would supposedly end. The point is that those obsessed with knowing the future don't always make the most reliable of connections, or think, today. Wilfred is apparently an exception, again affirming why Jesus asked us to love God with heart and mind, as well as soul.

Meditation Twenty-Two

Caesar, Capitalism & Christianity

"We do not have a theology of public life yet. So in the political sphere, we went from unthinking non-involvement to unthinking involvement....We do have public spokespersons like Jerry Falwell and Pat Robertson, but they really haven't thought these issues through."

Richard Mouw
President,
Fuller Theological Seminary

While much of our spiritual and financial poverty has been due to our proof-texting Scripture for our own financial interests, confusing politics for economics has likely caused even more.

During the time I worked with Larry Burkett, I never read or heard him quote anything from an independent economist or economic publication. On occasion, Larry would quote a politicized economist like Art Laffer and his simplistic "Laffer Curve." Laffer and my friend Jack Kemp shaped Reaganomics.

The curve famously said that government would have more and more money as it reduces taxes on the affluent and corporations. Turns out that was a curve ball for our economy, as well as political illusion, as the affluent and our corporations have most of our money today while most Americans are worried about governments going bankrupt.

Truth seems to be that most economic theories work in moderation. Lowering marginal tax rates may have increased tax revenue when rates were at 90%, but lowing them from where President Reagan took them hasn't worked so well. It's the same with preaching and teaching, particularly about money. We need to understand the merits of moderation in everything except passion for our faith and the love it teaches.

Larry's perspective was so highly politicized that he usually only quoted conservative politicians. Newt Gingrich, a fellow Georgian, was one of Larry's favorites. As most political scientists know, Speaker Gingrich ignited his 1994 revolution of "angry, white men," largely by sending nearly hourly faxes to influencers, or shadow-makers, depending on your worldview, like Larry. I suppose those angry men should thank God the Speaker didn't have email back then. I know several who let those faxes destroy their spirits. I'm not so sure how much financial good the faxes did for them either.

Political scientists also know the Republican National Committee once roasted Speaker Gingrich in a video. It showed one file cabinet after another. They were identical. At the end of the video, one file drawer looked different. A voice asked what all the cabinets were. Another voice replied they were the Speaker's ideas. The first voice then asked what the dissimilar file at the end was. The second voice replied those were Newt's good ideas.

Regardless, in one newsletter I keep on file for those who believe truth must be pessimistic, Larry said he was glad the Speaker was "telling the American people the truth." We now know the Speaker was deceiving us over his marital infidelities as surely as President Clinton was. While the Speaker was a one-termer, President Clinton actually survived the impeachment and re-election to leave a budget surplus. In 2000, America was projected by both public and private economists to have nearly paid the federal debt off by now.

So I still occasionally share another copy of Larry's Money Matters newsletter with anxiety prone clients. It is dated February 1996 and prophesied late in Gingrich's revolution that:

> *"The unhappy **truth** is: Even if every GOP proposal had been passed and signed into law with no changes, within 15 to 20 years Americans still would face the biggest economic crisis in world history. When the baby boom generation begins to retire around 2012, programs such as Social Security and Medicare, along with interest payments on the debt, will consume all tax revenue collected by the federal government. To support this level of spending, workers will need to pay lifetime tax rates of more than 80 percent! [Emphases mine)"*

It's now 2012. America balanced its budget under President Clinton and has conducted two costly wars under President "W" that Larry never anticipated. "W," who evangelicals helped put in office, ballooned the federal debt. Yet as we have seen, the federal government is taking a lower percentage of our GDP than at any time since I was born in 1950, at around 15%, rather than 80%. One half of all Americans are paying no federal income taxes, although they do pay payroll, property, sales and gasoline taxes. Interest payment on the debt is about 2.8% of GDP after being 4.2% during President Reagan's last year in office. Yet a lot of evangelicals still believe Larry was prophetic rather than politicized.

Apparently, Larry never had to study the great famines and depressions of history in engineering school. But since he claimed to teach "biblical principles" of finance, one would have thought he'd have known about the seven lean years of Egypt. Despite the legitimate issues we need to deal with as Americans today, I certainly wouldn't trade places with any of Joseph's contemporaries. Heck, I bet even Pharaoh didn't have automatic air conditioning for his car or palace!

If Larry missed "the truth" about the American economy, at least he got the "unhappy" part correct. Generally, **Christians who are members of the Religious Right have been among the most dispirited Americans I've tried to counsel the past twenty years**. That is undoubtedly a major contributor to the depression I have suffered. Studies tell us that women who carry fake designer handbags actually suffer lower self-esteem than do those who don't carry them as they know they'd be faking it. My guess is we Christians suffer from the same phenomenon. We look like Christians with our T-shirts, WWJD bracelets, crosses, and bumper stickers, but we worry about tomorrow more than our secular counter-parts.

Yet the beginning of anxiety is the end of faith. Economically anxious Christians can go to church, but they can't have true faith in God to provide for the future.

The irony is that Larry had his own struggles with depression, probably as his ministry was admirably founded on helping the financially struggling. He just never grew to understand the old Wall Street saying that, "we don't see reality as it is; we see it as we are." Of course, that's a violation of the first of Moses' Ten Commandments. God created reality and we aren't to mess with it by re-creating reality in our own image. Despite our wishes, we simply can't always see things from our own small perspectives. The biblical prophets always went to the mountain tops in order to see things more as God might see them. To do otherwise is humanism.

Unfortunately, Larry's pessimism was often the result of seeing the federal debt as being synonymous with the debts of those families he counseled. Larry could have avoided that humanistic mistake had he only read the February 10, 1996 issue of *The Economist*. It explained the federal debt is not like a household's debt and said two quite debatable assumptions made by pessimists like Larry were at…

"the heart of the debate about the burden of the national debt. The first is that all government spending is unproductive. The second is

*that government borrowing will always 'crowd out' saving that would otherwise have been invested, while taxation will reduce consumption alone. Both assumptions are questionable...**Public spending does not all take the form of wasteful consumption. Public investment, for example in infrastructure, will often yield a direct, sometimes measurable, return. Current spending on education or health care makes workers more productive. Defense too**: the return from Pitt's 'investment' in winning the Napoleonic wars was incalculable, as was Churchill's in the Second World War [when Churchill increased Great Britain's debt to GDP ratio to 240%, or three times where America's is today]. Today's generation would not thank its predecessors if, seeking to avert a national debt 'burden,' they had failed to win these wars."*

The spirits of millions of Americans might have avoided considerable politicized pessimism, if not paranoia, had Larry occasionally read *The Wall Street Journal*. Its legendary editor, now editor emeritus, Robert Bartley, wrote *Seven Fat Years* the same year Larry's book was published. Bartley's credentials as a devout conservative were impeccable. Yet his book said:

"The deficit is not a meaningless figure, only a grossly overrated one...Our *politicians* have conjured the deficit into a bogeyman with which to scare themselves. In symbolizing the bankruptcy of our *political* process, the deficit has become a *great national myth* with enormous power. But behind this *political* symbol, we need to understand the *economic* reality, or *lack of it*. In the advanced economic literature, the big debate is over whether deficits matter at all (emphases mine)."

Shortly thereafter, Casper Weinberger, the most conservative Secretary of Defense in the Reagan administration, wrote a full page editorial in Forbes that asked, "Is the federal debt all that bad?" It concluded it wasn't nearly as bad as politicians, and politicized media, had led tens of millions of Americans to believe.

My mentor Sir John Templeton, who was as economically conservative as anyone I've ever known, addressed the topic at an annual shareholder's meeting. Despite being famously anti-debt in his personal and corporate life, John said the federal debt would not even slow economic progress during the nineties.

Ironically, many political historians, including the most conservative, argue the federal debt that Larry so opposed was largely due to President Reagan, Margaret Thatcher and Pope John Paul II creating favorable conditions to end the Cold War. Conservatives always take credit for winning that war, just not for the debt that financed it.

My point is simply this: Modern Christians are often like those Hebrews trying to decide which of the twelve religious spies to believe. They were all twelve part of God's people. But two faithful spies said the giants could be handled. Ten said the fearsome giants would prevent the Hebrews from enjoying the milk and honey that God had promised for centuries. Note the ratio of fearful to faithful spies. Due to human nature, I doubt that reality will ever be different. Yet the Hebrews took the democratic path, rather than the faithful path, and heeded the majority of the spies, only to wander the desert the rest of their lives.

As Truth has never been a democratic proposition, we moderns need to be even more careful of who we follow in our age of even greater, more fearful shadow-making.

When it comes to economics, I believe that usually means listening to our Christian friends who *can* rather than those who simply teach. I honestly don't believe I've ever seen a Christian financial or media celebrity quoted on Wall Street, and it would follow a goat if it thought it knew how to make money. Yet John Templeton was a two-eyed economic king in the land of the seeing. He was also an advocate of "Austrian economics," perhaps the most conservative of economic philosophies. So he was famously anti-debt on the personal and corporate levels. Yet while Larry was writing his book, John was heavily buying U.S. stocks for the bull market ahead. Sure enough, the economy and stock market somehow managed just fine that decade.

Yet by the late nineties, the best-selling *Prayer of Jabez* promised evangelicals all we had to do to prosper after all was to pray for our stocks to go up. No need to study the economy or investing. God is a cosmic slot machine working through the stock market. But again, poor stewardship theology sold lots of books to the naive. Perhaps that's why the ancient *Didache* said Christians could identify false prophets as they always ask for more than their daily bread, as Jesus taught us to pray. We might also cut down on the number of false prophets if more of them reflected on the ancient teaching about stoning any would-be prophet who made an inaccurate prediction. The ancients understood God doesn't make mistakes, only humans expressing their own opinions do that.

Unfortunately, the Bible clearly explains that it's not human nature to learn by any means other than making a complete mess of things, often over and over. Then we only learn for a short time before we forget again. So by 1999, John was saying the U.S. stock market was highly over-valued and investors would likely make nothing from them during the coming decade. Sadly, perhaps due to our new-found political optimism over having a Republican back in the White House, and books like *Jabez*, the annual Paine Webber survey of investor expectations said Americans anticipated 18% a year from U.S. stocks over the first decade of the new century.

At the same time, Wall Street professionals were voting John, Warren Buffett and Peter Lynch of Fidelity Magellan fund fame, as the three greatest investors of the last century. Still, few in the mainstream or religious media told the public about John's most realistic new prediction. John had asked me to co-author an article for *Equities* magazine about why the Dow would stagnate a decade before resuming trend to the one million level during this century. That's actually only 5% per year, or half of what the market produced last century, but few believe it, even though they believe Y2K and the federal debt have ruined their futures. I also found that few Christians read Equities. And the mainstream media was then focused on the fears surrounding Y2K. John also completely ignored them. Perhaps John undoubtedly knew Japan had plenty of computers, but was making few preparations for Y2K.

Of course, Senator Hillary Clinton would soon run against Senator Obama and newspapers were running cartoons like the following:

Source Unknown

By the mid-nineties, John began to predict "financial chaos" due to the massive leverage on Wall Street. Notice he did not predict "economic chaos," and John was very precise with words. By 2008, Wall Street was leading our economy into the Great Recession.

Interestingly, Sir John died near the bottom of the Recession. I attended his memorial service at Princeton. John's son Jack, who has long managed the Templeton Foundation, sadly told me the sharp market decline had hurt the foundation's investments, which would hurt its grant-making. Jack asked me what I thought John would be doing at that most despondent moment. I suggested John would likely be buying some quality stocks that were suddenly very out of favor. Jack was skeptical, but asked if I'd summarize my views for the foundation's website at www.whatwouldjohntempletonsay.com. It published my article on February 24, 2009 if you want to read it.

I do not relate that story to brag about any sense of market timing on my part. I make my share of mistakes, as did John.

Yet John taught us that batting .600 in our stock picking would put us in the Wall Street hall of fame, assuming we had the *discipline* to avoid high-flying stocks that could really hurt us, as well as hold to our winning stocks for a while. As he and Warren Buffett taught, the first rule of investing is to avoid losing money; and the second rule is to never forget the first rule. Unfortunately, most people chase last year's winners, which means a lot of the appreciation potential is likely gone. There's also an old Wall Street saying that long-term investments are simply short-term trades that didn't work out.

I still make such human mistakes. But I make fewer of them after getting to know John. So I share that story simply to suggest that divine spirits in human form can indeed help us to overcome the fears, and the greed, impatience, and so on, that cost us so very dearly in this life, both spiritually and financially. If that's true with the very human John, with whom I disagreed on occasion, sometimes to my financial advantage, imagine how true it is when we focus on imitating the Son of God, with whom I've never had a disagreement that enriched me.

As wise old Solomon told us, there is nothing new under the sun. There probably won't be until the Good Lord returns. It has also been famously said that markets can remain irrational far longer than most of us can remain solvent. So that potential delay in the Good Lord's return may not be good news for your finances, assuming it will take his return for you to over-come your own fears, greed, and other spiritual disorders. It might be a wiser approach for you to create a richer future based on spiritual realities.

Part Three

*Trading the Compartmentalized Illusions of the Past
For the Holistic Realities of the Future*

*"We have it on authority of the Lord's own spokesmen
that He works in mysterious ways. Which may be why
modern economists have had such a grim time trying
to capture him in their equations. But if a recent, high-
powered conference held in Cambridge, Mass., is any
clue, it's not for lack of interest. Sponsored by the John
Templeton Foundation, the conference brought together
a star cast of economists and scholars to investigate the
public effects of religion - for good and ill alike - on larger
society and the economy....Believers, of course, cringe
whenever faith is measured by the yardstick of social
utility. After all, religion posits beliefs not on the grounds
that they are useful, but on the claim that they are true.
But surely believers ought to be the last to be surprised
that what's good for the soul might also help build a better
here and now. And they ought likewise to welcome the
attentions of economists who appreciate the disservice
to their own discipline done by reducing the richness
of human behavior to the one-dimensional, profit-
maximizing individual motivated only by his own gain."*
(Note: Your author was privileged to be included in this
conference entitled "Spiritual Capital.")

The Wall Street Journal
October 31, 2003

Meditation Twenty-Three

Is Capitalism Devouring Itself?

*"If I wanted to destroy a nation, I would give it too much
and I would have it on its knees, miserable, greedy and
sick."*

John Steinbeck
The Grapes of Wrath

*"I believe in God, family and McDonalds. And in the
office, that order is reversed. If any of my competitors
were drowning, I'd stick a hose in their mouth and turn
on the water. It is ridiculous to call this an industry. It is
not. This is rat eat rat, dog eat dog. I'll kill 'em, and I'm
going to kill 'em before they kill me. You're talking about
the American way - the survival of the fittest"*

Ray Kroc
Founder of McDonalds

When I was growing up on a working farm, which definitely wasn't one
of those beautiful horse farms, outside Lexington, Kentucky, some of my
neighbors and friends didn't always have enough to eat, to the point that I
knew some stole food from our fields. We had enough to eat, even if it was the
basics that we grew ourselves. So I considered myself to be most fortunate,
even if we would be considered poor today.

That's important to understand for your spiritual wealth. Sociologists and
psychologists tell us that anything but the very worst poverty of third world
variety rarely affects people spiritually and psychologically. What does affect
us negatively is relative poverty, or thinking we have things worse than
others. Considerable advertising is based on that reality. This may stimulate
the economy as we try to keep up with the Joneses, but it does little for our
spirits. I can remember a few pains of not feeling as affluent as some in our
community. But as I've gotten older, I've realized how very blessed I was that

my family had treasure chests full of spiritual wealth, even if our material wealth was far more limited.

Not only did I enjoy my mother's fried chicken, mashed potatoes and biscuits while growing up, I needed them. Despite her culinary skills, I had no excess weight when I left for college. There, I very much appreciated the fact that I could get two cheeseburgers, fries, a small Coke and three cents change for a dollar at McDonalds. I continue to believe that with a billion people hungry in this old world, there are greater concerns than we are creating chubby cherubs with Happy Meals.

Still, I've spent most of the past thirty years at my desk, writing and counseling investors. And a few months ago, I weighed almost eighty pounds more than I did upon graduation. Worse, I was taking two blood pressure medicines and still had high blood pressure. My regular doctor told me during my last annual physical that I had become diabetic. That shocked me. My mother, who is now in her eighties, has been virtually disabled by diabetes the past decade. Her family has a history of heart disease and mom had quadruple bypass surgery years ago. So like most humans who'd tried everything else and failed, it was time to do the right thing and lose some weight.

It was about the same time that a dear Christian friend, who happens to be my dental hygienist, told my wife about a doctor supervised diet that had helped her husband lose sixty pounds in a few weeks. She swore it had saved her husband's life. The real beauty was that he had never felt hungry during the process. Naturally, hearing financial claims of that nature each day, I was skeptical. But our friends had learned of the doctor, who had run the medical establishment at an Ivy League school, and diet from a pastor I know. He had also lost about the same amount of weight in the same time.

When we had lunch, over salads at Panera rather than burgers at McDonalds of course, he shared that he too had never felt hungry and now felt better than he had in years. I made an appointment with the miracle doctor. And six weeks later, I was forty pounds lighter than I had been at the peak. More importantly, I was off one blood pressure medicine and my pressure was back to normal. I was also off the diabetes medicine as my sugar level had dropped by half.

So what does that have to do with a book about morality and political-economy? Everything, once you pause to think about it. The October 28, 2011 issue of *The Financial Times* contained a chart that showed 34.9% of Americans were obese in 2002. By 2010, just eight years later, 46.3% of us were. And at root, today's budget debate in Congress is largely over health care and its costs. The Milken Institute recently estimated in *The Wall Street*

Journal that 70% of today's health care expenses are due to largely preventable disorders, like diabetes and heart disease. So we could avoid a lot of the political and economic stress in today's America if we would only learn to avoid rich and fatty foods, as Daniel proved way back in Babylon.

There are other huge economic ramifications however. The essence of the diet was to avoid processed foods and only eat that which grows naturally. None of my beloved potato chips, sandwiches made on white bread with mayonnaise, and so on. When I was finally able to accompany my wife to the grocery store without eating my arm off, I realized that essentially meant I had to avoid about 90% of the stuff there, not to mention McDonald's fries and my even more beloved Whoppers at Burger King and chicken sandwiches at Chick-fil-A. But what would happen to today's economy and particularly to jobs in the processed foods industry, if everyone suddenly adopted the diet recommended in the Bible that I've discovered is so good for the health and budgets of mankind?

I first began seriously thinking about those contradictions of capitalism, as Marx termed them, several years ago. Sir John Templeton, who eschewed consumer credit, suggested we buy the stock of MBNA, the largest credit card issuer in the world at the time. Perhaps it was only fitting that it was the very worst stock recommendation he ever gave to me. John also loved to tell the story about how he and his wife saved fifty percent of their incomes by furnishing their first home with second-hand furniture. Obviously, that would be quite bad for the furniture business, in which my wife worked at the time as a manager of three Ethan Allen stores. John also drove an old Lincoln when recommending the stock of Hyundai, or Kia, I forget which, as they were selling lots of new cars to consumers around the world. He did eventually buy one of those however when his old Lincoln literally fell apart.

In other words, I realized years ago that to be a successful capitalist, you largely have to avoid doing what many other successful capitalists suggest you do through their marketing and advertising, or shadow-making. Morally, that seems similar to those ministries who rail about the evils of credit cards but quickly accept them for their books and tapes. Economically, having half our population working in the fast food industry and the other half at Weight Watchers is like the government hiring some people to dig holes and others to refill them. Everyone works, but little of value is accomplished.

That worked just fine when only five to ten percent of the world's population subscribed to capitalism. But now the strains from most of the world's people now wanting what we have are growing rather evident, to anyone who wants to see. Jeremy Grantham of GMO has written that capitalism does a thousand things right but two or three things wrong. Unfortunately, he adds that any one of those two or three things can bring capitalism down and impoverish our grandchildren.

That's why I've long agreed with Peter Drucker and his prophetic mid-nineties book *Post-capitalist Society* that capitalism must become more "socially responsible," to use Peter's words. Perhaps our major corporations will one day grow less focused on being "efficient" or getting the most out of fewer and fewer people. Not only would that put more people to work, it might lessen the stresses on current employees. Maybe our stores could again close on Sundays and give people a time to re-create their minds, bodies and spirits by enjoying creation and each other. Maybe we'd live longer but healthier lives by consuming life-enhancing supplements and medications rather than simply avoiding the pains of illnesses. Perhaps that won't be as terrible for investors as we fear. Pepsi has shown that Diet Pepsi can be as profitable, or even more profitable, than regular Pepsi.

More importantly, a white paper from Merrill Lynch entitled "Values Based Investing Comes of Age" was issued in the summer of 2011. It documents there is virtually no difference in returns from socially responsible investing and the usual investing without our neighbors in mind. Even *The Wall Street Journal* has recently confessed a little religion can enrich the financial planning process.

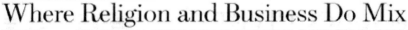

Where Religion and Business Do Mix

The Wall Street Journal, 9-19-2011

Meditation Twenty-Four

Political Economics with a Higher Bottom Line

*"The individual needs the return to spiritual virtues,
for he can survive in the present human situation
by reaffirming that man is not just a biological and
psychological being but also a spiritual being, that is
creature, and existing for the purposes of his Creator and
subject to him."*

Peter Drucker
Landmarks of Tomorrow

I have no need for gambling in my life. For twenty-five years, I've made a decent living for my family by working on "Wall Street," even if as far from it as one can imagine, both literally and figuratively. As some actors work "off-Broadway," you might say I've worked "off-Wall Street." Yet crucial to our understanding is what we call "Wall Street" is simply our collective activities to finance the future with our retirement funds, endowment funds, college funds, and other funds. But during my early years of working on Wall Street, I learned the considerable truth in that old joke that the easiest way to create a small fortune on the street is to begin with a large one. Actual studies say the typical stock investor earns about one-fourth of what the market produces due to fear and greed.

I also have a degree in political science and have likely been too close to politics until a few years ago for my spiritual and mental well-being. So I'd argue this philosophy at anytime:

Americans can elect as many extreme supporters of the welfare state or as many government-hating libertarians as we want. We can enact as much or as little government as we think will create even greater material prosperity. Absent a spiritual and moral reawakening however, most Americans will continue to believe our nation is headed in the wrong direction. We will remain dispirited about our economy, which will paradoxically slow our economy. Insider trading will continue to

characterize Wall Street and Washington. We will continue to worry about the nation we are leaving our children.

Despite teachings by some prosperity theologians, based on the Law of Moses, our GDP and Dow may actually continue to rise to new heights without that reawakening. Jesus said our most gracious Creator makes it to rain on the just and the unjust alike. That doesn't mean we will be any happier with Washington, Wall Street, corporate America, our churches and particularly ourselves. Simon Kuznets, the creator of our GDP, cautioned against such materialistic thinking with these words in 1932:

> *"The welfare of a nation can scarcely be inferred from a measurement of national income."*

Perceptions that our problems are material rather than spiritual are at least as old as Moses. The Bible tells us that when he was leading the Hebrews through the desert of despair toward the Promised Land of milk and honey, even that great man of faith had doubts about whether there could ever be enough for his tiny nation. His followers wanted to worship both Yahweh and Baal, a golden bull that was a symbol of virility that assured future plenty to nomadic herdsmen. They rebelled against the God they couldn't see and wanted to go back to Egypt, where at least they had meat to eat. Being a moral leader interested in eternal things, rather than a political leader interested in the latest poll, Moses urged them forward, grumbling all the way of course.

Since then, other great men of faith have had the same doubts about material sufficiency. A couple of centuries ago, The Rev. Thomas Malthus famously thought humanity was doomed as food production could not possibly keep up with population growth. Prophets of economic doom and gloom have come and gone since. Yet far more Americans today need to diet rather than increase their caloric intake. Many of our lives would actually be enriched by shedding a few pounds and material things.

That more spiritual approach to life was essentially the subject of a speech that John Bogle, the founder of the Vanguard mutual funds, gave at a university commencement ceremony in 2001. Jack said:

> *"A spirit of cooperation and togetherness is today more important than ever, especially in our urban areas where enormous wealth and grinding poverty exist side by side, and where, paradoxically, both extremes seem to lead away from the kind of community spirit that is at the core of the civility that makes community living so worthwhile. I am not at all embarrassed to mention the constructive role of religion in fostering these higher values. While I won't dwell now on the Christian values I cherish so deeply, I would note that virtually all religions preach the*

*existence of a supreme being and the virtues of a Golden Rule, and
standards of conduct that parallel the Ten Commandments. We thrive
as human beings and as families, not by **what faith** we happen to hold,
but by **having faith**, faith in something far greater than ourselves."
(emphases are Mr. Bogle's)*

Yet individualistic Wall Street traders have literally set up alters, complete
with candles and incense, to Alan Greenspan and the Federal Reserve, in
which so many investors still futilely place their hopes for the truly abundant
life. Most Americans also continue to vote their wallets election after election
as they continue to think our problem is truly, "the economy stupid." If we still
believe that after recent elections, we truly are stupid. *The Wall Street Journal*
has confessed:

> **"As the Bible says, we know that our redeemer liveth. And on
> Wall Street and Washington these days, the economic redeemer of
> choice is the Federal Reserve…It's a tempting religion, this faith in
> the magical powers of Ben Bernanke and monetary policy, but it's
> also dangerous. It puts far too much hope in a single policy lever,
> ignores the significant risks of perpetually easy money, and above
> all lets the political class dodge responsibility."**

There's another very practical reason the Fed cannot save us. Economists
call it "pushing on a string." Basically, there are two crucial components to
an economy like America's. The first is the amount of money in circulation,
which economists call the "money supply." The other is the number of
times each dollar turns over each year in our economy. Economists call
that "monetary velocity." If you multiply the money supply times monetary
velocity, you have a pretty good idea of the size of our Gross Domestic
Product. I say "pretty good" as about 12% of our economy is in the "informal
sector," or unreported and non-taxed.

So the Treasury Department can create dollars to put in our banks and the
Fed can create conditions, such as a low interest rate environment, that will
encourage Americans to borrow those dollars and invest or spend. But the
"animal spirits," typically fear or greed, of the marketplace will determine
whether people actually borrow those dollars.

As explained by economics professor Robert Schiller in Animal Spirits, when
such spirits are high, or people are confident that houses and stocks will
rise in value, they are more likely to borrow some of the money the Fed and
Treasury have provided. These spirits can also increase monetary velocity as
people spend. But when animal spirits are low, or people are afraid that house
and stock prices will fall, they obviously won't borrow money to invest.

Furthermore, if people aren't making money from houses or stocks, they won't spend as much as consumers. Economists call this the "wealth effect." It creates even more fear in the economy. It's a very interrelated, and spiritually contagious, matter. So the Fed has been expanding the money supply very quickly since the Great Recession. But due to our fears, we have been paying down debt and/or accumulating even more Treasury securities, which means returning the money to government. Others invest in government guaranteed bank deposits, and many banks simply invest the money in Treasury securities. Neither gets money flowing through the "real" economy of housing, stores, and so on.

This is where I believe Fed Chairman Alan Greenspan fell so terribly short by being purely rational and not understanding human nature is quite emotional and self-centered. As Paul Volcker, Greenspan's predecessor at the Fed, understood, the Bible is quite clear that easy money has always corroded character. So when the Fed increases the money supply too rapidly, which Greenspan always did when things began to slow for one reason or another, it essentially led to more speculation and unethical activity on Wall Street and in corporations. When the average American decided that he or she could no longer trust either, they began to tighten the grip on their money, drastically slowing monetary velocity.

What seems so difficult for humanistic leaders like Greenspan, academics, great champions of faith, and average voters alike, to grasp is that we are not simply rational consumers. We are wonderfully made in the image of the Creative Spirit, with hearts, souls and minds. However, that Spirit has told us that the more abundant life begins with understanding that character is more valuable than money and to count our blessings rather than our challenges, particularly our imagined challenges, as spirits can be animalistic, meaning fearful or greedy, as well as divinely prudent.

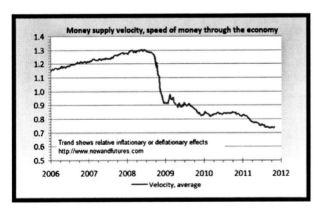

This spiritual challenge is as old as God telling Moses, to use the modern language of economics, to number his "human capital," or people. We have an account of that in the *Book of Numbers* from the Bible. Perhaps by noting such numbering, Joshua and Caleb were able to encourage their people into the Promised Land, despite the other ten spies scaring God's people about fearsome giants in their future. Those ten spies must have assumed God did not know about the giants when God described the land as a land of milk and honey.

So today, all of us, and maybe our religious leaders in particular, might meditate on these words from Mark Buchanan that I've treasured since reading them in *Christianity Today*:

> *"In the Garden of Eden, the first thing the serpent did was create in Adam and Eve a sense of scarcity. [They just had to have that last tree!] The serpent's trick, then as now, is to turn this staggering abundance and gracious protection into frightening scarcity. The serpent lied, and we got taken in. Now, despite the overwhelming evidence that we live amidst overflowing abundance, we always feel it's not enough. We sense it's running out...The deepest theological concept is thankfulness. Because to know God is to thank God."*

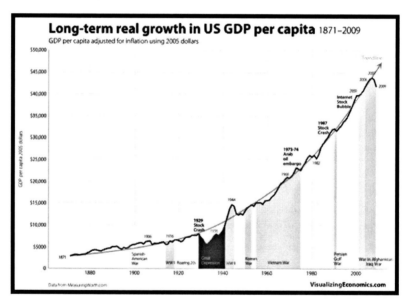

The *Book of Proverbs* also counsels: "Do not put your faith in any human leader. No human can save you." Yet decade after decade, many of us have put our faith in one political leader after another, from one political party and then another. As C.S. Lewis explained, a sick society must focus on politics as a sick man must focus on his stomach. Many libertarians have even put their faith in the human CEOs of our major corporations, as Ayn Rand encouraged. The Tea Party and Occupy Wall Street movement, as well as the low levels of trust in our leaders and our low level of confidence about the future, suggest that we might reconsider the Wisdom of Solomon at this time and begin to look up rather than left and right for true and enriching change.

We can love CEOs and politicians alike, but we should never put our faith in them.

The root of all evil hasn't really changed over the millennia. Thus we should understand the economists who most influence the politicians who, in turn, influence the media who influence us are often on the extreme ends of the political spectrum. These are economists like John Maynard Keynes on the left and Ludwig von Mises on the right. Those with more nuanced perspectives are more difficult for politicians, the media and the public to understand. Like President Truman, we all want a "one-handed economist" who won't always be saying "on the one hand but on the other hand" as extremes are a fact of reality.

Unfortunately, reality is seldom so simple. For example, economists are apparently correct that inequality increases material wealth. When we read the *Forbes* list of the four hundred richest Americans, we run a bit faster on that old treadmill in order to keep up. On the other hand, when we feel our cheese has been moved too far for us to ever catch up with it, what economists and sociologists call "social immobility," we simply quit trying, which is where far too many Americans are these days.

Rising inequality also has some rather unpleasant social consequences. *The Economist* has said:

> *"Within the rich world, where destitution is rare, countries where incomes are more evenly distributed have longer-lived citizens and lower rates of obesity, delinquency, depression and teenage pregnancy than richer countries where wealth is more concentrated."*

The words "obesity" and "depression" should give us pause as the political battle over the budget is primarily one over the costs of health care for ageing baby boomers. Those costs, particularly during surgeries, are made worse by the vast majority of Americans being so over-weight and despondent.

The words "teenage pregnancy" should give particular pause to those conservative Christians who simply vote their wallets each election. Doing so could mean policy decisions that increase material wealth, but also increase abortions and other social pathologies. When young women expect to have little more from life, they can always make a baby. If only all God's commands were as easy as "go forth and multiply."

To encourage policies that lead to the more abundant life for all, we need political, economic, and moral leaders who can see such connections, or think more holistically. Unfortunately, and ironically, while Americans have voted their wallets at least since President Clinton ran on the campaign theme "the economy stupid," we rarely send economists and sociologists to Washington. Lawyers and businesspeople rarely understand the connections to social consequences.

Alexis de Tocqueville, the French observer of colonial America who so ably documented our religious sentiments, predicted in *Democracy in America* that we would rarely have leaders of the caliber of Moses and Jesus, or even Lincoln, in the future. The simple reason is that Moses' people did not exactly vote for the Ten Commandments at the base of Sinai. Nor did the crowd prefer Jesus to Barabbas when Pilate conducted his opinion poll. As Edmund Burke told us, democratic people always get the government we deserve. We rarely notice the reality, but God didn't exactly depend on an opinion poll or election when the people demanded a king and Barabbas.

The more we think like "homo economicus," and vote our wallets, the more we will send politicians who think simplistically about economics to Washington. These politicians will continue to be drawn to simplistic notions like the "Laffer Curve" that drove Reaganomics beyond moderation and may not consider the moral and spiritual side-effects of their thinking. As a result, most voters will understand few solutions to resulting issues other than to simply "throw the bums out" once again.

Unfortunately, our problems are now systemic, so political change will change little as we'll simply elect more "bums." That's been a vicious circle since then-Governor Jimmy Carter said these words in *1976*:

> **"Our government in Washington now is a horrible bureaucratic mess. It is disorganized, wasteful, has no purpose, and its policies - when they exist - are incomprehensible or devised by special interest groups with little or no regard for the welfare of the average American citizen. The American people believe that we ought to control our government. On the other hand, we've seen our government controlling us."**

Former President Carter might say the same thing today, or even worse, if he were again looking to change the party in the White House. Challengers always put the most negative spin on things only to sound like Polly Anna once in office. With respect to President Carter, his "great malaise" speech sounded as if the Washington he presided over was just fine while we Americans were off-key. This is why *The Economist* observed: "Politicians earn much of their living by exploiting anxieties, encouraging people to feel worse than they should about the state of their country." Their ability to see things one way as candidates and another way once elected makes matters far more confusing.

My economic reply to the pessimism of politicians is that the Dow Jones Industrial Average is twelve times higher and, on average, per capita net wealth in America has tripled, since President Reagan took office. In the scheme of things, Washington may not be nearly as big an economic factor as Washington, and the politically obsessed, like to think. And our real problems may not be "the economy stupid" as politicians repeatedly insist.

In short, I simply do not believe five hundred senators, congressmen and a president will prevent three hundred million Americans from achieving financial success, regardless of how we define that, as long as we focus on milk and honey rather than giants. But yes, we can enable them to impoverish us by making us paranoid of real or imagined economic giants. Of course, millions would then blame our leaders for our own moral failings and again want to "throw the bums out." That's just human nature. I've never gained weight because I eat too much. I gain weight as my wife feeds me too much. My clients always buy those stocks that go up. I always sell them the ones that go down. Such is the human condition, at least the unredeemed human condition.

So, unless we look up during a moral reawakening in which we remember there are spiritual values just as important as GDP, we will remain spiritually poor, frustrated with today, and pessimistic about tomorrow. Any new bums we elect will inevitably disappoint us again once they are in the inner sanctums of Washington and Wall Street.

The classic little book, *Animal Farm*, by George Orwell described that reality decades ago. We less-than-scholarly types who pursued degrees in political science always reported on it as it was the shortest book a teacher would consider legitimate reading. But other than the Bible, it might be the first book you want to read after finishing this one. Yet odds are quite good that *Animal Farm* will only make you read again the Bible's argument about the kingdom of true peace and prosperity being an inner, rather than political, matter.

Spiritual riches may or may not eventually shape our economy in the same manner. Despite five decades of study and experiences, I honestly don't know. While the ethic personified by Jesus has enriched the lives of hundreds of millions over the millennia, I often wonder, in more realistic moments, how much he's really changed our world. Considerably I expect. Maybe more so in God's time. Or perhaps this world is indeed going straight to hell, as some television ministers suggest. We're a little more comfortable, cleaner and fatter than the ancients, but not much better off other than that.

As much as I'd like to believe God and believers will one day choose to do away with the giants that frighten us, my best guess is that this world will be our choice of a land of giants or a land of milk and honey for some time to come. Maybe God's plan is not to even do away with the giants as they create character when challenged and overcome, as the slaying of Goliath did for David. That is not for me to know either.

As a disciple rather than prophet, my job is to simply imitate David to the best of my ability by throwing a few stones at the real or imagined giants of our day. And today, most of us feel, rightly or wrongly, that those giants are economic. Fortunately, those giants are quickly brought down to size by even the smallest of God's creatures who have been armed with a little economic history and a few global statistics. I hope you will therefore go out and slay one of those economic giants who are intimidating your friends and neighbors.

Meditation Twenty-Five

Free Markets or Moral Markets?

*"It's been said that if you're not a socialist by the time
you're thirty, there's something wrong with your heart;
but if you're still one when you're forty, there's something
wrong with your head. I'd suggest that if you aren't a
steward by the time you're fifty, there's something wrong
with your soul."*

Gary Moore

The Wall Street Journal, 2-7-2009

Since burning out at my large Wall Street firm and thinking of seminary in
1986, I've thought extensively about a question that many Americans have
increasingly asked since Enron and the credit crisis of 2008: Is capitalism still
moral according to the Judeo-Christian ethic?

I realize it is moral if you accept the new morality of selfishness preached by Ayn Rand, called Objectivism, and believe the only purpose of an economy is to produce material wealth. But even some of our finest financial minds are no longer sure whether it is moral according to the Calvinist ethic that built our country's prosperity, the ethic that said there's a higher purpose to even our materialistic pursuits here on earth.

Like Noah, I'm always scanning the horizon to glimpse signs of hope above the seeming flood of financial immorality on Wall Street, in Washington, in corporate America and even in our churches. I recently glimpsed one such sign at Princeton University. My good friend David Miller who heads Princeton's Faith & Work Initiative interviewed John Bogle. The subject of their discussion was the Protestant foundations of our economy. Jack, as Bogle is usually called, graduated from Princeton in 1951 so the Calvinist ethic is in his DNA. Before the interview began, I told Jack about telling *Money* magazine it could better understand Sir John Templeton's thinking if it began with the fact that John was a Calvinist and it's often said Calvinists can make money as long as they don't enjoy it. Jack expressed the same amusement that John did when *Money* printed my quip over a full page picture of John. As he talked, it was apparent that Jack also found far more joy in giving money than spending money.

Still, as perhaps suggested by the names they went by during their careers, Jack and Sir John are different. Despite his humble origins, Sir John was comfortable with royalty and intellectuals. Jack meanwhile has the common touch. Interestingly, those orientations probably shaped their approaches to investing. Sir John essentially invested in the inefficient developing markets of the world by use of superior human reason and discipline. Jack invested in efficient developed markets through technology and sufficient humility to know that very few investors can out-perform efficient markets.

Having aspired to be a minister during his youth, Sir John could eloquently articulate his faith. Jack on the other hand, reminded me that St. Francis supposedly said to preach the gospel at all times and to use words when necessary. Scholars doubt Francis really said that but he should have as Jack personifies the notion. My point is that despite their differing approaches to our business and our faith, I expect John Calvin would have been quite proud of both Sir John and Jack. There's an enriching lesson for the Church and all its warring factions in Jack and Sir John being different, but equally faithful in their own ways.

As Jack spoke, it became quite apparent that the amazing success his company has experienced over the decades is a direct product of Jack's passion for putting the interests of investors before his own. Yet that also seemed a major reason Jack seemed rather despondent about the moral condition of America and Wall Street today. While he never mentioned Objectivism, Jack laments the shift from what he calls "stewardship to salesmanship" on the Street. And he was probably as critical of CEO compensation as anyone I've heard since Peter Drucker told *Forbes* that CEO compensation reminded him of pigs at the trough. Peter famously argued there is no justification for any CEO's salary to be more than twenty times that of the average employee of the company.

Jack had earlier given a speech to the business students at Columbia University. (You can find it by Googling the words "John Bogle.") **If Wall Street has a Jonathan Edwards today, it might be Jack Bogle.** Edwards was the president of Princeton and ignited the First Great Awakening with sermons such as, "Sinners in the Hands of An Angry God."

Jack didn't rise to quite that moral level during the discussion, but I left with the impression that he was capable of reaching those heights. I sensed it was only Jack's eighty plus years of experiencing grace that made his message palatable for the rest of us. I found that quite refreshing in our age when most pastors sound more like Dale Carnegie making friends than Jesus Christ making disciples, particularly when addressing the affluent and powerful.

Perhaps more interestingly, I happened to sit just behind Jack's wife Eve. It was clear from Jack's comments that she and Jack are true soul-mates. When I told Eve that Wall Street will truly miss the examples of John and Jack, she sadly said she couldn't advise any young person to go to work on Wall Street these days. Of course, I hope she wasn't talking about being an independent advisor specializing in ethical and spiritual investing. She was hopefully referring to Wall Street's sub-prime mortgage originators, proprietary traders, ruthless hedge funds, and so on. Yet each of us in financial services should think long and hard about Jack and Eve's comments. It is quite possible we are complicit in killing the goose that has laid the golden eggs for America by not insisting our largely self-regulated industry adhere to the highest possible standards of traditional morality.

The fact that a study said nearly 60% of Americans had sworn off stocks three years after the credit crisis might affirm that capitalism needs to be saved from the capitalists.

Of course, human memories are notoriously short, so they'll likely be back to stocks, and other investments like real estate, after they're risen in value for a while. And the cycle of fear and greed will be complete once again.

Jack's skepticism about the current moral order did not completely surprise me for two reasons: First, as I've noted before, but it bears repeating, Jack began his book *Enough* with this quote:

> *"The people who created this country built a moral structure around money. The Puritan legacy inhibited luxury and self-indulgence. For centuries, it remained industrious, ambitious and frugal. Over the past thirty years, much of that has been shredded...*The country's moral guardians are forever looking out for decadence out of Hollywood and reality TV. But the most rampant decadence today is financial decadence, the trampling of decent norms about how to use and harness money."

Second, Jack had earlier contributed to a conversation among thought leaders for the John Templeton Foundation and the subject matter was: "Does the free market corrode moral character?" Of course, answers ranged from conservative Senator Rick Santorum's "no" to progressive former Labor Secretary Robert Reich's "we'd rather not know." Responses depended greatly on how one read the question. The foundation's question was actually different than the more nuanced question I like to ask, "Does a *traditionally moral* market threaten economic freedom, or ensure it, as Moses and Jesus taught?"

From my perspective as a political science graduate, **a "free market" is simply one that operates relatively independently of government regulation. Freedom is a word long cherished by the Abrahamic faiths. But it's morally neutral. We can use our freedoms for good or ill,** which is why a recent survey by the University of Southern California found young Internet users thought big business was closer to being "big brother" than big government was. As Janis Joplin told us during the anarchic sixties, freedom can simply be "another word for nothing left to lose." A free market existed in Uganda when I taught there twenty years ago. The government of Idi Amin no longer existed but people were still trading fruits and vegetables in road side huts and so on.

When I say "capitalism," I mean a relatively mature market in which the small savings of many have been combined in a bank, mutual fund, and so on, so that more sophisticated businesspeople and governments have large sums to utilize for ideas of their own.

Crucially for stewards managing God's wealth, those ideas may or may not reflect the moral character of those who provided the savings. Historically, elites have tended to operate according to a different moral code than the rest of us. Hence so much frustration among the populace on Main Street

with how the elites on Wall Street and Pennsylvania Avenue use our money these days.

That is precisely the reason an increasing number of ethical and spiritual investors are looking for companies whose activities more accurately reflect what we aspire for the world we leave our children. Jack Bogle put our way of looking at things this way:

> *"The wellspring of the current financial crisis has less to do with the fundamental character of markets, or of people, than with relatively recent structural changes in the character of our financial and capital institutions. A little more than half-century ago, we lived in what could be described fairly as an ownership society, one in which corporate shares were largely owned by individual investors. In this society, the 'invisible hand' described by Adam Smith in the 18th century remained an important factor. The system was dominated by individual investors, who, pursuing their own self-interest, not only advanced the interests of society but exhibited such positive character traits as prudence, initiative, and self-reliance. But in recent decades we have become an agency society, one in which corporate managers hold control over our giant publicly-held business enterprises without holding significant ownership stakes. Call it managers' capitalism."*

Jack went on to add:

> *"The financial intermediaries that now hold voting control of corporate America are agents for the vast majority of individual investors. In the early 1950s, individuals held 92 percent of all U.S. stocks, and institutions held just 8 percent. Today, individuals hold only 25 percent directly while institutions hold 75 percent. But these new agents haven't behaved as agents should. Too frequently, corporations, pension managers, and mutual fund managers have put their own financial interests ahead of the interests of the principals who they are duty-bound to represent, those 100 million families who are the owners of our mutual funds and the beneficiaries of our pension funds. This failure is hardly a surprise. As Adam Smith wisely put it, 'managers of other people's money (rarely) watch over it with the same anxious vigilance with which...they watch over their own...They very easily give themselves a dispensation. Negligence and profusion must always prevail.'"*

Many prefer the term "stakeholder capitalism" to "shareholder capitalism" and "managers' capitalism" to signify that our employees, customers, the environment and future generations should also be consciously considered by those deciding where to invest our money. But Jack is correct that even shareholder capitalism was so much more broadly enriching to our nation.

America, and increasingly the world, might at least take a small step by going back to that future.

If you worry about the federal debt growing since President Reagan took office, you might put it in the context of the growth of mutual fund assets. *The Economist* **recently estimated global mutual fund assets have risen by** *thirty fold* **since the end of Reagan's first term. Both are clear indications of the securitization of our world's assets, and particularly the financialization of America.**

Sounding admirably like John Calvin and Jonathan Edwards, Jack went on to say:

> *"As for moral character, it is an absolute. One either has it or one does not...Not all that many decades ago, the rule seemed to be, 'there are some things that one simply doesn't do.' Let's call that moral absolutism. Today, the common rule is, "If everyone else is doing it, I can do it too.' There can be no other name for this view than moral relativism. This change helps to explain some of the recent aberrations in the free market...Our society has a huge stake in demanding higher moral values in a less fettered market system."*

Jack's solution? He largely encourages those professionals watching over our financial resources to reverse the process of what he calls "salesmanship to stewardship." That would be wonderful; but I expect a bit like expecting Washington to mend its own ways. I may now be too cynical. But I believe that setting Wall Street straight simply requires those of us on Main Street to assure those elites we entrust with the Creator's wealth consider ethics as well as risk/return. It's much the same with Washington.

That's all I've really meant over the years when I've used the word "stewardism" to distinguish it from "capitalism." Rather than being radical or revolutionary, as some conservative friends have suggested, stewardism is most conservative as it simply suggests there's something to be learned from the old ways.

U.S. Postage Stamp

Despite what ever-creative and ever-destructive capitalism tells us, the words "new" and "improved" do not always go together. That's particularly true when it comes to the historic concept of stewardship that guided Jack and Sir John and the new Objectivist morality that has guided junk-bond king Michael Milken, who re-read Ayn

Rand while in prison; Alan Greenspan, who literally sat at Rand's feet for years; Rush Limbaugh, the voice of the GOP for many years; Supreme Court Justice Clarence Thomas, who recently wrote the majority opinion that you cannot hold mutual fund companies liable if they mislead you with their prospectus; Glenn Beck, who's encouraged more investors to hoard gold coins than any man in history; Congressman Paul Ryan, who is heading the GOP's effort to cut entitlement spending and the former head of BB&T bank, who recently told the New York Times that Rand's philosophy would be the dominant philosophy in America, presumably replacing Judeo-Christianity.

That might already be true. I can only imagine the outrage if our government produced a stamp of Jesus Christ. But it had no problem producing one of Ayn Rand

***

A very personal note from your author.

During the mid-nineties, I wrote a book entitled *Ten Golden Rules for Financial Success*. It explained the financial and moral philosophy I had learned from Sir John Templeton. To be quite honest, John's thinking transcended anything this recovering fundamentalist had previously come across. While I didn't always understand John's thinking, a vast majority of it proved to be prophetic.

At the time, I was concerned that too many social conservatives in President Reagan's "big tent" were being influenced by the thinking of the economic libertarians in the tent, or were catching fleas by sleeping with dogs. I therefore contrasted John's theistic beliefs and spiritual priorities with the atheistic beliefs and material priorities of Ayn Rand. The chapter ended with me confessing that my greatest challenge in life would be learning to love Ayn Rand and her individualism, just as John's challenge had been to love Joseph Stalin and his collectivism. John approved every word I wrote.

John established the Templeton Foundation Press as he grew weary of having to be so negative in order to be of interest to the publishing houses. The Press later published a shorter version of *Golden Rules*. After that, John grew interested in my writing a book for our Christian colleges and seminaries about what the Bible actually says about political economy. As I spoke honestly about the confused thinking of several evangelical leaders, with whom John always disagreed over the economy and investing for the future, the staff turned the book down. John over-rode them. It too lamented the mixing of so many religions, including secular religions like Rand's, by American Christianity.

Fifteen years later, the September 2010 issue of *Christianity Today* contained a feature article I had written. It essentially suggested that Rand is today's Baal and we are now mixing her ideas with those of Christ as readily as the ancients did Baal and Yahweh, creating enormous confusion and stress in the process. A couple of evangelical leaders, like Chuck Colson and Marvin Olasky, took note. But most ignored my caution as libertarian influences within the Tea Party were primarily responsible for creating stale-mate after stale-mate in Congress.

But what really hurt was that just as I am putting the finishing touches on this book, the Templeton Foundation, which is now headed by John's son Jack, who I've long described as more "solidly evangelical" than his dad, has just announced that it has funded, and is giving away one hundred thousand copies of, a book by Rand's disciples entitled *Capitalism Is Moral*. Not "could be moral with sufficient integration of the Calvinist ethic," which I believe John believed, or "should be moral," but "is" moral. One chapter describes how Christianity slowed material growth in the past and how the ideas of Ayn Rand will lead America into the future.

I was so broken-hearted that I literally had to visit my doctor after a few days. He informed me of a new study out of Japan that proves people can suffer heart ailments due to grief. He advised me to focus on "the things that are good and deserve praise," as Saint Paul termed them. So I began to remember pleasant moments I had with John, and I realized, from conversations that I had with Jack, that I may have known things about John that John kept from even his children. My father was also of that stoic, "John Wayne" mold, so it wouldn't surprise me.

For example, as John neared age ninety, I often kidded him about his lady friends. He had lost his second wife but still enjoyed the company of interesting ladies at dinner and so on. I often asked how it was that he always seemed to have a pretty lady on his arm at our foundation meetings. Despite his reputation for humility, John just winked and said that it had been that way his entire life!

Perhaps that's why he called me one day. He never did that as there's an annoying delay in the telephone when speaking to someone in the Bahamas, so he usually sent faxes. So I told Sherry that she must be mistaken when she said John was on the phone. But she wasn't. John had actually called to see what I would think if he began dating a considerably younger, and very beautiful, lady of fairly high profile. He explained that she had called to inquire about money management but he thought she really wanted to date. I suggested that would be wonderful for him. But being a Calvinist, he explained she lived in the states and he would have to pay for her plane fare. Again, I suggested there were worse ways to spend a few of his dollars.

I have no idea what John decided to do. But I do know that when we hung up, Sherry said we sounded like two eighth graders discussing who had a crush on whom. I couldn't disagree. And I remembered that as we get older, we seem to grow more child-like, with which Jesus seemed to suggest would help us to be more spiritually mature.

John couldn't show that side of himself to the public, and I'd guess his children, too often, if at all. Wall Street values rationality and finds emotions quite suspect. So John often came across as human as a computer. That's why a senior staffer of the foundation and I once discussed over dinner how he seemed to be a religious Ayn Rand. She essentially cut the heart and soul out of humankind and relied entirely on the mind, whose thoughts are not usually God's thoughts.

But John wasn't really that way. He may have reasoned but he reasoned with the mind of Christ rather than the mind of Rand, as Rand's disciples do. So his mutual funds refused to finance companies primarily engaged in alcohol, tobacco and gambling, as they still do by the way. John also spoke fondly of having transferred billions of dollars from affluent North Americans to the developing nations of the world. Of course, had he done so as a ministry, he'd be a saint by now. But since he did it through the markets, many "America firsters" feel he was unpatriotic. Such is the compartmentalized mind of many conservatives. Small wonder they rarely understood, much less appreciated, John's holistic thinking. In addition, John's many writings, which are solidly Judeo-Christian if you read them in their entireties, display a big heart and a bigger soul, which also made him hard for some to understand.

While Rand died lonely and depressed, John had thousands attend his memorial services whose lives had been so enriched by what he believed and lived. While Rand thought mankind can live by bread alone, John knew Tocqueville was right that we were created with a taste for both earth and heaven. That's why I have to believe John would be saddened that the foundation, which has long been a major funder of traditionally religious causes, has joined many religious conservatives in mixing the religions of Christ and Rand to create a new religion, simply as Rand despised the government that Christ asked us to render unto and St. Paul told us to "honor and respect."

Meditation Twenty-Six

To Change Institutions, Change Hearts And Minds

"Good people make good institutions."

James W. Frick

*"What's been lost is the idea that a banker has some
responsibility to protect the client's interest."*

Daniel McFadden
Nobel Laureate, 2000

During seminars, I sometimes use two graphs to describe the primary
change I've witnessed since joining Wall Street during the late seventies. In
my opinion, they go a very long way in explaining the Occupy Wall Street
movement, and perhaps the Tea Party, and concerns of Americans in general.

I've labeled the first graph "Early Wall Street." Imagine a piece of pipe lying on
its side. On one end of the pipe are people with money but no good ideas for
using it. On the other end are people with good ideas, but no money. In the
middle of the pipe, there is a pump that I have labeled "Wall Street." Its job is
to keep money flowing thru the pipe. During the early eighties, Wall Street
received about 10% of corporate earnings to keep that money moving. It was
a difficult but achievable job to keep those on both ends of the pipe happy,
and earn a decent living in the process, with a modicum of ethics.

But due to human nature being created higher than the animals but lower
than the angels, it's tempting to watch all that money flow by on its way
elsewhere and not want ever more of it. So the second graph, labeled "Current
Wall Street," shows several spigots on the pipeline.

One spigot might be the "proprietary trading desks" inside the big, publically-
traded investment firms and banks. Essentially, they use money, usually raised
from investors on Main Street, to literally trade in the markets, often against
the very same people on Main Street who provided the money. Those people
on Main Street usually have productive jobs that demand most of their time,
as well as minimal experience and resources to judge the market. The traders

have all day to do nothing but trade. And they have enormous capital, again supplied by those on Main Street, with which to buy the most advanced technologies, research, and so on.

If successful in trading for our money, the big institutional traders often earn bonuses of half their annual trading profits, so they are very aggressive. If unsuccessful, the institutions too often get our money anyway in the form of a tax-payer subsidized bailout. That arrangement, immoral to capitalism as imagined by Adam Smith, as well as any decent notion of stewardship, is precisely why former Chairman of the Federal Reserve Paul Volcker has proposed changing the system with his so-called "Volcker Rule." Naturally, the banks, who are usually led by CEOs who've been taught that their only social responsibility is to take care of their banks, are resisting.

A second spigot might be "proprietary products." These are mutual funds and other investments that are not only sold by Wall Street firms for fees and commissions, but are managed by the same firms for additional management fees. The concern about these is that brokers and planners have too often been encouraged to give those products priority over a non-proprietary investment that might have a better track record of prudence, ethics and performance for investors and society. Anyone who's watched the many Wall Street firms disappear since the bull market began in the early eighties knows those firms were far better at selling securities than managing wealth.

A third spigot might be those hedge funds that are outside the big firms but are still partially owned by the big firms. Again, the capital made available by investors on Main Street can be used against them in the markets. The list goes on. So when the market peaked in early 2000, financial services companies were taking in almost 30% of our corporate profits. And financial professionals were making more money than similarly educated professionals, often far, far more money. As the Tax Justice Network quipped on October 12, 2011 about the so-called 1%:

> "Who's in that top 1%? Are they heroic entrepreneurs creating jobs [as Ayn Rand imagined in her fictional books]? No, for the most part they are corporate executives. Recent research shows that round 60% of the top 0.1% either are executives in nonfinancial companies or make their money in finance, i.e., Wall Street broadly defined. Add in lawyers and people in real estate, and we're talking about more than 70% of the lucky one-thousandth."

One does not have to be an egalitarian, or believe everyone should make the same incomes, to understand that is clearly inequitable, which is the major reason both the Tea Party and the Occupy Wall Street movement have been protesting. All that money being drained off the nation's money supply is also a major reason politicians from both parties have been so friendly toward Wall Street. But all that drained money, in my opinion anyway, is why your retirement plan has stagnated for years.

Nobel economist Milton Friedman, and therefore many CEO's today, liked to argue our publicly-traded corporations are in the "private sector." But like our governments, they are actually funded with money from the public. One might assume publicly-traded Wall Street companies that have been funded with the public's money would hesitate to bite the hand that feeds them by trading against Main Street. But as the old saying goes:

"It's hard to get people to see the truth when they're paid a small fortune not to see it."

Still, those spigots are like the Spanish Moss that hangs in the trees outside my office window. When there is a small amount, it doesn't matter much. But when it gets too thick, it can kill the trees on which it depends, so I have to kill it.

It's the same way with Wall Street. Its younger members will never understand this as they've not reached the age to understand toxic self-absorption. But more seasoned and less biased heads know Wall Street is in real danger of killing the money flow, as evidenced by the credit crisis that preceded the Great Recession. Yes, it is indeed easier to see that once someone is affluent, as I am these days; but that doesn't change the fact of the matter, which anyone with a semblance of a social conscious knows.

Consider the example of my sister. When she became disabled, she stopped working as an attorney for the state of Kentucky more than a decade ago. Her retirement plan was frozen at that point. Though invested in some very high quality equity mutual funds chosen by the plan's trustees, she has made nothing during the years since she quit working. Obviously, that will greatly affect her future. And most Americans are in the same boat. Very simply, trading wealth around and draining it from the pipeline accomplishes very little wealth creation. Yes, it creates jobs and income on Wall Street; but so does prostitution and dealing black jack in Las Vegas. The primary difference is that Las Vegas provides a moment of pleasure when taking your money.

The sad part is this ethic has infected the Christian community. I used to attend Bible study each week in the home of affluent and conservative Christian friends. Their son graduated from college a couple of years ago and went to work with a hedge fund. He made over $100,000 per year right out of college. But that wasn't enough. So he bought a few computers and sat up shop in my friends' home. He now makes far more by simply letting his computers siphon a little off the stock market each day, which means the money you have in your IRA, your church's endowment fund, and so on. More sadly, this is conscious. He has told his parents that he knows he's doing nothing useful for society, but the money is too good to ignore.

The task at hand is therefore to essentially save capitalism from the capitalists. That is why Paul Volcker has been strongly advocating change. Mr. Volcker killed inflation during the eighties when we feared it as many now fear Wall Street and Washington. His rule would greatly limit the amount of such parasitic activity on the part of our investment firms. There are other ideas floating around, such as the "Tobin Tax" on high frequency traders, to discourage speculators like my friends' son. Naturally, they are fighting such measures. If you are a true investor, you might support them.

One of the things rarely mentioned by the press about Mr. Volcker is that he is a devout Christian and serves on the board of a Christian college that I considered attending. As such, he undoubtedly knows there is little, if anything, in Judeo-Christianity about easy money being a virtue. He was therefore willing to stop the easy money practices our nation engaged in after the Vietnam War. As the old saying used to go, it is the Federal Reserve's job to take away the punch bowl just when the party gets really rolling.

Unfortunately, Alan Greenspan apparently believed Ayn Rand's teaching that the moral purpose of our lives is to make money. So in the opinion of many, he further spiked the punch bowl when the party of the nineties had grown over-heated, eventually causing the economy to catch flames during the Great Recession. My clients used to wonder when he would eventually tighten credit. I replied that due to his moral reasoning, the odds of him stopping the printing of dollars were as likely as Billy Graham stopping the printing of Bibles.

Source Unknown

The other thing to understand is that Greenspan apparently passed his mantle on to Ben Bernanke. Mr. Bernanke was once asked what he would do if he printed money for the banks but Americans were reluctant to borrow it as they are over-burdened with debt or America needs so little more material wealth. Economists call that "pushing on a string" and the Japanese have experienced it for years. Anyway, Mr. Bernanke replied that if he had to, he'd print hundred dollar bills, rent a helicopter, fly across America and throw the money out. He's since been known as "Helicopter Ben." And he's essentially tried to provide free money by keeping interest rates near zero, for our banks anyway.

The point, for the Tea Party and Occupy Wall Street movement, as well as Congressman Paul, is that it is not necessary to rid ourselves of the institution called the Federal Reserve. We simply need to have it managed by people with the proper moral perspective, whether that puts more money in the pipeline for Wall Street to siphon or not.

Good people make good institutions, even in Washington.

Meditation Twenty-Seven

Beyond Simply Saying "God Owns it All"

"Many people think the church asks too much of
its members. In reality it asks too little...Frankly,
many churches have dumbed down church until it
has no meaning at all. We are afraid to ask men for
commitment, so they think we're after their wallets, not
their hearts."

David Murrow
Why Men Hate Going to Church

I was a member of the Rotary club for years. When my last club disbanded, I suppose I became one of those increasing number of Americans who are "bowling alone." But I still can't say that I've missed it. It often seemed that all we did was get together weekly, listen to a boring speaker tell a joke or two, and too often argue a while.

Still, we had to attend every week or find another Rotary club at which to "make up." We were strongly encouraged to become Paul Harris Fellows by giving at least $1,000 to the Rotary Foundation in its effort to eliminate polio around the world, which it has virtually succeeded in doing. Finally, we were expected to recite the Four Way Test each week. That is a statement of ethics that might have been quite beneficial to Washington, Wall Street, CEOs, and even the church in recent years. Still, most of us wondered at times if attending weekly was worth our time, talent and treasure.

I tell you that as I've long suspected most churches demand even less of members, and men in particular. If you can make it, fine. If you give anything, even better. And if you've memorized the historic creeds, you're extraordinary. And of course, no one wants services going for longer than our Rotary Club met.

So the most consistent comment I receive about my writing is that it is too long. Every editor for every religious publication for which I've written, and every religious organization I've spoken for, has asked if I can't shorten my insights. I virtually always decline as words to an author and speaker are like children to a mother. And then the editors and hosts shorten my insights for me. I always reflect that when I visited Uganda, their church services would go on for hours as they had nothing "better" to do. I have also grown to believe that is a major reason Chuck Colson has written American Christians are gravitating toward "a religion that is easygoing and experiential rather than rigorous and intellectual."

I'm afraid that is going to be the case for the foreseeable future. We live in a media-saturated world of three second sound bites. Politicians therefore offer microwave solutions to our nations' problems. But I'm going to stick to my guns anyway. The simple reason is that I believe the concept of stewarding the Christian life is far more important than any of those six page analyst reports that brokers are expected to read each day. One of my favorite money managers, Jeremy Grantham of GMO, recently published his "shortest ever" quarterly letter to shareholders. It was four pages long.

Pepper . . . and Salt

THE WALL STREET JOURNAL

"I do have strong moral values, but I don't let them rule my life."

I also believe these articles are even more important than the three newspapers I read each day and the five financial magazines I read each week. Even those often leave me thirsty for a fuller explanation of matters than they have provided. That's why I believe God gave us a Bible comprised of sixty-six books rather than a *CliffsNotes* pamphlet. It's simply impossible to explain the connections between politics, economics, faith and our personal finances in a two minute commentary, as I unsuccessfully tried to do for UPI Radio and the Skylight Radio Network.

Yet I even had the same issue when friends supposedly watched a ninety minute video of a seminar I did in the Twin Cities entitled, "Meditations on November 2012." It contains political, economic and spiritual information that a devout former congressman, who served on the Financial Services committee of the U.S. House of Representatives, found enlightening. A primary thesis is that the popular media loves conflict and therefore polarizes culture into far left and far right. Politicians must play to that polarization to win primaries, even if they then disappoint their bases by moving to the middle to win general elections and govern our multi-cultural society. I argued true religion unifies by moderating our relatively small differences so we can live in peace, rather than the anxiety that impoverishes, both spiritually and financially. In essence, life is like those see-saws we rode as kids. You could sit on the far ends and have a thrilling ride. Or, you could stand peacefully in the middle.

My thesis was solidly affirmed two weeks later when *The Economist* magazine's cover story was, "The Missing Middle: The Woeful Gap in America's Politics." As did my video, the article suggested the primary hindrance to Washington solving any problems rested largely with conservative Christians. We often confess to "certainty of belief" about fundamental religious matters, which is fine perhaps. But too often, we also seem incapable of nuance in mundane matters of economics, politics and our faith. We even saw that over the extraordinarily mundane matter of Y2K, when many were most certain a computer glitch would end our world. For decades now, others have believed the same of "liberals," and the federal debt in particular. We just can't seem to understand Washington isn't the sum of America and the federal government can run a deficit without our country running one, which is why America's net wealth has risen along with Washington's debt.

Of course, some viewers did not appreciate that perspective, as gracious but honest as I tried to make it. Those with libertarian, or far right, views were quite critical. The reason is that I began by quoting a recent report from *Christianity Today* about a new Baylor University study. It said frequent Bible reading can turn the most conservative Christians more progressive in some ways. Of course, as I was trying to transcend politics and speak morally, I confessed frequent Bible reading might also turn those on the far left more conservative.

The point was that one reason politics and the media frustrate us so much is that the moderating ethos of Judeo-Christianity seems to have less and less influence in our culture. Meanwhile, cultural Christianity simply reflects America's polarization rather than heals it. If one wants to be a social progressive, he or she can find a mainline church that shares his or her views. And those who want to be economic progressives can always find an evangelical church that adheres to prosperity gospel, or a Baptist or independent church that ignores economics. God knows there are plenty of both.

The result is that few Christians in the West, whether progressive or conservative, have any idea anymore what the faith has taught over the millennia. *Christianity Today* recently noted that phenomenon when it said evangelicals often think of Billy Graham as a church father. Yet that was also evident recently when the Archbishop of Canterbury, the head of the Anglican Church, which is related to America's Episcopal Church, attempted to talk about economics in the *Financial Times of London.*

While the *Times* printed his letter, it also followed up with an editorial about how little moral guidance the church had provided to members during the economic crisis. Among the few specifics the archbishop endorsed was the "Tobin Tax," a small tax on stock transactions which some believe would discourage high frequency traders. That didn't set well with some readers either as the Times printed a letter to the editor suggesting guidance on taxes is beyond the church's moral authority.

I found that response interesting as the Bible clearly says Moses, Jesus and Paul disagreed. As I reviewed in my seminar, Moses, who we might remember was a law giver as well as prophet, actually taught this concept, as recorded in Exodus 23:10: "For six years, plant your land and gather in what it produces. But in the seventh year let it rest, and do not harvest anything that grows on it. The poor may eat what grows there, and the wild animals can have what is left." Even when I hear that passage quoted, it's usually in the simple context of environmentalism, which is what it's largely about. But by that one verse, Moses also made it law for the Israelites engaged in farming to devote one-seventh, or 14% of their income, to what we might call social spending today.

And that was just the beginning. Moses also said the landless who were hungry could walk through the wheat fields and vineyards belonging to others and pick what they needed for their current meal (Deuteronomy 23:24-25). That was limited as the poor were instructed to not take any away in a doggy bag. But the landless Jesus was apparently taking advantage of that law when challenged by the Pharisees about working on the Sabbath. That concept is more important than we think.

Christian planners interested in evangelizing the world should pay particular note that *The Wall Street Journal* wasn't overly impressed with the small difference they could find between the country's best known "Christian financial planners" and secular planners. It was simply that the Christian planners prompted clients to give to ministries, which may be why some ministries feature their views so often, even if there's little evidence those views have been particularly enriching to listeners and readers. Yet the *Journal* noted those planners used the same investment vehicles as secular planners. Which means there was likely no consideration of the poor or environment in those modern "fields" of wealth creation.

There's no reason to imitate the Pharisees by suggesting any of us know what Christians should or should not invest in. Other than the tobacco industry, in which I grew up, I'm not aware of any industry's products that are deadly if its products are used in moderation. There is a case to be made for personal responsibility in such matters. But there's also no reason for investors to be blind to the major problems such industries cause, often to the "least of these." The April 26, 2011 issue of *The Wall Street Journal* detailed:

> *"Nearly half of all cigarettes sold in the U.S. are smoked by people with a serious mental illness, according to a study in the Journal of The American Medical Association in 2000. People with schizophrenia, bipolar disorder and other mental illnesses are twice as likely to smoke as the general population, and they tend to smoke about 50% more cigarettes per day."*

Substantial profits of other industries, like the alcoholic beverage companies, are reportedly heavily dependent on addicts who do not use those products in moderation. And some products and services are simply more enriching for those producing them than for those consuming them. For example, I've been known to enjoy a good cigar even though my doctor would prefer I not. That's where even disciplined consumers need to exercise wise personal responsibility. Yet all investors should discern whether they want to invest in such companies. At the very least, all companies, but particularly those managed by professing Christians, should exercise social responsibilities toward competitors, employees, contractors, future generations by caring for the environment, and so on, when marketing their products.

We should also understand that even Moses, whose Ten Commandments primarily said we "shalt not," went considerably beyond simply avoiding harm. Jesus was far more proactive by saying "love." Even though the afore-mentioned Mosaic laws may have affected 15% or more of Israel's GDP, none had anything to do with tithing, which was also mandatory, or giving, which went beyond the mandatory tithe to volunteerism. That reality was reflected in the writing of the great Hebrew theologian Maimonides in his principles of tzedakah, which, unlike philanthropy, were also mandatory. His Eight Levels of Giving, as expressed in the *Mishneh Torah*, Chapter 10:7-14, were:

1. Giving an interest-free loan to a person in need; forming a partnership with a person in need; giving a grant to a person in need; finding a job for a person in need; so long as that loan, grant, partnership, or job results in the person no longer living by relying upon others.

2. Giving tzedakah anonymously to an unknown recipient via a person (or public fund) which is trustworthy, wise, and can perform acts of tzedakah with your money in a most impeccable fashion.

3. Giving tzedakah anonymously to a known recipient.

4. Giving tzedakah publicly to an unknown recipient.

5. Giving tzedakah before being asked.

6. Giving adequately after being asked.

7. Giving willingly, but inadequately.

8. Giving "in sadness."

Now that we understand keeping a person from needing charity was considered far more important than giving to that person once he or she does need charity, we can talk about tithing...as the Bible does. Theologians often note there were actually multiple tithes in the Bible. The first was called the festival tithe, as described in Deuteronomy 16:10-11. It essentially says to get together after harvest and have an all-inclusive party. We Lutherans note that passage says to "buy beer;" but having been one, I know the Baptists will stipulate it must be non-alcoholic.

Then there was the tithe of the "first born of the cattle and sheep" described in Deuteronomy 12:6. It was a time of communal feasting and celebration hosted by the cattlemen and shepherds. Finally, there was the third year tithe for the priests, foreigners, widows and orphans described in Deuteronomy 14:28. All together, these tithes may have amounted to another 20% of GDP.

And that was before the Temple tax was instituted later. It was a flat tax, apparently as God didn't want the affluent wielding more influence over the country's moral institutions than the poor had. Interestingly, one of my more experienced and insightful ordained friends insists most churches eventually hire pastors who share the worldviews of the most affluent members. I doubted that at one time, but the more I look at the composition of search committees and such, the more I believe he may have a point.

Also interestingly, while many conservative ministers advocate a flat tax for federal taxes, I've never heard a minister advocate the biblical principle of the affluent and poor of our churches paying the same. That's obviously as our churches, just like politicians, are quite dependent on the affluent. But overall, it's quite likely that ancient Israel looked more like Northern European countries than most conservatives, like myself, and libertarians in particular, care to admit.

One might assume that Christian leaders would be quite happy with all that social spending and giving, even if relatively less of it was routed through the churches. One would be wrong. During decades of working with churches and non-profits, I've grown to believe that many of our leaders don't mind the popular but false perception that all help for the poor should be done through institutions. Maimonides may have recommended giving through institutions, but conservative leaders often exhibit a double-mindedness when arguing care for the poor is impersonal and ineffective when done through government without realizing it can be the same when done through religious institutions.

The fact Jesus never said to sell what we have and give it to the Temple or the evangel is essentially the theme of a new book entitled *Toxic Charity*, which was bravely and favorably reviewed by the November 2011 issue of *Christianity Today*. It too will upset a lot of cultural Christians but anyone who has served on as many non-profit boards as I have can attest the author has a point. Clearly, the ancients who knew it was better to prevent poverty, rather than simply give to relieve it, were onto something. I say that hard truth despite knowing the old saying:

"When I gave to the poor, people called me a Christian; but when I asked why there are so many poor, they called me a socialist."

Many of my critics' emails regarding my talk and videos were more theological than practical. That's apparently as many believe Jesus transformed the Law of Moses into spirituality, where all care for the needy is motivated by love, as described in the *Book of Acts*. Having a degree in political science and having worked on Wall Street, I just can't be that idealistic about the state of humanity. That's one reason I'm now Lutheran. I know I desperately need all the grace I can get. I therefore realistically believe that Jesus was quite Jewish, which is why he said every detail of the Law of Moses would endure forever.

I therefore believe Jesus simply freed his true disciples of the legalism of the Law with his law of love, which results in a decidedly more joyful way of life. But that does not mean cultural Christians and non-believers have been freed of law for anarchy, greed on Wall Street, shadiness in Washington, and so on. I now call those cultural Christians CHINO's, meaning Christians in Name Only, in imitation of libertarians who call moderates RINO's, or Republicans in Name Only. My experiences with Christians and money suggest CHINO's rather than atheists may be the single largest cause of the decline of the church today. Mother Teresa used to say that over and over.

The strongest objections were actually from two Christian leaders who live in quite affluent and libertarian areas. As the gospels say about Jesus' encounters with the Pharisees, of which I confess to being one of the worst, neither was directly confrontational but each resisted the teachings of the video by splitting theological hairs. The first is a financial leader of a large church in California. It is no coincidence the Ayn Rand Institute is located nearby. It is an area known for generous giving to symphonies, art galleries and churches but of little giving to the needy. And of course, the area doesn't generally believe taxes are the price of civilization.

I had said in the seminar that the Bible says no man knows the future and we should therefore not be unduly stressed over projections of the federal debt. To me anyway, that sounds very close to Jesus' teaching about worrying about tomorrow, or C.S. Lewis writing in *The Screwtape Letters* that God's job is to keep us focused on today while Satan's job is to keep us worried about tomorrow. So I reminded those in attendance that many conservatives thought the debt would prove earthshaking during the early nineties but by the time President "W" took office, official and private projections said the debt would be nearly paid off by now. Two wars and tax cuts took care of that rosy projection. So we're now projecting disaster again. Anyway, my friend from the church said the Bible says no such thing, that there are places in the Bible where God speaks through prophets. Of course, he's right...and wrong.

Ecclesiastes 8:7 does indeed say "none of us know what is going to happen, and there is no one to tell us." Having ninety minutes to explain America's political economy and various cultural religions that influence it, I didn't take the time to nuance the fact, as I did in my last book, that God does know the future and on very rare occasions may choose to speak through prophets. My point is that we will all be richer if we learn God may not be as interested in speaking through religious celebrities about the federal debt, Y2K, the stock market, and so on, as many of us think.

The second critic was a devout Catholic who is a leader of a libertarian publication in another very affluent community. Of course, I was critical of the economic perceptions our media create as I generally find more editors have degrees in journalism than economics. But this critic, who apparently didn't make it past the slide of Sir John Templeton advising investors to avoid the mainstream media, split another theological hair. He noted that St. Paul did not counsel "moderation in all things." Again, he was right...and wrong. Paul did not use the words per se. Some believe they came from Aristotle, something Paul would have likely known as he was an educated man. But Paul did teach moderation in drink, eating, and most importantly, a moderate approach to politics that "honors and respects" government, even if it's barbarous Nero (Romans 13), without growing dependent on government.

The Amish and Mennonites may have that most correct among American Christians. They so care for one another, they have historically been able to claim exemption from governmental programs, like Social Security, suggesting we can limit government through love, if not politics. That was the part that actually bothered my friend as he publishes anti-government diatribes almost weekly. Yet St. Benedict understood Paul so clearly that Benedict made moderation a central teaching of the Benedictine Order. That's why the ascetic St. Francis and his Franciscan Order had to beg and borrow from the Benedictines from time to time. That too is a practical matter that I believe the Occupy movement might keep in mind.

That more holistic thinking in the political arena may also result in more holistic thinking about the markets. The Mennonites may invest in stocks and bonds, but they do so within fairly strict moral guidelines.

Anyway, the next time the popular media asks our religious leaders if God wants us to be rich or poor, I hope they'll remember that Psalm about God doing us a favor by giving us neither too much nor too little. For the human tendency is that we might grow independent of God if we are too rich, but we might dishonor God if we do not have what our families truly need. The same is true of nations. That is one reason everyone planning to again vote their wallets might want to spend ninety minutes, or the time most people watch television each evening, with my video at www.youtube.com/watch?v=mFMHpz7vyas.

Meditation Twenty-Eight

What Would Jeremiah Do?

"Most people who time the market are terrible at it:
Cash flows into stock funds hit peaks in early 2000 and
ebbed as the market hit bottom. This kind of activity is
incredibly costly. From 1989 through 2008, the S&P 500
gained a bit more than 8% a year, but the average equity
fund investor earned less than 2% thanks to lousy market
timing."

Fortune

You've finally listened to the wisdom of ministries telling you to pay off your credit cards. You're giving more. Like the typical American, your savings rate has increased from 2% to 6%. You read *The Automatic Millionaire*, as suggested by a major ministry a couple years ago and have even prayed for the stocks in your IRA to go up, as suggested by *The Prayer of Jabez*. How's that working for you?

If your IRA is no larger than it was a few years ago, despite adding to it regularly, you may be asking if you faith has failed you. It hasn't. You've simply learned the hard way what humanity has insisted on learning the same way since Plato taught his metaphor of life in the cave.

Unfortunately two things prevent our following more enlightened approaches, i.e., we are bound to our chairs by the fears that have bound us since our mothers first said, "Don't go in the street or you'll get hit," and "Don't talk to strangers," as well as those people making the shadows usually kill the enlightened ones. Remember the fates of Jesus, Peter, Lincoln, Gandhi, Bonhoeffer and Martin Luther King? The shadow makers like having their power over you. Their incentives can be political, which is usually about money sooner or later, but it's usually about money directly, particularly in a capitalist society.

For example, *The New York Times*, which had a Florida group of papers that I worked for at one time, used to run a very effective advertisement. It was striking in its simplicity: a full page with a small world with a crack running through it. A tiny man was cringing on top of that world. The caption below simply read "The Times Demand the *Times*." The implication was that American's couldn't survive the problems of life unless we subscribed to their publication.

But my mentor Sir John Templeton was a bit more enlightened than the typical American and was telling us that we'd never invest wisely if we read the popular press. He even suggested most newspapers would soon go out of business as they were almost exclusively focused on the bad news that enriches the papers, rather than the good news that enriches readers.

Of course, we Christians know "the world," operates that way. That's why we can depend on religious leaders we know. Wrong. One of the very most important teachings of the Bible is that too many devout and well-intentioned religious leaders, like the Pharisees, make so many shadows that Jesus never had time to fight with political and business leaders. But surely we know that as we know the biblical Truth. Wrong again. The more you listen to Christian media the more you are likely to think the Bible, our real source of Truth, is about how life was, rather than is.

For example, the January 2010 issue of *Christianity Today* contained a story entitled "Chicken Little Was Wrong." It began by cautioning cave dwellers that: "The statistics we most love to repeat may be leading us to make bad choices about the church." It then quotes a leading religious sociologist as saying: "

> *"Why do evangelicals recurrently abuse statistics? My observation is that they are usually trying desperately to attract attention and raise people's concern in order to mobilize resources [money again] and action for some cause [power again]....Evangelical leaders and organizations routinely use descriptive statistics in sloppy, unwarranted, misrepresenting, and sometimes absolutely preposterous ways."*

We've witnessed that reality the past two decades. Christians, who are typically among the "99%," have worried over the federal debt and credit card debt while the "1%" has grown increasingly wealthy. Sure, there are far more reasons than our perceptions those debts are giants in our Promised Land. But it surely hasn't helped the typical Christian to believe our nation and those attending our churches are bankrupt.

I'm also not saying credit management isn't highly important. But it's not enough. We need to be more holistic in our teaching and understanding. It's in our interests, as well as the interests of the Kingdom. If God's people had heard as much from true economists and investment counselors, like John Templeton, as radio credit ministries, they might have more money to give today from having invested wisely.

Unfortunately, we won't accomplish that if we simplistically ask, "What would Jesus do?" He'd always sell anything he had and give it to the poor, as he advised the rich young ruler who was seeking perfection. Pretending we're investing as Jesus would might boost the egos of some Christian investment advisors and bring a few naïve dollars into their firms. But it more resembles the Pharisees than Christ and dramatically distorts the nature of God by creating God in our own image. God knows any human investment advisor, and any company of humans that those counselors might invest in, have fallen far short of the perfection of Jesus Christ.

But Jesus was realistic about human imperfection, respectful of the prophets and clearly, according to the Bible, had a few affluent disciples who somehow managed to get through that old eye of the needle. So I believe Jesus wouldn't mind if we imperfect investors ask, "What would Jeremiah do?" You may remember that Jeremiah once invested in a field (*The Book of Jeremiah*, chapter 32). But he didn't do so when things looked sunny. He invested when things looked very, very cloudy. That took a lot of faith. That's why he did it at that time, rather than hoard his money until things looked sunnier. Still, I'm sure that he, as John Templeton famously preached, understood that prices are usually their very lowest when things look their very worst. If you understand markets, and their law of supply and demand, it simply cannot be otherwise.

The corollary is that prices are usually their highest when things look their sunniest, as during early 2000. The political shadow makers were talking about Washington running surpluses that would allow it to pay off the federal debt by now. The financial shadow makers were talking about the "automatic" riches to be made in Internet stocks as the Dow streaked toward 36,000, or even 100,000. There were actually best-selling books of both those projections. So investors were telling the Paine Webber annual survey they expected to make 18% annually during the coming decade. But of course, when the market bottomed in March 2009, surveys revealed investors were their most pessimistic in history.

That's when I wrote an article for the Templeton Foundation that Sir John would likely be buying stocks. While the past is never a guarantee of the future, the following chart from J.P. Morgan shows the merits of investing when others are despondent. It seems simple enough but the media and Wall Street will be giving you dozens of reasons not to invest just when you should.

They will then give you many reasons to stay invested when confidence returns and you should sell.

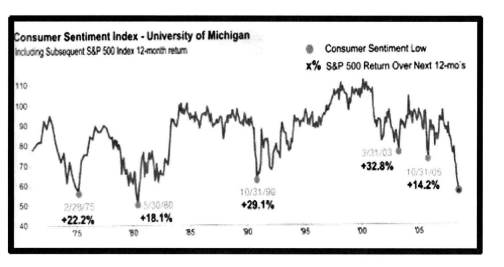

It works much the same way if you're a real estate investor. For example, around 2006, investors had been making steady returns from income-producing real estate investment trusts (reits) while stocks had been on a roller-coaster. So many people wanted reits for the equity portion of their portfolios. But real estate is quite dependent on financing and when the financial crunch hit before the Great Recession began, the same clients who wouldn't consider anything but real estate suddenly wanted to sell their reits.

That brings up another important point for investors. There are times to own reits that are listed on a stock exchange, so they can be easily bought and sold, and there are times when valuations are better in "non-traded" reits that cannot be easily bought and sold. As the Bible assures, there is a time for every purpose under heaven.

I also believe there are some investors, generally emotional investors, who should invest in the non-traded reits. The reason, as Warren Buffett says, "Liquidity is just the ability to do the wrong thing at the wrong time." That was certainly the case during the Great Recession. After those once "greedy" investors turned fearful at the bottom of the markets, reits have been the best performing asset class of the past three years, recovering almost all of what they lost during the recession. By having twenty percent or so on their portfolios in illiquid investments, as most sophisticated institutional investors do, those emotional investors were spared selling when they should have been buying even more.

So how do you know in our media saturated world who is being prophetic and who is selling shadows? Begin by reflecting on Jeremiah 11 and 12. They talk about the plots on Jeremiah's life just before he asks God why wicked men always prosper and succeed on this earth. Then remember Jesus' caution to religious leaders to be careful when everyone speaks well of them as our Gospel of love is irritating to both those who want to fearfully hoard and/or greedily get rich quick. That is, Christianity's hard but most enriching truth is that popular, successful shadow makers are very rarely prophets. If you want a more truly abundant life, you're going to have to think for yourself. I believe it was General Patton who cautioned that when everyone is thinking the same thing, someone isn't thinking.

As this book has tried to convey as clearly as possible, successful investing requires for your mind to work in conjunction with your heart, while controlling the fearful and greedy emotions of your heart. Lose your heart over a spouse; never lose it over an investment. Or, as my dad was fond of saying, "A man who names his pigs is broke and don't know it." That was a farmer's way of advising to remain quite rational about your investments. It's no different when investing in stocks, bonds, real estate and other investments.

Over the decades, I've found a few use tools that can help true investors keep their heads when all those around them are losing theirs. Importantly, none of these is perfect, but combined they may greatly increase your odds of investing wisely. Each is like a pressure gauge for tires. If your tires are supposed to have thirty-two pounds of pressure, and the gauge says you are at thirty or thirty-four, it doesn't mean the tire will blow. It simply means conditions are not ideal, and in the markets, conditions are rarely ideal. That's why wise old Solomon wrote that, "If you wait for the wind and the weather to get just right, you will never plant and never harvest" (*The Book of Ecclesiastes*, chapter 11, verse 4).

Warren Buffett has said his favorite stock market indicator is to compare the total value of American stocks to the Gross Domestic Product of our nation. Mr. Buffett can do that for himself but there's a website that does it for the rest of us. It's at www.gurufocus.com/stock-market-valuations.php. Gurufocus even estimates the potential return for the stock market based on that ratio. You don't really need to understand how that works, just that it's a useful tool for checking your emotions, which will shift from fear to greed as the markets grow ever more expensive. Unlike most everything else in life, people want to buy investments the more expensive they become.

Value investors might also appreciate two "pressure gauges" manufactured by the investment firm Smithers & Co at www.smithers.co.uk/page.php?id=34.

One gauge, called "q," measures the value of stocks verses what has been invested in those companies, or book value. The originator of q won a Nobel Prize but it essentially tells you that you don't want to pay $500,000 for a house if you could build one identical to it for $250,000 on a lot next door.

The other gauge, called "CAPE," measures the current value of stocks verses the "cyclically adjusted price earnings" ratio. This essentially smoothes the short-term ups and downs of corporate earnings so you won't be fooled by emotional panics and peaks. Again, you don't need to understand all that. Just understand that the simple chart Smithers calculates can help the conservative investor avoid buying and selling at the wrong times due to emotions.

Finally, regardless of whether you're interested in stocks, bonds, or otherwise, you might occasionally go to www.GMO.com. GMO manages over $100 billion of the Good Lord's wealth for God's children. And it has an outstanding, though not perfect, record of measuring value and predicting which asset classes have the greatest value. From the Homepage, go the "Seven Year Asset Class Forecast." Notice that forecasted returns are real, or after inflation.

Don't be surprised if it and particularly Jeremy Grantham's quarterly letter to investors are not in agreement with the majority view. When the Dow Jones was around 14,000 around 2006, Jeremy told investors that he'd be interested when it fell to 7,000. Most thought he was nuts. But when it did drop to 7,000, he bought while everyone else was selling. Jeremy and GMO remain as "contrarian" as John always famously was, though John liked to call it being "accommodative." As he explained it, when everyone is being greedy and wants to buy your stocks, be accommodative and sell your stocks to them. And when everyone is fearful and wants to sell you their stocks, be accommodative and buy them.

This may sound a bit unchristian, as if you're taking advantage of your neighbors, and I've struggled with that notion. But reality is that if there are no prudent people of faith around when everyone is panicking, or being greedy, our economy would implode. When people are greedy, we could waste vast sums of money on unproductive endeavors, like ill-conceived Internet companies. In reality, the prosperity of our nation depends of us being "salt" and prudently behaving in a counter-cultural fashion.

That could be quite important. As I do my final edit in the spring of 2012, most investors are still fearful and are therefore bunkered down in "safe" bonds. But GMO's forecast calls for bonds to produce negative real returns during coming years. Similarly, Warren Buffett has just told his investors that bonds are among the most dangerous of asset classes and "should come with a warning label." I too remember during the early eighties, when the Federal Reserve allowed interest rates to rise, that investors lost fortunes in "safe" government bonds.

Beyond your personal financial interests, hoarding "safe" investments may also not be good for society. In essence, Washington is being financed by banks and individuals lending to government by buying treasury securities, and very low paying treasury securities at that. That flow of money into treasury securities allows our politicians to avoid dealing with difficult budget matters. We could encourage those politicians to act more responsibly if we, first, stopped financing their intransigence and, second, enacted a law that says the congress and president cannot be re-elected anytime our budget deficit exceeds three percent of GDP.

I'm no prophet but I'm willing to predict the second will never be enacted. So the first idea may be our only option.

Meditation Twenty-Nine

Why Love "All the Little Children of the World?"

*"Nationalism: One of the effective ways in which the
modern man escapes life's ethical problems."*

Reinhold Niebuhr

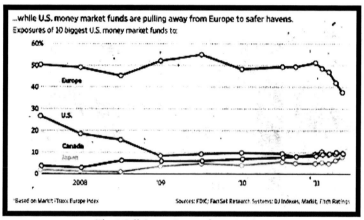

The Wall Street Journal, 11-3-2011

One of the ironies of Wall Street these days is that many investors hoping to
avoid the economic problems of Europe are bunkered down in money market
funds. Yet the graph above shows that while American money market funds
have been pulling away from Europe due to its crisis, fully forty percent of the
money in our largest money funds is still invested in Europe.

That reminds me of two things – how the ancient Hebrews seeking to avoid
the giants of the Promised Land wandered the desert for forty years, and
how so many investors during the nineties who feared the federal debt would
bankrupt Washington were also encouraged by fear-filled prognosticators to
invest in Treasury securities. Of course, those securities were the federal debt
that was to be defaulted. Seems we humans continue to be tempted to turn
our worst fears into reality. That is why true religion moderates fear, as well as
greed, into prudence.

The amount our major money funds have invested in Europe is four times that invested in the United States. The reason for so much is that European assets pay a higher interest rate due to their problems, or risks. And because of the Federal Reserve's policy of keeping U.S. interest rates as near to zero as possible, largely so our banks can recapitalize their past mistakes, money market funds have needed more interest than American securities pay in order to earn their management fees and have any interest remaining to pay investors. European securities have kept our money market funds from "breaking the buck," or earning negative returns for investors. Should a major fund do so, and the industry not prop it up, it could have a dramatic effect on the psychology of the markets if investors lose faith in even money market funds.

That's only one reason that no one should experience any happiness over the economic problems of the world, even if it does send hot money to America in search of a "safe haven." In the short-term, that can seem good for Washington as it can borrow from around the world for nothing, especially when inflation is considered. But in the long-term, nationalism can only be harmful to America's economy, as we supposedly learned during the Great Depression. This includes the most nationalistic of American politicians, like Pat Buchanan who once wrote an editorial in *The Wall Street Journal* that we should only invest in America,

Our corporations are sitting on two trillion dollars of cash, supposedly in case another credit freeze should occur. I don't completely agree with that rationalization, but it's a factor. Obviously, a lot of us have been hoping that cash might create some jobs in the United States. In turn, the unemployment rate promises to play a major role in the next election. So our economy and politics are very much like the Bible describing the Body of Christ: distinct fingers that had better work together for the good of the body.

Pragmatically, there's no way for anyone with a pension fund, mutual fund or endowment fund to avoid the interconnections of our world, which is one reason I've always detested Wall Street promising anyone "financial independence." The Franklin Templeton mutual funds have published this chart about how much of their profits America's major companies earn overseas:

I mention all this as the December 10, 2011 issue of *The Economist* contained a lengthy article entitled "There Could Be Trouble Ahead." It was

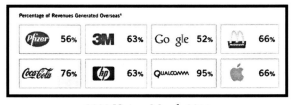

Percentage of Revenues Generated Overseas*

Pfizer	56%	3M	63%	Google	52%		66%
Coca-Cola	76%	hp	63%	Qualcomm	95%	Apple	66%

2020 Vision, March 2011

about the parallels between the Great Depression and the problems in Europe. It said:

> *"For in two important - and related - areas, the rich world could still make mistakes that were also made in the 1930's. It risks repeating the fiscal tightening that produced America's 'recession within a depression' of 1937-38. And the crisis in Europe looks eerily similar to the financial turmoil of the late 1920s and early 1930s, in which economies fell like dominoes under pressure from austerity, tight money and the lack of a lender of last resort."*

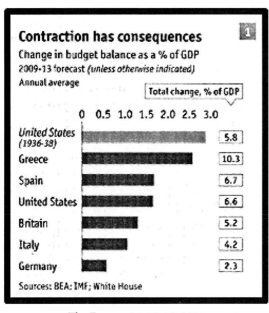

Contraction has consequences

Change in budget balance as a % of GDP
2009-13 forecast (*unless otherwise indicated*)
Annual average

Total change, % of GDP

	Total change, % of GDP
United States (1936-38)	5.8
Greece	10.3
Spain	6.7
United States	6.6
Britain	5.2
Italy	4.2
Germany	2.3

Sources: BEA; IMF; White House

The Economist, 12-10-2011

While the article made it clear that today's America is not Greece, as is often said, the article did feature the following chart comparing today's Greece with the America of the 1930's. *The Economist* is obviously concerned about the new fondness for fiscal austerity among Tea Party politicians:

The article concluded:

> *"The situation is not yet beyond repair. But the task of repairing it grows harder the longer it is delayed. The lessons of the 1930s spared the world a lot of economic pain after the shock of the 2008 financial crisis. It is not too late to recall other critical lessons of the Depression. Ignore them, and history may well repeat itself."*

The Federal Reserve and the European Central Bank have been quite stimulating since *The Economist* provided that caution. But the lesson remains. The Great Recession was simple affirmation that God obviously knew there would always be giants in the Promised Land but that they can be conquered as we are children of that God. The slave mentality of the Hebrews, and the ten fear-filled spies who told the people the giants were too fearsome to handle, simply never understood God's plan all along was for the children to manage the giants, as David did Goliath. So be prudent out there; but keep the faith.

Meditation Thirty

Can't We Just Love One Another For Enriching Change?

*"For at least another hundred years we must pretend to
ourselves and to everyone that fair is foul and foul is fair;
for foul is useful and fair is not. Avarice and usury and
precaution must be our gods for a little while longer still.
(But) the day is not far off when the economic problem
will take back seat where it belongs, and the arena of
the heart and the head will be occupied or reoccupied,
by our real problems--the problems of life and of human
relations, of creation and behavior and religion."*

John Maynard Keynes
1883-1946

Not long ago, a libertarian paper asked me to write for it. But after I began by writing about the social responsibility of business, the publisher and editor stopped answering my e-mails.

I understand. As a conservative who agrees with the biblical notion that wealth creators have a responsibility to neighbors and the needy, I've learned that this old notion now strikes many on the far right as very progressive, even new age. And I think it illustrates the emerging chasm between true conservatives, who value what humankind has learned over the millennia, and today's libertarians, who value new and radical ideas that prize self-interest and denigrate all but the narrowest forms of responsibility.

I attribute this largely to the current infatuation, among many on the far right, with the ideas of Milton Friedman (for business) and Ayn Rand (for individuals). Dr. Friedman, a Nobel laureate, taught that the only social responsibility of a corporation was to make money for shareholders. Ms. Rand, who wanted to be remembered as the greatest enemy of religion ever, once wrote "it is only in emergency situations [like shipwrecks] that we should volunteer to help strangers." She added we owe them nothing upon reaching shore. But before Dr. Friedman's libertarian business philosophy and Mrs. Rand's similar new morality of atomistic individualism became fashionable, other conservatives were writing about social responsibility in a positive way.

Perhaps chief among them was Peter Drucker, legendary management consultant and author, who conservative magazine publisher Steve *Forbes* once described as having an "uncanny" ability to foresee the future. In his 1993 book entitled *Post-Capitalist Society,* Peter, as he preferred to be called, predicted the concept of responsibility, both personal and social, would replace power as our central organizing principle once we grew weary of selfishness on the part of politicians and CEOs. "There is no one else around in the society of organizations to take care of society itself." But Peter prudently added: "Yet they must do so responsibly, within the limits of their competence, and without endangering their performance capacity." I might note that balanced approach of loving neighbor as self is precisely what Sir John Templeton aspired to accomplish during his brilliant career.

That nearly 20-year-old vision of Drucker may finally be coming true today, though not for traditional moral reasons. *Forbes* magazine has seemed to favor Friedman over Drucker in recent decades. But its September 26, 2011 cover story was entitled: "Social power and the coming corporate revolution. Why employees and customers will be calling the shots." Regarding the social media, which has organized the Occupy Wall Street movement in recent months, *Forbes* told CEOs:

"This social might is now moving toward your company. We have entered the age of empowered individuals, who use potent new technologies and harness social media to organize

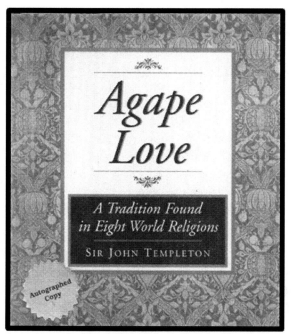

An autographed book by and from Sir John Templeton to Sherry Moore, wife of your author

themselves. You'd better get out of their way – or learn to embrace them."

Forbes added that all companies will soon become "social enterprises," so, contrary to Friedman, CEOs had better concern themselves with interests beyond their own and that of shareholders.

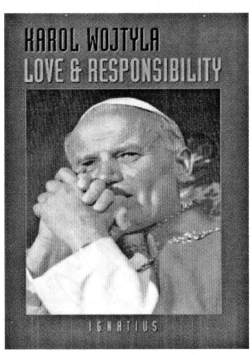

An Early Book by John Paul II

Responsibly managed, a revolutionary return toward ancient moral sentiments might actually reduce animosity among America's political leaders. That's a crucial element in our political economy as trust was the lubricant of pre-Friedman and pre-Rand capitalism. Today's selfish activities by elites are grit in that lubricant. So here are a couple of modest examples of how we might get ahead of the curve in rebuilding trust in our institutions.

America's global corporations are aggressively lobbying their friends in Congress to reduce or eliminate the taxes on what they earn overseas. They currently keep that money overseas to keep it from being taxed. Some CEOs have publicly echoed Friedman by arguing they are simply acting in the best interests of shareholders. Such corporate moves irk many progressives, including President Obama, because they see such acts as socially irresponsible in an age of federal deficits, joblessness, and record poverty coinciding with record corporate profits. They also argue that the last tax amnesty on such "repatriated" profits did nothing to curb CEOs from reaping big bonuses by laying off even more Americans in the name of productivity and efficiency.

But what if progressive politicians and conservative business leaders agreed to a deal that would help America without punishing shareholders with supposedly onerous taxes? Corporations might repatriate their profits with the 5 percent tax rate used during the last amnesty...as long as they used the money to create jobs in the United States. Companies, not government, would decide what new jobs make economic sense. If it made no sense for a company to hire in the U.S., it wouldn't repatriate any profits, creating more wealth overseas, which is socially responsible in the larger sense. Or, we might raise the tax rate on the affluent but give them a tax deduction for hiring the unemployed.

The benefits of such arrangements might be spread far and wide. More working Americans might then have money with which to buy, a favorite cause of progressives. Small US businesses, which used to be important engines of job creation, but can no longer get financing for such, might win as major corporations could invest in more capital goods to equip those workers. Or major corporations might make loans to capital starved small businesses that are critical suppliers.

The federal government might actually benefit as more people escape welfare and pay taxes. That broadening of the tax base is a favorite cause of conservatives. [While I am no fan of taxes, I've long believed *all* Americans should pay a modest "freedom fare" when our nation is at war.] Our young people might begin to believe America has a future after all. Our older people might invest in the future of our children and grandchildren again.

The cost for all this? There might be some short-term taxpayer subsidy, since the Internal Revenue Service might have gotten more money (in theory, at least) from repatriated profits, assuming corporations had a change of heart and repatriated it despite the taxes. But the major cost would simply be surrendering the radical and selfish moralities of Friedman and Rand for the old conservative tradition of both personal and social responsibility.

Peter Drucker understood that loving one's neighbor as oneself in business and politics is actually a sound organizing principle for any society. We could do worse than to listen to him. As *Forbes* said, Peter had an uncanny ability to see the future.

Conclusion

Never, Never, Never Lose Faith in Love

"Only love makes great political movements. Movements based on resentment, anger and public rage always fade, they rise and fall, they never stay. If you came to play, get serious."

Peggy Noonan
The Wall Street Journal

"As the world enters the third millennium, we may hope that the church, after some generations of loss of nerve, rediscovers its old confidence in the economic order. Few things would help more in raising up all the world's poor out of poverty. The church could lead the way in setting forth a religious and moral vision worthy of a global world, in which all lie under a universally recognizable rule of law, and every individual's gifts are nourished for the good of all... Capitalism must be infused by that humble gift of love, called caritas, described by Dante as 'the Love that moves the Sun and all the stars.' This is the love that holds families, associations and nations together. The current tendency of many to base the spirit of capitalism on sheer materialism is a certain road to economic decline. Honesty, trust, teamwork and respect for the law are gifts of the spirit. They cannot be bought."

Michael Novak

By this point, you may have concluded that I am rather pessimistic about America. You would be wrong.

I am now more hopeful for the future than I've been during the forty years that I've studied political science, worked on Wall Street, and done stewardship work in the church. Very simply, I believe the Bible, and my experiences on the Street, affirm the old saying that it's always darkest just before the dawn. It seems we humans simply have to mess things up pretty badly before we learn. While we will undoubtedly forget the expensive lessons we've learned during recent years, there is considerable evidence, from rather quite disinterested parties, that America might soon remember why our money is imprinted with the phrase, "In God We Trust."

The twelve step programs tell us, the first step to sobriety is understanding you get intoxicated too often. Drunkenness too often occurs in our political economy as, due to the negativity of politicians and the media, even Christians are so materialistic we never seem to have enough. Yet the following chart from the November 19, 2011 issue of *The Economist* showed America is still filing more patents than any nation on earth, at nearly a half million per year. To me anyway, that doesn't sound like the pitiful has been giant many perceive America to be.

There is also evidence developing that we may yet handle such positive economic developments more responsibly than in the past few decades.

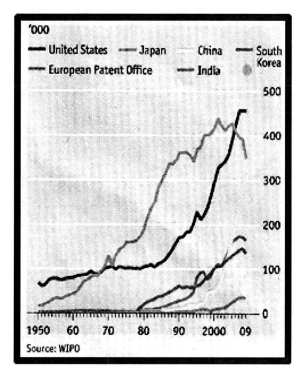

Consider for example that *The Wall Street Journal* recently said:

"*The Benefits of the Bust: The financial crisis is leading to a new model of capitalism... The propensity of modern economic theory for unjustified and over-simplified assumptions allowed politicians, regulators and bankers to create for themselves the imaginary world of market fundamentalist ideology, if government will only step aside. **Although the academic recommendations from the Left and Right differed in almost every particular, including on stimulus spending, they had***

one striking feature in common - a detachment from reality that
made them completely useless for all practical purposes."

Professor Robert Fogel, a Nobel laureate in economics and a religious skeptic, has written a book entitled *The Fourth Great Awakening*. It predicts that due to the failures of both right and left, we are at the dawn of another awakening that will not only be spiritual, as many in the church even seem to believe, but traditionally religious. He adds:

> **"One cannot understand current political or ethical trends,**
> **or properly forecast future economic developments, without**
> **understanding the cycles in religious feelings in American history."**

It might also be good news for both the church and the economy that the two senior editors of *The Economist*, only one of which is a believer, recently co-authored a book entitled *God Is Back*.

Professor James Buchanan, another Nobel laureate in economics, echoed this change recently when he told *The Wall Street Journal*:

> *"The loss of faith in politics has not been accompanied by any demonstrable faith in markets. We are left, therefore, with what is essentially an attitude of nihilism toward economic organization. There seems to be no widely shared organizing principle upon which persons can begin to think about the operations of a political economy."*

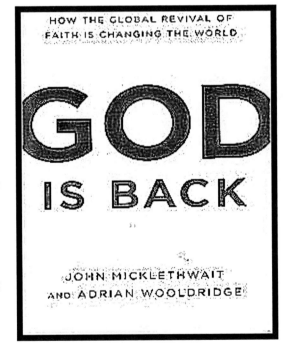

Peter Drucker, being ever prophetic, anticipated Buchanan's frustration during the mid-nineties when Peter wrote *Post-Capitalist Society*. He wrote:

> **"Every few hundred years in Western history there occurs a**
> **sharp transformation. We are currently living through just such**
> **a transformation... Political and social theory, since Plato and**
> **Aristotle, has focused on power. But responsibility must be the**

principle which informs and organizes the post-capitalist society. The society of organizations, the knowledge society, demands a responsibility-based organization."

Perhaps you've noticed that many companies selling alcoholic beverages are now urging us to, "Drink responsibly." [Now all we have to do is to convince them to market their products more responsibly.] Liberty Mutual Insurance Company is using the slogan, "Responsibility is our policy." The leaders of Citicorp have even spoken of "responsible banking."

As economically encouraging as that might be, those in ministry should remember that not only was Peter Drucker a prophetic management guru, he once taught theology. So his statement was likely far more religious than most of us might assume. Peter understood human nature must be transformed into something more divine. That is why theologian Richard Niebuhr wrote a book entitled *The Responsible Self.* It said:

"There are doubtless as many ways of associating Jesus Christ with the responsible life as there have been ways of associating him with the ideal life or the obedient or dutiful one... The Christian ethos so uniquely exemplified in Christ himself is an ethics of universal responsibility."

Very simply, most Americans essentially believe Christ never created a single problem on earth, or committed a sin, yet he accepted responsibility for all the world's sins on the Cross. Due to humanistic philosophies interested in secular results only, that is exactly the opposite of what we have gotten from Wall Street and Washington recently. I have yet to hear anyone accept the smallest responsibility for anything that has gone wrong.

That's the easy confession however. The much more difficult one is that I have also never heard a major Christian leader accept responsibility for any of our economic problems. But we surely have many sins of omission, and even commission, to confess. We can help to put America on the right path again by making that confession and re-assuming our God-given responsibilities for creating the more abundant life, which is both spiritual and material. After all, that's why Jesus himself said he came to earth. Christian leaders could do worse than imitate him.

But what about you? Yes, you too have responsibilities to assume. In fact, I can think of what we might call the "Ten Responsibilities" to provide a timely complement to the Ten Commandments. If you adopt them, I believe your odds of prospering, in the fullest sense of that word, will be greatly improved if Warren Buffett again proves correct about the future of America. In his letter to shareholders in 2011, Mr. Buffett wrote:

"No matter how serene today may be, tomorrow is always uncertain. Don't let that reality spook you. Throughout my lifetime, politicians and pundits have constantly moaned about terrifying problems facing America. Yet our citizens now live an astonishing six times better than when I was born. The prophets of doom have overlooked the all-important factor that is certain: Human potential is far from exhausted and the American system for unleashing that potential remains alive and effective."

Assuming you don't want to avoid your responsibilities by pretending all is hopeless, you make no difference, or the world is about to end, those ten responsibilities are:

First, assume the responsibility to count your blessings. The media and politicians, as well as the church apparently, are unlikely to help you. You will be spiritually blessed by doing so. And if Jesus was correct that if we "seek first" spiritual resources and the material things we need will be added unto us, and I believe he was, odds are at least fifty-fifty in a prosperous land like America that you will also be blessed financially, assuming that is one of your goals in life, which it need not be.

Second, assume the responsibility of bringing our nation back together. We've been assured a house divided cannot stand. We've also been assured that peace-makers will be blessed. Our grandchildren will be as well.

Third, understand all God's children are a unique combination of progressive and conservative ideas. Our politicized world insists on dividing good and evil with a vertical line between left and right. But Jesus divided it with a horizontal line between higher and lower. There is bountiful room for progressives, independents and conservatives in the Kingdom. Libertarians will have to decide if they can live with the "honor and respect" for government and rendering unto Caesar that goes on there.

Fourth, particularly if you are a Christian leader, assume the responsibility to know what you are talking about. The Bible says Jesus himself promised it would be better if we had millstones hung about our necks and tossed into the sea than to mislead another child of God. We also increasingly live in a rational and scientific world where facts are important and verifiable. We know the human mind is quite limited and there will always be such a thing as evil genius. But we claim to know the Truth about life. Without losing touch with our hearts and souls, we should always know the facts about mundane matters like Y2K and the federal debt. Otherwise, we should be humble enough to remain silent.

Fifth, assume the responsibility for preferring churches that teach social and economic justice. Despite what Glenn Beck, who famously and most confusedly recommended both Ayn Rand and Jesus Christ to viewers, has also counseled, any church that does not teach those subjects simply isn't fully Christian. You are unlikely to be fully human and our nation won't be fully great, until you do.

Sixth, that implies you will assume personal responsibility for your neighbors and particularly those in need. Yes, give to your church and favorite ministries. Allow the government to provide a safety net if you wish. But also give to someone who is truly needy as you develop a loving relationship with that person. You will get back far more than you give.

Seventh, assume the responsibility of knowing how your savings are used. If they are being used irresponsibly, move to a local credit union, community bank or seek out an institution that is dedicated to serving America's poor, Native Americans, and so on. You might go to www.cdfi.org if you need ideas.

If you believe in financing small businesses, which are increasingly starved for capital in America, you might look into a "business development corporation," or "BDC." There are an increasing number of these being introduced on Wall Street to considerable fanfare. You might think of them as a mutual fund where the manager was the business lending desk in a commercial bank. He makes loans to businesses that are smaller than the S&P 500, but considerably larger than a mom and pop business.

For example, one fund I've looked at lends money to companies like Outback Steakhouses, a company most people know. The loans are usually "secured" by the companies' assets of one nature or another, which is typical with small business loans. As those assets are crucial to the business, such loans have historically had a solid record of returning the investor's money, along with above-average earnings for a relatively conservative investment.

If you want to finance mom and pop businesses, you might look into a "micro-lending" fund and/or "community development institution." You can usually find several of those by Googling those phrases.

Eighth, assume the responsibility for knowing what your money is doing on Wall Street. That can be quite complex, even legalistic, but even simple approaches will help to refocus Wall Street. Simply obtain a *Morningstar* report or recent quarterly report on your stock funds. Glance at the major holdings and see if you're proud to own them. If not, you might go to www. socialfunds.com for a list of funds that strive to be socially responsible.

If you are a pastor, assume the responsibility of assuring your congregation is economically literate, in a moral sense. You don't have to do that personally any more than you lead the choir. Understand that you may have several financial professionals in your church and there will inevitably be conflicts of interest. You'll need to accept the responsibility of managing those conflicts, as most businesspeople have to each day. The future greatness of the church depends on your accepting that responsibility for our money culture. That might even help you better understand the moral dilemmas faced by your members.

My view is that no church member should ever profit personally from managing resources for his or her own church. But like pastors themselves, they might care for their own families by assisting affluent members in need of financial services. Be assured that some deeply conflicted members will feel that members should purchase such services from non-Christians, thereby helping to divest the kingdom. Some will object to any talk about money. Seek the applause of heaven rather than your squeaky wheels. You might appoint a knowledgable lay leader, as Stephen Ministries does in my church, to assure those laity are more interested in the finances of members than their own finances. That responsiblity should be aligned with the power to discipline any counselor who displays unbalanced self-interest. But do not expect those members to resemble Mother Teresa and serve the affluent for nothing, which the affluent will likely most demand. That will never spread the Christian ethic. Not only might that realistic approach enrich our members and our faith, it would teach the Great Commandment to those professionals who should live it from Monday to Saturday.

If you like to invest in real estate trusts, look at the businesses they will house as you judge their financial merits. For example, the Wells real estate trusts have long sought to only rent to businesses with which a Christian might be comfortable.

The Hines real estate trusts might be considered by the environmentally conscious as it has long believed, according to its marketing materials, that "a sustainable approach to real estate can improve the bottom line, help the environment and create better places for people to live and work." Many of its buildings are Leed certified. That stands for "Leadership in Energy and Environmental Design," which is "a nationally accepted benchmark for the design, construction and operation of high-performance green buildings."

Be prudent when investing, as that's a central Christian ethic. It implies that God loves you just as much as God loves your neighbors and future generations. There simply are no exceptions to the old sayings that

investing is a risk/reward proposition, as well as if it looks too good to be true, it is.

Ninth, avoid speculation. Look at the "turnover ratio" on the first page or two of the quarterly report or *Morningstar* report to see if your manager is speculating, trading or investing. If it says "100%," it means the manager is trading your stocks on average each year, which is about the norm. If it says "200%," he or she is only holding your stocks about six months on average. It isn't unusual to see numbers over 300%. Obviously, the manager could care less if the companies are behaving responsibly if they are going to buy and sell their stocks each three or four months. Truly responsible managers will hold your stocks two or three years at a minimum.

Even the Bible cautions, "If you're in a hurry to get rich, you're going to be punished." That's not to say the financial returns you get from a high-turnover fund must be lower. But John Bogle at Vanguard has produced studies that say they will on average, particularly after-tax, as long-term investors receive a nice tax break. And punishment can be indirect and not immediately visible when the owners of our nation's great businesses, meaning us, do not pay attention to what corporate managers are up to. **Who in their right mind would buy a small business, hire a manager and expect to profit if the owners paid no further attention? That is being the exact opposite of a responsible steward.**

Finally, for the good of our faith and our children's futures, assume the responsibility of teaching your children, even grandchildren, how to live responsibly. There are many ways of doing so but teaching them about money is a good one. As Billy Graham said when echoing the biblical prophets, most things in life seem to fall in line if we just get our money right.

I'm most grateful that my mother took me to see Rev. Graham over fifty years ago. Since then, I've never believed any preacher has been able to top him, even if he has really only had one sermon: humanity's deep need for God's graceful love. So this would normally be a great place to stop. But Rev. Graham essentially spent his life teaching about the truly abundant life. And the recent *Financial Times* series "Capitalism in Crisis," essentially suggested we all reflect on Sir John Templeton's core belief, "How little we know, how eager to learn." The *Times* shared this sentiment, with which Solomon might heartily agree, from Harvard professor of economics Carmen Reinhart:

"One absolutely essential prerequisite is: educate, educate, educate. It is really hard to see another way out of the growing sustainability problems that capitalism has given us. We must focus on the inadequacies of primary and secondary education, as well as the need to re-educate and retrain adults. I would take the point much further: Societies need to find ways to make adult education, including economic and financial literacy, far more available and far more compelling.

> *If voters are uninformed and easily swayed towards demagogues peddling short-term ill-considered policies, there is little hope for righting the course of capitalist countries.* The idea that the masses are indifferent to education, and that any broader notion of literacy beyond the three R's is a hopeless cause, is nonsense. As someone who has spoken to all kinds of people in the wake of the financial crisis, my sense is that most citizens are starved of information, and would consume it hungrily if offered in a palatable form. Without such, it is hard to see a long-term cure for contemporary capitalism's many political problems."

This is why we put this book together, as well as established our website, which is always free as the Gospel really can't be sold, and probably shouldn't be, at www.financialseminary.org. We trust the book has been enriching, if not always all that enjoyable, and hope you join us in life-long learning at The Financial Seminary.

Blessings, both spiritual and material, as they are inextricably linked. And keep the faith, by always looking up!

CPSIA information can be obtained at www.ICGtesting.com
Printed in the USA
BVOW011051030412

286745BV00001B/7/P